INSPIRE / PLAN / DISCOVER / EXPERIENCE

SCOTLAND

SCOTLAND

CONTENTS

DISCOVER 6

EXPERIENCE 56

NEED TO KNOW 206

Left: Scottish Parliament, designed by Enric Miralles
Previous page: Kilchurn Castle, Loch Awe

DISCOVER

Neolithic Ring of Brogdar, Orkney

WELCOME TO
SCOTLAND

Rugged shores and wild Highland glens. Stern castles and haunting battlefields. World-class museums and internationally renowned festivals. Scotland offers enough bucket-list experiences to draw visitors back year after year. Whatever your dream trip entails, this DK Eyewitness Travel Guide is the perfect companion.

1 Wild red stag grazing in the frosty moorlands of the Scottish Highlands.

2 Visitors admiring the view from the top of Calton Hill, Edinburgh.

3 Twilight over Eilean Donan Castle on Loch Duich.

Small but spectacular, Scotland is famed for its majestic mountain landscapes, tranquil lochs and windswept moorland, all fringed by thousands of miles of dramatic coastline. The undulating farmlands of Angus, Ayrshire and Aberdeenshire and the verdant sheep pastures of the Borders are a haven of tranquillity, while pocket wildernesses like the Cairngorms, Rannoch Moor and the Trossachs are but a stone's throw from bustling towns and cities such as Edinburgh, Glasgow and Inverness.

This richly varied hinterland is a joy for outdoor enthusiasts, offering a vast array of activities from gentle country strolls to long-distance hill walking, rock climbing and whitewater kayaking. Meanwhile, the museums and art galleries of Scotland's cities are temples to art and culture, and a plethora of bars and clubs serve up a buzzing nightlife comprising live gigs, impromptu folk sessions and comedy. Old-school inns abound, but cool cocktail bars and gastropubs offer an exciting new take on food and drink while still honouring the country's local produce and culinary tradition.

With so much on offer, it is easy to feel overwhelmed. This guide breaks Scotland down into easily navigable chapters, with detailed itineraries, expert local knowledge and comprehensive maps to help you plan your perfect trip. Whether you're here for a flying visit or a grand tour, this Eyewitness Travel Guide will ensure that you see the very best the country has to offer. Enjoy the book, enjoy Scotland, and *haste ye back*.

REASONS TO LOVE
SCOTLAND

Dramatic coastlines, soaring mountains and spirited cities, each with their own rich and multifaceted culture. There are so many things that make this vibrant country irresistible. Here's a round up of a few of our favourites.

1 DRAMATIC HISTORY

Explore ancient strongholds such as Edinburgh Castle *(p68)*, or be transported to medieval times as you wander the winding, cobbled closes and hidden courtyards of the Royal Mile *(p70)*.

MAJESTIC LANDSCAPES *2*

Venture through the iconic Highland landscapes of Glencoe and the Isle of Skye, and explore rolling moorlands and ravishing coastlines in Torridon and the northwest.

3 HOGMANAY

Party your way into the New Year with world-class bands and awesome midnight pyrotechnics at Edinburgh's famous Hogmanay, then join locals in a "Loony Dook" to blow the cobwebs away.

A FLOURISHING FOODIE SCENE 4

Scotland is in full culinary bloom thanks to creative chefs across the country working their magic with the best locally sourced ingredients.

CITIES OF CULTURE 5

Admire Renaissance gems at Glasgow's Kelvingrove Art Gallery *(p126)* or cutting-edge design at Edinburgh's National Gallery of Modern Art *(p88)* and the V&A, Dundee *(p156)*.

DISTILLERIES GALORE 6

Scotland is a whisky-lover's paradise. Sip ancient malts in distilleries such as Glenlivet in Speyside *(p148)*, or try a new breed of Scotch at an artisan spirit house or cocktail bar.

HIGHLAND CULTURE 7

Experience Highland heritage, tartan pageantry, pipe music, Scottish dance and caber-tossing muscle-men (and women) at Highland games and clan gatherings.

ISLAND GETAWAYS 8

Admire a Hebridean sunset from Saligo Bay on Islay *(p189)*. As otherworldly shadows dance across the sand, you'll see why the island is called Queen of the Hebrides.

9 WILDLIFE SPOTTING

Spot seals, whales and dolphins in the chilly waters of the Moray Firth *(p199)*, meet puffins on Handa Island *(p202)*, or go on a Highland safari where you can see red deer and wildcats.

10 CEILIDH TILL THE WEE HOURS

Tap your feet to the rhythms of traditional Scottish jigs and reels at a lively ceilidh, or even better, join in. Just about anyone can get the hang of an Orcadian Strip the Willow.

OUTDOOR ACTIVITIES 11

Ride whitewater rapids on the River Tay, cycle in Galloway Forest Park *(p114)*, or ascend summits like Ben Nevis *(p166)* and Lochnagar while walking the West Highland Way.

WORLD-CLASS GOLF 12

Play a breezy round of golf at the iconic St Andrews Links, birthplace of golf and home of the famous Royal and Ancient Golf Club *(p156)*.

EXPLORE
SCOTLAND

This guide divides Scotland into five colour-coded sightseeing areas: Edinburgh, Southern Scotland, Glasgow, Central and Northeast Scotland and the Highlands and Islands, as shown on this map. Find out more about each area on the following pages.

Atlantic
Ocean

Outer Hebrides

Stornaway

Lewis

Harris

Rudel

North
Uist

Quiraing

Isle of Skye

Portree

South
Uist

Inner Hebrides

Kilbride

Canna

Cuillins

Sleat

Barra

Rhum

Eigg

Muck

Coll

Tiree

Iona

Mull

Colonsay

Oronsay

Jura

Islay

Gigha

IRELAND

Londonderry
(Derry)

NORTHERN
IRELAND

BELFAST

WESTERN EUROPE

SCOTLAND

NORWAY

North
Sea

SWEDEN

UNITED
KINGDOM

DENMARK

IRELAND

ENGLAND

WALES

GERMANY

CZECH
REP.

Atlantic
Ocean

AUSTRIA

FRANCE

SWITZ.

ITALY

PORTUGAL

SPAIN

GETTING TO KNOW
SCOTLAND

Stretching from the rich farmlands of the Borders to a chain of isles just south of the Arctic Circle, the Scottish landscape is distinct and diverse. There is plenty to discover here, from tranquil lochs and rugged hills to clan castles and vibrant cities, each with their own unique charm.

PAGE 58

EDINBURGH

Replete with sights and cultural treasures, Edinburgh is the gateway to Scotland. Dominated by the ramparts of Edinburgh Castle, the Royal Mile runs through the heart of a uniquely intact medieval quarter of the city. To the north, the gracious Georgian New Town is filled with upscale shops, boutique hotels, restaurants and café-bars. Beyond the city lie urban villages, such as Stockbridge and Leith, that have a charming character of their own.

Best for
Sightseeing and culture

Home to
Edinburgh Castle, National Museum of Scotland, Scottish National Gallery

Experience
Panoramic views over the city and beyond from the summit of Arthur's Seat

PAGE 94

SOUTHERN SCOTLAND

Stretching between the North Sea and the Atlantic, Scotland's southern regions are bound in the north by the Firths of Clyde and Forth. Fertile farmlands contrast with upland moors and riverside valleys, while baronial mansions stand alongside evocative ruins of historic abbeys and castles. The delights of this region are within an hour's drive of Edinburgh or Glasgow.

Best for
History and scenery

Home to
Culzean Castle, Abbotsford

Experience
Taking the ferry to Arran and climbing Goatfell, the island's highest peak

→

GLASGOW

PAGE 116

Scotland's biggest city, straddling the River Clyde, buzzes with energy. A legacy of the 18th- and 19th-century mercantile and industrial revolutions, the city centre is studded with several handsome buildings, including the City Chambers and Kelvingrove Museum and Art Gallery. But it is also a city that is constantly reinventing itself, with a lively and youthful nightlife, trendy shopping districts, and a cosmopolitan array of places to eat and drink.

Best for
Art, shopping and nightlife

Home to
Kelvingrove Museum and Art Gallery, Glasgow Science Centre

Experience
A waverley paddle-steamer cruise on the River Clyde

PAGE 134

CENTRAL AND NORTHEAST SCOTLAND

Encompassing wild uplands and tamer lowland landscapes, Central and Northeast Scotland is a patchwork of farmland and forest, fringed by sandy shores. Each of its cities has a unique history, from the medieval splendour of Stirling Castle and the austere architecture of Aberdeen's St Machar's Cathedral to the industrial heritage of Dundee and Falkirk. Loch Lomond, the Trossachs and Tayside offer a range of outdoor activities and experiences, while Royal Deeside combines natural beauty with regal splendour.

Best for
Royal heritage and whisky

Home to
Aberdeen, Scone Palace, Loch Lomond, Stirling Castle

Experience
Whitewater rafting and canoeing on the River Tay

THE HIGHLANDS AND ISLANDS

For many, the Highlands and Islands epitomize Scotland. This is a vast and sparsely populated region of innumerable lochs, rivers, glens and moors dotted with majestic clan castles and ancient standing stones. Hundreds of islands lie off the coast, many of them within sight of shore or an easy ferry ride from Oban, Mallaig or Ullapool. Inverness, the Highland capital, is an excellent starting point for exploring Loch Ness and the Cairngorms, while Fort William holds the key to Ben Nevis, Britain's highest peak.

Best for
Outdoor adventure and majestic mountains

Home to
Ben Nevis, Cairngorms National Park, Loch Ness

Experience
Walking in the shadow of Ben Nevis or island-hopping on the west coast

1

2

2 WEEKS
Around Scotland

| Day 1

Start your day at the National Museum of Scotland *(p76)*, then stroll to the Royal Mile *(p70)*, pausing for a quick snap of Greyfriars Bobby and a lunch stop at one of the many restaurants on George IV Bridge. Deacon Brodie's Tavern, where an effigy of the famous 18th-century villain lurks in a corner, is a favourite for a pie and a pint. After lunch, walk up the Royal Mile to Edinburgh Castle *(p68)* and admire the mighty Mons Meg in the castle grounds. Walk down The Mound to the Scottish National Gallery *(p78)* to admire works by Scottish masters. Finish the day with a climb up Calton Hill *(p74)* for a sunset panorama, then descend to lively Broughton Street for drinks, dinner and live music at The Barony.

| Day 2

A half-hour drive west on the M9 will take you to Falkirk, where The Helix *(p153)* is home to two colossal equine heads that rear above the canal. A further 25-minute drive brings you to Stirling *(p144)* and its legendary castle. Explore within the castle's ancient walls, then head for the nearby Wallace Monument, an unmistakable landmark. Climb this Gothic spire for an impressive view of the Castle and learn about Scotland's national hero, William Wallace. Spend the evening in the quaint town of Dunblane, where Chez Roux at Cromlix House offers a light, nouvelle, French-influenced menu.

| Day 3

Visit the iconic Doune Castle *(p148)*, then drive a further half-hour to Perth *(p150)* where you can pause for lunch and visit the Fergusson Gallery. After lunch, cross the River Tay to Scone Palace *(p140)* a stately home crammed with precious antiques. Stretch your legs in its wooded gardens before embarking on a short drive to your final destination of the day: Dundee *(p156)*. Dine in the city's arts quarter, and enjoy live entertainment nearby at Dundee Rep Theatre.

1 Calton Hill at sunset.

2 Modern exterior of the V&A Dundee.

3 Macallan whisky barrels, Speyside.

4 Crathes Castle, Deeside.

5 Skye Bridge, connecting the town of Kyleakin to the mainland.

Day 4

Begin the day with a visit to Dundee's V&A Museum of Design, where the original interior of Charles Rennie Mackintosh's Oak Room is a highlight, then board RRS *Discovery* and learn about Captain Scott's polar voyages. After a spot of lunch, head north to the haunting ruined clifftop fortress of Dunnottar Castle *(p146)*. Spend the night in Aberdeen *(p138)*, where you can feast on Black Angus steak and North Sea lobster at The Brasserie at Malmaison Aberdeen, which also has stylish rooms.

Day 5

On your way to Royal Deeside, stop at Crathes Castle to explore its walled garden and nature trails – a perfect spot for a picnic lunch. Then on to the famous Balmoral Castle and Estate *(p148)*, where you can walk through delightful pine-scented grounds and admire the Baronial architecture. Carry on through the Cairngorms *(p168)* and admire rugged mountain landscapes on your way to Aberlour for the evening.

Day 6

Follow The Malt Whisky Trail® *(p149)* through Speyside to Craigellachie for a fascinating tour around the The Macallan Distillery and Visitor Centre. En route to Inverness, stop off for an afternoon tour of the infamous Culloden Battlefield *(p200)* to imagine the clash of claymores that took place here in 1746. A jumble of friendly pubs and atmospheric restaurants welcomes you to Inverness.

Day 7

First stop Drumnadrochit to join a Loch Ness Monster "research cruise". Admire the ruins of Urquhart Castle *(p170)* from the water, then eat at the Loch Ness Inn's Lewiston Restaurant, which serves local produce with a contemporary twist. Follow the banks of Loch Ness through breathtaking Glenshiel *(p202)*. Pause for a stroll around the magnificent Eilean Donan Castle – Scotland's most photogenic castle – on Loch Duich, then on to Kyle of Lochalsh. Cross the bridge to the Isle of Skye *(p172)* where a fine dinner and cosy room await at Kinloch Lodge. →

Day 8

Visit the dinky town of Portree for a colourful snapshot, then head for Dunvegan Castle, stronghold of Clan MacLeod for over eight centuries. Just off the main road from Portree to Staffin is the start of a fantastic walk along the Trotternish ridge, leading to The Old Man of Storr, which rewards hikers with fantastic views across the island and beyond. Don't miss a quick stop at the Talisker Distillery for a sip of the whisky nicknamed "the lava of the Cuillins".

Day 9

Take the short ferry crossing from Armadale to the pretty town of Mallaig (p194), famed for its fresh seafood. Stop off at the Sands of Morar and take a stroll where this idyllic sweep of white sand meets aquamarine water. Continue your drive through Glenfinnan to pay your respects to Jacobite warriors at the Glenfinnan Monument and see the iconic Jacobite Steam Train, which doubles as the Hogwarts Express in the Harry Potter movies, as it chuffs along the Glenfinnan

Viaduct in a billow of smoke. You can even ride the train – a regular service runs between Mallaig and Fort William. Arrive in Fort William in time to dine at The Crannog while watching a glorious sunset over Loch Linnhe.

Day 10

A short trip from Fort William is Glen Nevis, where you can get a great view of Scotland's highest peak and stretch your legs on many a woodland stroll, or a more energetic munro. If you wish to conquer Ben Nevis (p166), start the day early, and ensure that the weather conditions are right, and that you are well prepared for the demanding ascent.

Day 11

The drive south from Fort William through Glencoe (p196) is real stunner. You'll find great views of Buachaille Etive Mor from the Glencoe Visitor Centre. From here, follow the A82 for an hour and a half, skirting heather-covered Rannoch Moor, to Loch Lomond (p142). Don't miss

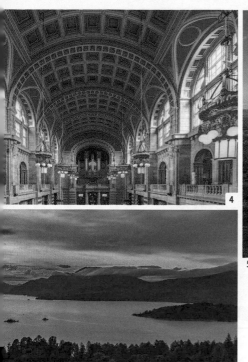

1. The Old Man of Storr, Skye.
2. Jacobite Express crossing the Glenfinnan Viaduct.
3. Loch Lomond at sunset.
4. Main hall at Kelvingrove Art Gallery and Museum.
5. Hikers exploring the Eildon Hills.

a stop in the picturesque town of Luss. Enjoy dinner and drinks overlooking the loch and Ben Lomond at Colquhoun's at the Lodge on Loch Lomond, where the menu features grilled steaks, local game and exquisite seafood.

Day 12

Start your day of exploring the beautiful Trossachs National Park aboard a Victorian paddle-steamer boat cruise on Loch Katrine. Spend the rest of the day taking advantage of some of the many activities on offer in the Queen Elizabeth Forest Park, be that biking, walking sections of the West Highland Way or even ziplining above the treetops. Set off on the 45-minute drive to Glasgow in the early evening to arrive in time for dinner out in the bustling city centre.

Day 13

Stroll through Glasgow's Kelvingrove Park to Kelvingrove Art Gallery and Museum (p126) where works by the Scottish Colourists and the Glasgow Boys steal the show. To refuel, visit quirky Ashton Lane where your taste buds will be spoilt for choice. From here, it's a short walk to the Riverside Museum (p131) where you will be wowed by gleaming vintage vehicles. Relax at The Winged Ox at St Luke's, next to the famous Barrowlands music venue, where you'll find an eclectic menu of food, drink and entertainment.

Day 14

Take a slight detour through the rolling Borders countryside on the way back to Edinburgh, stopping at literary legend Sir Walter Scott's favourite viewpoint of the triple-crowned Eildon Hills (p110). Head north to the last sight on your tour, the enchanting Rosslyn Chapel (p105). Admire its intricately carved stonework, then walk through leafy Roslin Glen before embarking on the short drive back to Edinburgh city centre.

7 DAYS

On the North Coast 500

Day 1

Starting in Inverness *(p198)*, a short drive along the south shore of the Beauly Firth (keep an eye open for dolphins) then north through Dornoch, will take you to Dunrobin Castle *(p201)*, seat of the Earls of Sutherland and one of the north's great fairytale stately homes. Stop at the Golspie Inn for a light lunch before continuing north to John O'Groats *(p203)*, then on to windswept Dunnet Head. From there, Scrabster is just 35 minutes away. Catch the 7pm ferry to Stromness *(p176)*, then dine at the Merkister Hotel's Skerries Restaurant, which specializes in Orkney beef and fresh seafood.

Day 2

Explore the wonders of Neolithic Orkney *(p176)*, including the ancient tomb at Maeshowe and the stone megaliths at Stenness and the Ring of Brodgar. In the afternoon, visit Kirkwall to admire St Magnus Cathedral, a 12th-century masterpiece in red and yellow stone.

Day 3

The next morning, return by ferry to the mainland, and begin the winding route along the A836 across the windswept, rugged expanse of Scotland's northern coast, stopping to admire stunning viewpoints and sheer clifftop vistas as you go. Veer off to the aptly named Côte du Nord (open Mar–Sep only) for a lunch that fuses the finest local Scottish produce with French cuisine. A mile before you hit Durness, venture into the eerie caverns of Smoo Cave *(p203)*.

Day 4

As a welcome break from driving, park up and join a ferry and minibus tour from Durness to Cape Wrath *(p203)*, where waves crash beneath savage grey cliffs and hundreds of aquaking seabirds perch on sea stacks just offshore. Stop here for a snap of the white stone lighthouse on the very northwest tip of mainland Britain, with views that seem to stretch to the edge of the world.

1 Visitors exploring the Ring of Brodgar, Orkney. ↑

2 Stunning interior of St Magnus Cathedral, Kirkwall.

3 Lighthouse, Cape Wrath.

4 Red grouse among the heather at Handa Island.

5 Road to Loch Maree.

Day 5

The route down the West Coast, heading south from Durness, is where the magic really kicks in. First, head to Tarbet, where you can hop on a ferry to the tiny Handa Island (p202) where the air is filled with the cries of tens of thousands of seabirds. On your return to the mainland, head south to Eddrachillis Bay, a mirror-calm natural anchorage dotted with heather-tufted islets where seals bask and yachts anchor in summer. Then follow the road that passes through an undulating series of peaks known as the Quinag, and the impressive Ben More Assynt and Conival munros. This wild expanse of mountain and moorland, sliced up by long narrow lochs, is only 18 miles (30 km) from Ullapool (p203), where you can enjoy a night of foot-tapping fiddle music at the Ceilidh Place.

Day 6

Follow the shore of long, narrow Loch Broom, then double back west on a remote road overlooked by the breath-takingly wild summits of Sgurr Mor and An Teallach. Visit the meticulously preened Inverewe Garden (p203) on Loch Ewe, where vivid red and purple rhododendrons bloom spectacularly in their very own unique microclimate.

Day 7

Continue on this road alongside the beautifully serene Loch Maree, then fork left at Kinlochewe to drive inland through the desolate but stunningly beautiful moorland of Torridon in Wester Ross to Achnasheen, then return by way of Strathpeffer (p200). Stop en route for a view of the foaming cascades of thundering white water at Rogie Falls, 2 miles (3 km) west of Contin on the A835. Continue along this road to return to Inverness, where a warm welcome in one of the lively Highland capital's many cosy pubs and restaurants awaits.

Adventures at Sea

Scotland's coastal waters offer endless possibilities for water-based adventures, from sea kayaking to deep-sea diving. Qualified scuba divers can discover vast underwater kelp forests and ghostly shipwrecks such as Scapa Flow in Orkney *(p177)*.

←
Scuba diver exploring an eerie shipwreck at Scapa Flow, Orkney

SCOTLAND FOR
OUTDOOR ADVENTURES

Adventurous visitors to Scotland will enjoy a plethora of adrenaline-pumping activities. Long hours of daylight make summer the perfect season to get out and about, but the great Scottish outdoors is open all year round. The winter sports season lasts from December until April.

TOP 5 WINTER SPORTS AREAS

Cairngorm Mountain
Home to some 19 miles (30 km) of pistes and cross-country trails.

The Lecht
Pistes for all levels at 2,900 ft (645m).

Glenshee Ski Centre
Britain's largest ski area with 36 slopes.

Glencoe Mountain
Scotland's steepest ski run with views of Buachaille Etive Mor and Rannoch Moor.

Nevis Range
A huge network of slopes and back-country routes within sight of Ben Nevis.

A Hiker's Haven

Scotland has a vast network of long-distance walking routes, and almost nowhere is out of bounds. The West Highland Way and the hills and glens of the Cairngorms National Park *(p168)* are favourites among keen hikers.

→
Hiker walking The Cape Wrath Trail in Torridon as sunset descends upon the valley

Inland Waters

Scotland's many rivers and stunning lochs offer plenty opportunities for thrilling whitewater kayaking, rafting and canoeing through breathtaking scenery. More easy-going activities are available on calm stretches of water – ideal for young families and novices. Aberfeldy, on the upper reaches of the River Tay, and Aviemore are hubs for river experiences of all kinds. For a day out on calm waters, sailing dinghies can be hired on inland lochs.

$\rightarrow$

Kayaker descending rapids on the scenic River Tummel

Pony Trekking

Pony trekking is another great way to experience moorland and mountains, from day trips in the Pentlands, the Cairngorms and the hills of Skye to longer trekking holidays.

$\leftarrow$

Horse riding on the sandy bay at Dornoch in Sutherland

Cycling and Mountain Biking

Networks of well-surfaced bike paths abound in Edinburgh and other cities, often along former railway lines. More energetic riders will find off-road trails in Galloway Forest Park, the Trossachs and, outside winter sports season, Nevis Range and the Lecht. Off-road and urban bikes rental is widely available.

$\rightarrow$

Mountain biker jumping at speed on a forest mountain-bike trail

Wild Deer

With over one million wild red deer in Scotland, deer stalking is a popular pursuit, but rather than harming the deer, why not join a four-wheel-drive safari in the Cairngorms *(p168)* to capture a photo of the magnificent stags with your camera. The best time to see them is during the autumn rut and in colder weather.

→

A red deer stag standing in front of a snow-capped mountain in the Highlands

SCOTLAND FOR
WILDLIFE
ENCOUNTERS

The wide, open spaces of the Highlands, rugged cliffs and tidal firths of the coasts and rocky shorelines of the isles shelter a rich variety of birds and animals. But you don't have to travel far to encounter amazing wildlife. City parks and waterways provide havens for birds and small mammals such as red squirrels, while dolphins and seals can be spotted from urban shores.

Whales, Seals and Dolphins

The waters around Scotland's northern shores and the northern and western islands provide refuge for numerous marine mammals. Take a boat trip from Aberdeen or Inverness to see bottlenose dolphins and harbour porpoises, or explore the waters around Mull to spot minke whales, basking sharks and killer whales (orcas). Grey seals and common seals are a frequent sight in the sea lochs and sandbanks of the west coast, in the Firth of Forth and in the Firth of Tay.

←

Grey seals being observed and photographed on a sandy riverbank near Aberdeen

Puffins and Seabirds

Seabirds can be spotted from just about anywhere on Scotland's coastline. See the world's largest colony of northern gannets on Bass Rock *(p102)* and, for a close encounter with puffins, head to the remote Handa Island Wildlife Reserve *(p202)* between May and July.

$\longrightarrow$

An Atlantic puffin, with its distinctive brightly coloured bill, on Handa Island

Migrating Geese

Visit Islay or the Solway Firth between mid-September and late April to see huge flocks of migrant waterfowl. More than 80,000 barnacle geese and white-fronted geese migrate to Scotland from the Arctic each winter.

$\longleftarrow$

Barnacle geese flying over the Wildfowl and Wetland Trust Reserve, Caerlaverock

REWILDING SCOTLAND

Re-establishing native species to Scotland has had positive results, but has also proved controversial. White-tailed sea eagles and beavers have been successfully reintroduced to Scotland, despite objections from farmers and gamekeepers who claim eagles prey on young lambs and beavers damage riverbanks. There have been even more strident objections to imaginative proposals to reintroduce lynx and even wolves to Scottish hillsides.

$\uparrow$ Bison roaming in the Highland Wildlife Park in the Cairngorms

Highland Wildlife Park

Bison, wolves, lynx and bears that were once native to Scotland roam free in the spacious open-air enclosures at the RZSS Highland Wildlife Park *(p169)* in the Cairngorms National Park. Highlights include the extremely rare Scottish wildcat, which is now almost extinct in the wild.

Eilean Donan

On a tiny island in Loch Duich, Eilean Donan *(p202)* is surely Scotland's most photogenic castle. Its owners, the MacRae chieftains, were notorious for mounting the severed heads of their foes along the ramparts. Their keep was demolished after the 1715 Jacobite rising and painstakingly rebuilt by John MacRae-Gilstrap between 1912 and 1932.

INSIDER TIP
Explorer Pass

The Historic Environment Scotland Explorer Pass gives unlimited access to castles and historic sites all over Scotland.

→
Evocative Eilean Donan Castle on its tiny island in Loch Duich

SCOTLAND FOR
SPECTACULAR CASTLES

From imposing fortified strongholds to ghostly shells crowning sea-girt crags, pocket-sized keeps of Highland and Border lairds, and the fanciful 19th-century inventions of imaginative Victorians, each of Scotland's many castles has its own secrets, legends, and often bloody history.

Dunnottar Castle

Ruined Dunnottar is a perfect natural fortress. Waves crash at the foot of its crag where a thin neck of rock links it to the land. Scotland's crown jewels, kept here when Cromwell invaded, were smuggled out before Dunnottar fell to his Roundheads, and were hidden in a nearby church until the monarchy was restored *(p146)*.

→
Ruins of Dunnottar Castle perched on a craggy outcrop near Stonehaven

← Dramatic lighting illuminates the ramparts of Edinburgh Castle at night

THE EVOLUTION OF THE SCOTTISH CASTLE

Dating back to the 12th century, Scotland's first castles were simple towers of wood or stone surrounded by a ditch. By the 13th century, Scottish lairds and chieftains were building fortified tower houses designed to withstand raids. In the peaceful years of the 17th-century tower houses became more comfortable and decorative. The 18th and 19th centuries saw the appearance of aristocratic palaces like Dunrobin, influenced by Renaissance and Gothic revivals, while Victorian plutocrats opted for country retreats in Scottish Baronial style, replete with turrets and mock battlements.

Edinburgh Castle

Overlooking the capital, Edinburgh's iconic castle *(p68)* has changed hands many times during its tumultuous, and at times gruesome, history. Its imposing position on the crags of Castle Rock has been of strategic military importance since the 12th century, and it remained the Scottish Royal residence until the Union of the Crowns in 1603. Many of the buildings within the castle walls date back to the 16th century, but its formidable ramparts were heavily reinforced in the 18th century against the very real threat of a Jacobite rebellion.

Dunrobin Castle

This romantic 19th-century re-creation of a French chateau in the Scottish Highlands is built around a 15th-century keep founded by the earls of Sutherland, whose descendants still live here *(p201)*.

↑ Beautiful ornate baronial turrets of Dunrobin Castle

Edinburgh International Book Festival

Scotland's capital has inspired over 500 novels, and was named the the the first UNESCO City of Literature in 2004. In August it hosts the world's largest International Book Festival, where publishers from all over the word present new titles and leading authors take part in readings and book signings at events throughout the city.

$\rightarrow$

Robin Mair speaking at Unbound, Edinburgh International Book Festival

SCOTLAND FOR
BOOKWORMS

Scotland has a remarkable literary heritage, and has produced more than its fair share of acclaimed writers and enlightened thinkers. Bookworms will enjoy the wealth of bookish festivals, events and experiences on offer that honour the country's most celebrated literary luminaries.

MEAN STREETS AND TARTAN NOIR

With *Laidlaw* (1977), Scots author William McIlvanney kicked off Scotland's "tartan noir" crime fiction genre, a pantheon including likes of Ian Rankin's gloomy Inspector Rebus, Christopher Brookmyre's roguish investigator Jack Parlabane, and Denise Mina's DI Alex Morrow, a rare female protagonist in the crime fiction world. Val McDermid's novels were adapted into a cult TV series, *Wire in the Blood*, and Kate Atkinson's Jackson Brodie stars in *Case Histories*.

Burns Heritage Trail

One of Scotland's most celebrated and prolific writers, Robert Burns has made his mark all over the country. There are numerous museums and exhibitions in his name. For hard-core fans, the Burns Heritage Trail *(p112)* is a comprehensive tour of where he lived and wrote and the places that inspired him most.

Scotland's National Book Town

Book-mad Wigtown in Dumfries & Galloway is a book-lovers paradise. Home to more than 20 bookshops and literary cafés, this quaint town hosts a lively literature festival over ten days every autumn, featuring over 250 literary events for adults, kids and young people, and welcoming numerous high-profile Scottish authors and guest speakers.

→

Decorative entrance to one of many second-hand bookshops in Wigtown

The Beatrix Potter Exhibition, Dunkeld

Childhood summers spent in rural Perthshire were a strong influence on *The Tale of Peter Rabbit* author Beatrix Potter, and fostered in her a keen interest in the natural world. Stroll through the Beatrix Potter Garden at Birnam Arts *(p151)* and see if you can spot Peter Rabbit.

←

Small scupltures hiding in the Beatrix Potter Garden at Birnam Arts, Dunkeld

Edinburgh Literary Pub Tour

This award-winning and light-hearted walking tour takes you through the cobbled streets, secret closes and hidden courtyards of Edinburgh's Old Town to the old haunts of some of Scotland's greatest authors and poets, most of whom favoured down-to-earth boozers over posh salons.

↑ The Auld Brig in Alloway, Ayrshire features in Robert Burns's famous poem *Tam O'Shanter*

↑ The popular White Hart Inn, the oldest pub in Edinburgh

◁ Duff House

William Adam, founder of a dynasty of great Scottish architects, designed this grand country hideaway for the First Earl of Fife in his signature style, fusing Palladian and Baroque elements. Works by Ramsay and Raeburn sit alongside European masterpieces such as El Greco's *St Jerome in Penitence*.

▷ National Gallery of Scotland

The *grande dame* of Scotland's galleries stands on The Mound in Edinburgh. Opened in 1859 to a design by William Henry Playfair, the Neo-Classical building is a landmark in its own right. Within is a world-class collection that includes Scotland's own master painters and works by medieval, Renaissance and later artists from Titian, Raphael and Botticelli to Vermeer, Monet, Gauguin and Van Gogh.

SCOTLAND FOR
ART LOVERS

Scotland's art galleries celebrate the vivid colours of 20th-century moderns and the ground-breaking work of 21st-century artists from around the world. Many Scottish painters and sculptors have earned worldwide acclaim and are well represented in the country's shrines to art and culture.

◁ V&A Dundee

Designed by Japanese architect Kengo Kuma, Scotland's newest and boldest aesthetic gallery opened on Dundee's regenerated waterfront in 2018. While focusing on modern and contemporary design by new and up-and-coming artists, the centrepiece here is the Scottish Design Galleries, where the gem of the collection is Charles Rennie Mackintosh's carefully reassembled 1907 Oak Room, unseen by the public since it was dismantled in the 1970s.

▷ Glasgow Mural Trail

Street artists such as Smug and Rogue-One have made city walls their canvases for eye-catching and vibrantly colourful works scattered along this open-air trail. They celebrate every aspect of Glaswegian life and culture, from depictions of revered local heroes like comedian and musician Billy Connolly to urban wildlife.

◁ Scottish National Gallery of Modern Art

Bronzes by Eduardo Paolozzi, a sweeping landscape work by Charles Jencks and pieces by Henry Moore and Barbaba Hepworth dominate the sculpture gardens surrounding the two grand 19th-century buildings that house this collection. Dada and Surrealist art rules the permanent collection at Modern Two, while Modern One hosts changing exhibitions by titans of modern and contemporary art.

TOP 4 SCOTTISH ARTISTS

Henry Raeburn (1756-1823)
Royal portraitist knighted by George IV.

Samuel Peploe (1871-1935)
A leading light of the post-Impressionist "Scottish Colourists".

Anne Redpath (1895-1965)
Star of the acclaimed "Edinburgh School".

Eduardo Paolozzi (1924-2005)
Pop art pioneer and creator of massive bronze sculptures.

△ Kelvingrove Museum and Art Gallery

The stars of the Glasgow Style and Scottish Colourist movements share hallowed spaces with European masters such as Salvador Dali, Rembrandt, Monet, Renoir and Van Gogh within the halls of this triumphal red sandstone palace. Encrusted with Spanish Baroque spires and turrets, it opened in 1901 and is a much-loved cultural landmark.

Listen in on a Pub Session

Visiting musos can sit in on sessions in folk music bars like the legendary Sandy Bell's *(25 Forrest Rd)* in Edinburgh and the Taybank Hotel *(Tay Terrace)* in Dunkeld. When the Shetland Fiddle Frenzy is in full swing there are jam sessions in just about every pub in Lerwick. Looking for something different? Most places have at least one bar serving up anything from pub rock and old-school rockabilly to acoustic sessions, indie-pop and even electronica.

←

Musicians playing at the world-renowned Sandy Bell's bar, Edinburgh

SCOTLAND FOR
MUSIC LOVERS

Scotland is a nation of music lovers. Plaintive pibrochs recall bygone battles and fiddles set feet tapping at events and venues all over Scotland, while newer rock and pop traditions are represented by guitar-based indie bands and DJs who perform to packed theatres, concert halls and giant stadiums.

TOP 4 LIVE MUSIC VENUES

King Tut's Wah-Wah Hut, Glasgow
w kingtuts.co.uk
Many legends launched their careers here, among them Oasis.

Barrowland Ballroom, Glasgow
w glasgow-barrowland.com
Glasgow's best venue for up-and-coming bands.

The Jazz Bar, Edinburgh
w thejazzbar.co.uk
Scotland's only dedicated jazz venue has up to five gigs daily.

Fat Sam's, Dundee
w fatsams.co.uk
This vast club hosts DJs, bands and theme nights.

Pipers and Pibrochs

For centuries bagpipes have been the traditional sound of the Highlands, and are now one of the most recognized emblems of Scotland. During the summer, Edinburgh's Royal Mile *(p70)* is awash with kilted pipers competing for tourists' attention. Some play lesser known pibrochs – slow, melancholy melodies.

→

The Inveraray & District Pipe Band parading through the town

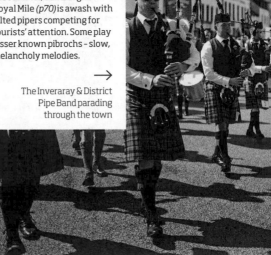

Head to a Traditional Music Festival

Scotland's traditional music festivals attract visitors from all over the world. Scottish folk music embraces not just Celtic sounds but global rhythms and harmonies too. Glasgow's Celtic Connections festival (p48), is the year's biggest folk event. In the Northern Isles, Fiddle Frenzy, held in July, is Shetland's celebration of the most enduring fiddling tradition in Scotland.

→

A folk band performing at the Celtic Connections festival, Glasgow

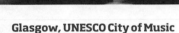

Glasgow, UNESCO City of Music

Glasgow was the UK's first UNESCO City of Music and its musical history runs deep; today it is home to a vibrant and eclectic music scene. Learn about the city's musical heritage on a fascinating walking tour of Glasgow's Music Mile (www.glasgowmusiccitytours.com).

←

The Barrowland Ballroom, one of Glasgow's famous music venues

Dance the Night Away at a Ceilidh

Traditional Highland dancers compete in front of judges at formal events, but there's nothing formal about a Scottish ceilidh. It's surprisingly easy to pick up the steps of communal dances like Strip the Willow, and locals are always happy to teach the basics. Ceilidhs are held in pub back rooms, village and church halls and in farm barns in summer. Look out for posters or ads in local newspapers.

→

Dancers learning the steps to a traditional Scottish reel

Edinburgh Food Festival

At the end of July, the Edinburgh Food Festival takes over George Square for a week-long celebration of all that's best in Scottish produce. With cooking demonstrations by some of the country's top chefs, it's the perfect place to discover the variety of traditional and contemporary flavours that Scotland has to offer.

→

Food vans serving up a plethora of treats at Edinburgh Food Festival

SCOTLAND FOR
FOODIES

Scotland's humble gastronomic beginnings are very much a thing of the past. Swapping deep-fried Mars Bars for Michelin stars, it is now a top foodie destination, home to a plethora of acclaimed fine-dining restaurants and a wealth of talented chefs working with great local ingredients.

Wild Dining

Pop-up wild-dining experiences offer visitors the chance to try expertly curated fine food and drink (such as wild-foraged mushrooms and "wild wine") in the most unexpected of settings, from walled castle gardens to serene woodlands. **Find out More:** *www.the madmarchhare.com*

←

Beautiful table setting at a woodland wild-dining experience

Fruit Picking in The Borders

A summer day spent picking gooseberries, raspberries, redcurrants, blackcurrants and sweet Scottish tayberries (a unique bramble and raspberry hybrid) is great fun. Border Berries, on Rutherford Farm near Kelso *(p106)*, is one of the few remaining berry farms that ripens its fruit in the open air. After fruit-picking, visitors can refuel at the farm café. Visit in July to late August, when the berries are ripe and juicy.

←

Picking fresh raspberries at a fruit farm in the Scottish Borders

TOP 5 **SCOTTISH DELICACIES**

Haggis
Scotland's most famous dish, consisting of spiced sheep's offal, oats and seasoning, is traditionally eaten at a Burn's supper with "neeps" (swedes), "tatties" (potatoes) and a dram of whisky.

Stovies
A mix of potatoes, onions and beef cooked in dripping (fat).

Cullen Skink
Creamy soup made from smoked haddock, milk and potato.

Arbroath Smokies
Haddock split open, salted and smoked.

Venison
The meat of wild red deer is dark, gamey and full-flavoured.

HIDDEN GEM
Underneath the Arches

East meets west at Glasgow's Argyle Street Arches, where street-food vendors serve all manner of fusion snacks to tantalize your tastebuds.

Scotland's Foodie Trails

Themed foodie trails showcase Scotland's unique flavours, from Arbroath's smoked haddock to the tangy, heather-infused real ales of Islay. Surprises include Scotland's Chocolate Trail, where chocolatier Iain Burnett creates delights like salted raspberry chocolate with Szechuan pepper salt in his artisan shop.

→

Arbroath smokies cooking on a fire pit on Auchmithie beach, Arbroath

Lowland Whiskies

Lowland whiskies tend to be smooth and their palate gentle. Until recently lowland distilleries were few and far between, but new ones are cropping up, many producing spirits that replicate the light, grassy style of the region. **What to try:** Glenkinchie (p105) is made near Edinburgh, while Auchentoshan is triple-distilled in Clydebank. Bladnoch, in the small town of Wigtown, is Scotland's most southerly distillery.

$\rightarrow$

Casks at the Glenkinchie distillery, a long-standing whisky producer

Did You Know?

Whisky stored in casks evaporates at a rate of around 2% per year. This is called the "angels' share".

SCOTTISH
SPIRIT

No special occasion is complete without a dram of the drink that is the pure essence of Scotland. Although global brands have industrialized whisky-making, their dominance is being challenged by artisan distilleries that produce exciting new malts using age-old skills. Meanwhile, new distillers are creating gins and other spirits such as rum, vodka and absinthe.

Speyside Malts

Many of Scotland's famous malt whiskies come from Speyside, where distillers claim there is a perfect balance of climate, terrain and water from Highland springs. **What to try:** Glenlivet and Glenfiddich, matured in Bourbon casks to give them notes of light vanilla and orchard fruits, or sherry-matured, Macallan, the "Rolls Royce of single malts", has notes of dried fruits and sweet spices. Don't miss a visit to the Macallan distillery as part of The Malt Whisky Trail® in Speyside (p149).

$\leftarrow$

Glenlivet whisky, one of Speyside's most famous malts, being poured into a glass

Highland Malts

Due to the Highlands' vast and diverse terrain, its single malts can vary considerably. Some are rich and full-bodied, others sweet and fruity. **What to try:** Glenmorangie, Scotland's biggest-selling single malt, is light and flowery taste, while Edradour makes a minty, creamy whisky.

$\longrightarrow$

A glass of single malt whisky, served "on the rocks" over ice

New Make Spirits and Gins

Gin has become Scotland's trendy tipple of choice alongside "new make" spirits that side-step the ageing process of traditional whisky production. **What to try:** Rascally Liquor at Annandale Distillery or go on a "gin jolley" at Pickering's in Edinburgh's Summerhall.

$\longleftarrow$

Edinburgh's hand-crafted Pickerings gin served with tonic and a slice of orange

HOW WHISKY IS MADE

Whisky is traditionally made by toasting freshly sprouting barley grains, then fermenting the malted barley to create a "wash" from which the raw alcohol that becomes whisky is distilled. To add complex flavours, it is usually aged for 5, 10, or 12 years or longer in oak casks that have held sherry, whisky or other wines. Malt whisky may be made only with spirit distilled from malted barley, while blends can combine different types of whisky.

↑ Laphroaig distillery produces a distinctively smoky single malt

Island Malts

The malt whiskies of the Hebrides are redolent of heather and peat smoke, while some claim to detect a hint of seaweed and iodine in some island malts. For many they are an acquired taste. **What to try:** Islay malts like Laphroaig, Lagavulin and Bowmore, Tobermory from Mull and Talisker from Skye.

Furry Friends

Get up close and personal with chimps, pelicans, creepy-crawlies and giant pandas at Edinburgh Zoo *(p89)*. Home to over 1,000 animals with a vast expanse of space to roam, it makes for a great day out for animal lovers of all ages. The zoo places strong emphasis on conservation, and many animals here are rare or endangered species. Fun activities and talks take place throughout the day to teach children about the animals.

→

Playful penguins at Edinburgh Zoo cooling off under the sprinklers

SCOTLAND FOR
FAMILIES

With an abundance of castles, country parks and exciting museums Scotland is a veritable playground for kids. Even in big cities, you're always close to parks and gardens where tots can romp around safely. Most attractions are family-friendly, leaving the weather as your only worry.

Adventures in Science

Young visitors to Glasgow Science Centre *(p124)* can take an incredible voyage inside the human body, walk among the planets or travel to the far reaches of outer space at exciting interactive exhibits like BodyWorks and the Planetarium.

 INSIDER TIP
Kids Go Free

ScotRail allow up to two children to travel free anywhere in Scotland with the purchase of an off-peak adult return. Tickets can be bought at ScotRail ticket offices and online, and also include free child entry to some of Scotland's top attractions.

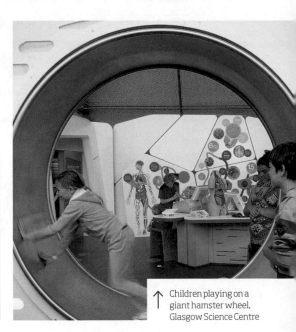

↑ Children playing on a giant hamster wheel, Glasgow Science Centre

Swing From The Treetops

Go Ape offers treetop-level high ropes and zip-wire adventures at outstanding locations throughout Scotland, including the grounds of Crathes Castle near Aberdeen, Queen Elizabeth Forest Park in the Trossachs *(p142)*, and Glentress Forest *(p106)*.

→

Child exploring the tree-top canopy on a zipwire at Go Ape

Hit The Slopes

Tobogganing, snowboarding, skiing and ice climbing are among the adrenaline activities on offer at this year-round indoor winter sports centre just 10 minutes from central Glasgow. There is also a soft play area for little ones who aren't quite ready to hit the slopes.

←

Youngsters learning how to snowboard at Snowfactor

TOP 4 RAINY DAY ACTIVITIES IN EDINBURGH

Camera Obscura and World of Illusions
Mind-boggling fun for all the family.

Scottish Storytelling Centre
Storytelling events encourage participation and creativity.

Museum of Childhood
Kids are amazed by this museum's collection of primitive playthings.

Our Dynamic Earth
An electrifying exhibition about our fascinating planet.

Get Lost in Traquair Maze

In the grounds of a fabulous historic mansion, this miniature labyrinth of lovingly tended Leylandi Cyprus trees is the longest maze of its kind in Scotland and is a guaranteed child-pleaser.

↑ Visitors entering the labyrinthine Traquair Maze, the largest hedged-maze in Scotland

Sand in the City

Scotland's biggest cities are never far from the coast, and each has, within a manageable distance from the city centre, their own seaside resort. Once teeming with holidaymakers, these city beaches now offer a quiet escape for both locals and visitors alike. Stroll along the sand, eat fish and chips and ice cream, paddle in the shallows or, if you're feeling brave, swim further out. Portobello Beach offers a breath of fresh sea air only 8 km (5 miles) from central Edinburgh, and it hosts a summer sandcastle competition and sand sculpture festival. Gullane, 35 km (22 miles) from the city, offers long breezy walks on a vast stretch of sand. On the west coast, Largs has been a great escape for Glaswegians since the 19th century.

→

People walking their dogs on the sandy bay at Portobello on a winter afternoon

SCOTLAND FOR
BEACHGOERS

Scottish holiday spots and seaside resorts fell from favour in the 1960s, when affordable air travel lured Scots to the Mediterranean. But seaside thrills now attract sporty visitors back to beaches in towns and cities and even further afield to the white sands and windy bays of the west coast.

Surf's Up

The Atlantic rollers that sweep Tiree's shores make this tiny Hebridean island a surfers' mecca. Year-round Atlantic swell and the sheer variety of surf on offer – from those elusive barrel waves to gentler whitewater beach breaks – make this an ideal destination for both seasoned surfers and beginners. What's more, the island claims more hours of sunshine than anywhere else in Britain, and with waters warmed by the Atlantic Gulf Stream, you may well forget you're in Scotland.

←

Surfer catching a wave on the windy island of Tiree, a surfing hotspot on the west coast

Arrive in Style

In the Outer Hebrides, the island of Barra's impressive Traigh Mhor (big beach) doubles as the island's airport, with tiny planes from the mainland scheduled to arrive at low tide so they can land on its flat sandy bay. For even more spectacular strands you must cross the causeway that links Barra to Vatersay. Its crescents of white sand may be the most beautiful of all Scotland's beaches.

← Plane landing on Traigh Mhor, Barra

TOP 5 **SEASIDE EATERIES**

The Espy, Portobello
Aussie gastropub right on the seafront. Their homemade ginger beer packs a punch.

Cromar's Classic Fish and Chips, St Andrews
Twice acclaimed as Scotland's finest chippie, and serving up a quality fish supper since 2013.

The Carron Fish Bar, Stonehaven
Birthplace of the notorious deep-fried Mars Bar, a uniquely Scottish delicacy.

The Lobster Shack, North Berwick
This seasonal beach hut serves is famed for its fresh locally caught lobster (p103).

Nardini's, Largs
This classic ice-cream parlour has been an Art Deco landmark on Largs esplanade for more than 100 years.

↑ Beautiful and remote Seilebost Beach on South Harris

Miles of Isles

The thousands of beaches scattered around Scotland's 10,000-mile (16,500-km) coastline range from tiny, hidden coves to endless white sandy bays and turquoise lagoons that, on a sunny day, can look more like the Caribbean than Scotland. Morar, north of Fort William, is famed for its chain of pink and silver beaches, while Hebridean beauties like Seilebost on Harris astound with stunning aquamarine colour palettes and dazzling white sands.

◁ Trainspotting (1996)

Edinburgh city council was so shocked by Irvine Welsh's gritty, realistic and somewhat gruesome tragi-comedy of Edinburgh low-life that it refused permission to shoot the movie in Leith, where the original novel was set. It was filmed instead in the more film business-friendly (and less shockable) Glasgow.

▷ James Bond's Scottish Roots

It will come as no surprise to true 007 fans that Britain's most suave secret agent has Scottish roots, with his native homeland featuring heavily in the Bond movie franchise. Drive through Glencoe's stunning mountain pass to James Bond's family home as depicted in *Skyfall* (2012), or visit Eilean Donan Castle, which starred as the Scottish headquarters of MI6 in *The World is Not Enough* (2012).

SCOTLAND
ON SCREEN

From gritty urban realism to fantastic sagas of dungeons and dragons, Scotland's spectacular landscapes, picturesque castles and quaint villages have inspired directors and producers the world over. Take a cinematic journey round Scotland to see iconic movie and television backdrops for yourself.

◁ Outlander (2014)

The much-loved time-travel series *Outlander* was filmed against some of the most evocative historic buildings and landscapes in Scotland. Castle Leod, near Strathpeffer, serves as Castle Leoch, a key setting for the series. Other locations include Aberdour and Falkland in Fife (which doubled as 18th-century Inverness), Blackness Castle, Kinloch Rannoch, the Cairngorms and the Highland Folk Museum at Kingussie.

◁ Harry Potter and the Hogwarts Express

The multi-arched Glenfinnan Viaduct railway bridge features in the eight Harry Potter movies, carrying the Hogwarts Express on its way to the now legendary school of witchcraft and wizardry. In summer, you can ride the Jacobite Express steam train, which doubled as the Hogwarts Express in the films, on its way across the viaduct from Fort William to Mallaig. Standard trains also cross it daily all year round.

◁ Braveheart (1995)

With an Australian-American starring as Scots hero William Wallace, *Braveheart* was shot almost entirely outside Scotland. This is because the scenes of Wallace's great battles against the English are now engulfed in the urban sprawls of Stirling and Falkirk. However, a mock-medieval village was built in Glen Nevis for early scenes, some of which were shot against the spectacular backdrop of Glencoe, the Mamore hills and Loch Leven.

TOP 5 SCOTTISH MOVIE STARS

Sean Connery
The original and best James Bond.

Ewan McGregor
McGregor was young Obi-Wan Kenobi in the *Star Wars* prequels.

Robbie Coltrane
Best known as Hagrid in the *Harry Potter* movies.

Kelly MacDonald
MacDonald played Renton's girlfriend in *Trainspotting*.

James McAvoy
McAvoy starred in the *X-Men* chronicles.

△ Doune Castle, Perthshire

The majestic Doune Castle *(p148)*, on the fringes of the Trossachs, is a particular favourite among location scouts and has starred in *Monty Python and the Holy Grail* (1975), *Ivanhoe* (1952) and *The Bruce* (1996), plus TV drama *Outlander*. The castle also posed as Winterfell in the pilot episode of *Game of Thrones* (2011–present), but was dropped in favour of cheaper locations.

A YEAR IN
SCOTLAND

JANUARY

△ **New Year's Day** (1 Jan). Hardy bathers plunge into the North Sea at various locations.
Celtic Connections (last 2 weeks in Jan). Glasgow's famous festival of Celtic music.
Burns Night (25 Jan) This is celebrated all over Scotland. Dumfries hosts Big Burns Supper.

FEBRUARY

Glasgow Film Festival (mid-Feb–early Mar). See the best of local and international cinema at venues throughout the city.
△ **Six Nations Rugby Tournament** (Feb–Mar: varying Sat and Sun). One of the highlights of Scotland's sporting calendar.

MAY

△ **Beltane Fire Festival** (30 Apr/1 May). This spring festival features bonfires and a torchlight parade in Edinburgh.
Spirit of Speyside Whisky Festival (1st week in May). A celebration of Scotland's national drink.
Perth Festival of the Arts (3rd week in May). Perth Concert Hall and Perth Theatre stage opera, classical music, drama, dance and rock shows.

JUNE

St Magnus International Festival (last week in Jun). A lively celebration of music, drama, dance and literature in Kirkwall, Orkney.
△ **TRNSMT Festival** (last weekend in Jun and first weekend in Jul). Scottish rock and indie music is performed by top bands and emerging artists on Glasgow Green.

SEPTEMBER

△ **Braemar Gathering** (1st Sat in Sep). Celebrates Highland pageantry at Princess Royal and Duke of Fife Memorial Park, Braemar.
Wigtown Book Festival (last week in Sep). Held in Wigtown, Scotland's National Book Town, with readings by authors, signings and book launches.

OCTOBER

△ **The Enchanted Forest** (throughout Oct). A spectacular sound and light event set in Highland Perthshire's Faskally Wood.
Tiree Wave Classic (mid-Oct). Held on the island of Tiree, this is the longest running professional windsurfing event in the world.
Samhuinn Fire Festival (31 Oct) Edinburgh's Hallowe'en event has fire displays and acrobatics.

MARCH

Whyte & Mackay Glasgow International Comedy Festival *(2nd fortnight in Mar)*. Internationally renowned comedy festival.

△ **Aberdeen Jazz Festival** *(3rd week in Mar)*. A five-day festival featuring a range of musicians and performances at the city's top venues.

APRIL

△ **Edinburgh International Science Festival** *(1st fortnight in Apr)*. This two-week festival offers a diverse range of educational and innovative events and experiences for adults and children.

Highland Haggis Festival *(1st Sun in Apr)*. A celebration of Scottish produce and Highland culture, with a particular focus on the much-loved haggis, held in the Highland town of Spean Bridge.

JULY

Edinburgh International Film Festival *(2nd fortnight in Jul)*. Presents award-winning new releases, classic cinema, arthouse films, blockbusters and independent productions at venues throughout the city.

Edinburgh Jazz and Blues Festival and Glasgow Jazz Festival *(2nd week in Jul/3rd week in Jul)*. Live jazz, blues and soul performances held in Glasgow and Edinburgh.

△ **Glasgow Mela** *(3rd weekend in Jul)*. Celebrates multicultural Scotland with live music, dancing and exotic street food from around the world.

AUGUST

△ **Edinburgh International Festival and Edinburgh Festival Fringe** *(throughout Aug)*. Events take place at every venue in the city.

The Royal Edinburgh Military Tattoo *(throughout Aug)*. Held at Edinburgh Castle with military parades and fireworks every night during Edinburgh International Festival.

NOVEMBER

Saltire Festival *(30 Nov)*. Festival of music, culture, sport and heritage celebrates St Andrew's Day with a range of eclectic events at venues throughout East Lothian.

△ **Edinburgh's Christmas** *(mid-Nov–early Jan)*. Princes Street Gardens become home to an ice rink, a reindeer garden and a Christmas Market.

DECEMBER

△ **Edinburgh's Hogmanay** *(31 Dec)*. Celebrations around the Royal Mile and throughout Scotland well into the early hours.

Stonehaven Fireball Festival *(31 Dec)*. This ancient tradition sees 60 local fireball-swingers parade down the town's high street on the stroke of midnight.

A BRIEF
HISTORY

Scotland has been torn apart by religion and politics, coveted by a powerful neighbour, and wooed and punished for 400 years in the power struggles between England, France and Spain. The country has risen and fallen through the ages, but has always demonstrated an irrepressible spirit.

In the Beginning

Stone Age settlers arrived in Scotland in around 7000 BC. By 2000 BC their Neolithic descendants were erecting impressive megalithic stone structures like those at Callanish (p183), which were to become a focus for ritual activity during the Bronze Age, and stone villages like Skara Brae (p176). By around 800 BC they had learned to forge iron, evolving into what Tacitus called the Picts, the "painted people". Often regarded as savage warriors, recent studies suggest that the Picts were in fact a sophisticated people who could read, write and convey their culture and history through art.

1 Antique map of Scotland. ↑

2 Depiction of Pictish warriors circa 300 BC.

3 Ancient remains of Hadrian's Wall.

4 Painting of William the Conqueror.

Timeline of events

7000– 2000 BC
Mesolithic and Neolithic eras

82 AD
First Roman incursion into Caledonia

121
Roman withdrawal from Caledonia and construction of Hadrian's Wall

800 BC
Dawn of early Celtic Iron Age culture

563
Columba founds a monastery on the island of Iona and spreads Christianity

Romans and Caledonians

The Romans invaded Scotland in AD 82–84, but by AD 121, after several defeats at the hands of the Picts, they were forced to retreat to Hadrian's Wall, which marked the northwest frontier of the Roman Empire for nearly 300 years. The traditional view is that Hadrain's Wall was constructed to keep the Caledonians from raiding and pillaging the civilized Roman Empire; however, some historians believe its real purpose was much less noble: that it was designed to intimidate and extract taxes from tribes on both sides of the border. A later attempt to secure Rome's frontier in the form of the Antonine Wall, between the Clyde and Forth, failed and the Romans abandoned Britain in AD 410.

New Invaders

In 1072 William the Conqueror led the first Norman incursion into Scotland, with little success. The border between Scotland and England was already under dispute, and centuries of conflict were still to follow. At this time, Scotland was made up of a number of loosely connected regions lead by Scottish kings and clan chiefs who gave lands to Anglo-Norman barons in return for serving in Scotland's wars.

BIRTH OF A NATION

The Scottish nation emerged from centuries of conflict and warfare between Picts, Scots, Britons, Angles, Norsemen and incomers from Ireland and even the Roman Empire, who could not conquer the land they called "Caledonia". In 843 AD the Scots and Pictish realms merged to form the Kingdom of Alba, and by the 11th century this included most of what we know today as Scotland.

794
The first Vikings cross the treacherous North Sea to raid, trade and eventually settle in Scotland

843
Union of Scots and Picts creates the Kingdom of Alba

1040
Macbeth rules over the Kingdom of Alba until 1057

1154
Loss of "southern countries" to England

1124
King David I imposes a Norman feudal system. A clan system prevails in the Highlands

1

The Wars of Independence

After the death of Alexander III in 1286, Edward I of England installed a puppet king by the name of John Balliol. When the Scots rebelled, King Edward's army invaded. In pursuit of independence from the English crown, rebels rallied behind a commoner, William Wallace, who lead them in their fight for independence as Guardian of the Kingdom of Scotland. After he was captured and executed, their support shifted to the now famed warrior, Robert the Bruce. Scion of a Norman-Scots dynasty, and with a claim to the throne, Bruce forged nobles, commoners and clansmen into an army that won a decisive victory at the Battle of Bannockburn in 1314, successfully resetablishing Scotland's status as an independent country.

The Unlucky Stuarts

The Stuart dynasty began with Robert the Steward, who became king in 1371. They were an ill-fated line: James I and James III were assassinated, James II was blown up by one of his own cannons, James IV died in battle, and James V died after another defeat at English hands. His baby daughter became Mary Queen of Scots and was executed on the orders of

1 Robert the Bruce rallying his troops at the Battle of Bannockburn.

2 Mary, Queen of Scots.

3 Battle of Dunbar.

4 Wedding portrait of William of Orange and Mary II.

Did You Know?

The name Steward was changed to Stuart to make it easier for the French to pronounce.

Timeline of events

1320
The Declaration of Arbroath affirms Scotland's status as an independent country

1326
Meeting of the first Scottish Parliament

1287
Edward I of England and his troops are defeated by Scots at the Battle of Stirling Bridge

1314
Scots defeat Edward II of England at the Battle of Bannockburn

1513
10,000 Scots including James IV die at the Battle of Flodden

2

3

4

Elizabeth I of England, the last monarch in the Tudor dynasty. Mary's son, James VI, was luckier, inheriting Elizabeth's throne in 1603, uniting the crowns and reigning until 1625 as James VI of Scotland and James I of England.

The Reformation in Scotland

The Reformation arrived during Mary, Queen of Scots' reign, creating a deep and long-lasting religious divide during which Catholicism was purged, albeit with revivals and impregnable strongholds in the Highlands and islands. Scotland's most vociferous leader of the Reformation was the preacher John Knox (p73), who fearlessly denounced Mary, Queen of Scots.

Open war between Scottish Presbyterians and King Charles I merged with England's Civil War, when Scots fought for both sides. Charles II, crowned at Scone after his father was deposed and beheaded in 1649, was driven into exile. Scotland became part of Cromwell's Commonwealth until Charles's restoration in 1660. Protestant Scots Covenanters resisted the Catholic-leaning Charles and his successor, James II, who was ousted in 1688 by the anti-Catholic Whig faction in favour of his daughter Mary II and her Dutch husband, Prince William of Orange.

THE JACOBITES

The first Jacobites were mainly Catholic Highlanders who supported James VII of Scotland (James II of England), who was deposed in 1688. Their desire to restore the Catholic throne led to uprisings in 1715 and 1745. Their failure led to the demise of the clan system and the suppression of Highland culture for more than a century.

1542
Mary, Queen of Scots becomes Queen of Scotland when she is just six days old

1559
John Knox leads the Reformation

1603
James II of Scotland succeeds Elizabeth I to become King of both Scotland and England in the Union of the Crowns

1641
Cromwellian occupation of Scotland

1692
Clan Campbell murder 38 MacDonalds on the King's orders in the Glencoe Massacre

1

2

The Union with England

James VI had reigned for 36 years when he became heir to the English throne, but it was bankruptcy that finally forced Scotland into union with England in 1707. With this Act of Union came the dissolution of the Scottish Parliament. Eight years later the last Stuart monarch, Queen Anne, was succeeded by her cousin George, Duke of Hanover. Defeat at Culloden after Jacobite risings in 1715 and 1745 finally extinguished support for the exiled Stuarts. It was followed by brutal pacification of the Highlands. Peace, however, fostered a new mercantile economy. Trade with England's colonies enriched merchants whose capital eventually financed a steam-powered industrial revolution. Glasgow became a great manufacturing city, Edinburgh an intellectual powerhouse and Dundee a thriving centre of the textile industry.

The Road to Devolution

Scotland's newborn proletariat became a fertile recruiting ground for socialism and trade unionism. Glasgow's industrial heartland was nicknamed "Red Clydeside". Working-class areas like Fife and Dundee were also strongly left-wing. Industry

BONNIE PRINCE CHARLIE (1720-88)

The last of the Stuart claimants to the Crown, Bonnie Prince Charlie marched his army as far as Derby, only to be defeated at Culloden. Disguised as the loyal maidservant of a woman called Flora MacDonald, he fled to Skye and sailed back to France in 1746. He later died in Rome. Flora was buried in 1790 on Skye, wrapped in a bedsheet of the "bonnie" (hand-some) prince.

Timeline of events

1707
Act of Union creates United Kingdom of Great Britain

1745
Bonnie Prince Charlie leads the second Jacobite Rebellion

1848
Queen Victoria's first visit to Balmoral

1914
Glasgow's shipyards are of vital importance to the war effort

1929
Worldwide depression leads to huge unemployment and deprivation

1943
German air raids during WWII result in the deaths of more than 1,000 Scots between Glasgow and Clydebank

suffered as the British Empire declined after World War II but discovery of North Sea oil in the mid-1970s boosted the economy. It was also a gift to the Scottish National Party, which adopted the slogan "It's Scotland's Oil". The majority of Scots voted in favour of the creation of a Scottish parliament in the Scottish devolution referendum in 1977.

Scotland Today

Scotland in the 21st century is a cosmopolitan society. Many Scots are descendants of 19th-century immigrants from Ireland and Italy. Others originate from Commonwealth countries, notably Pakistan, Bangladesh and India, or from EU countries. There are also substantial Turkish and Chinese communities.

The SNP has dominated politics since devolution, but their battle for independence was lost by a thin margin in the 2014 referendum. In the 2016 Brexit referendum, Scots voted to stay in the EU. England's vote to leave, however, means Scotland, as part of the UK, must follow against its will, which in turn has reignited calls for a second vote on independence. Whether this vibrant nation chooses to go its own way or stay within the UK is yet to be seen.

1 Jacobite Express on Glenfinnan Viaduct.

2 North Sea Oil Rig.

3 Campaigners during "Indyref", 2014.

4 Modern exterior of the Scottish Parliament in Edinburgh.

Did You Know?

The Scottish Parliament reconvened in Edinburgh almost 300 years after it was dissolved by the Act of Union in 1707.

1975
Exploitation of the newly discovered North Sea oilfields begins

1996
The Stone of Destiny is returned to Edinburgh Castle

2014
Nicola Sturgeon becomes the first female First Minister of Scotland

1999
Scottish Parliament reinstated after 292 years

2016
62% of Scots vote for Britain to remain in the EU referendum

2018
A fire destroys Glasgow School of Art and the V&A Dundee opens

EXPERIENCE

Cooper moving heavy whisky casks

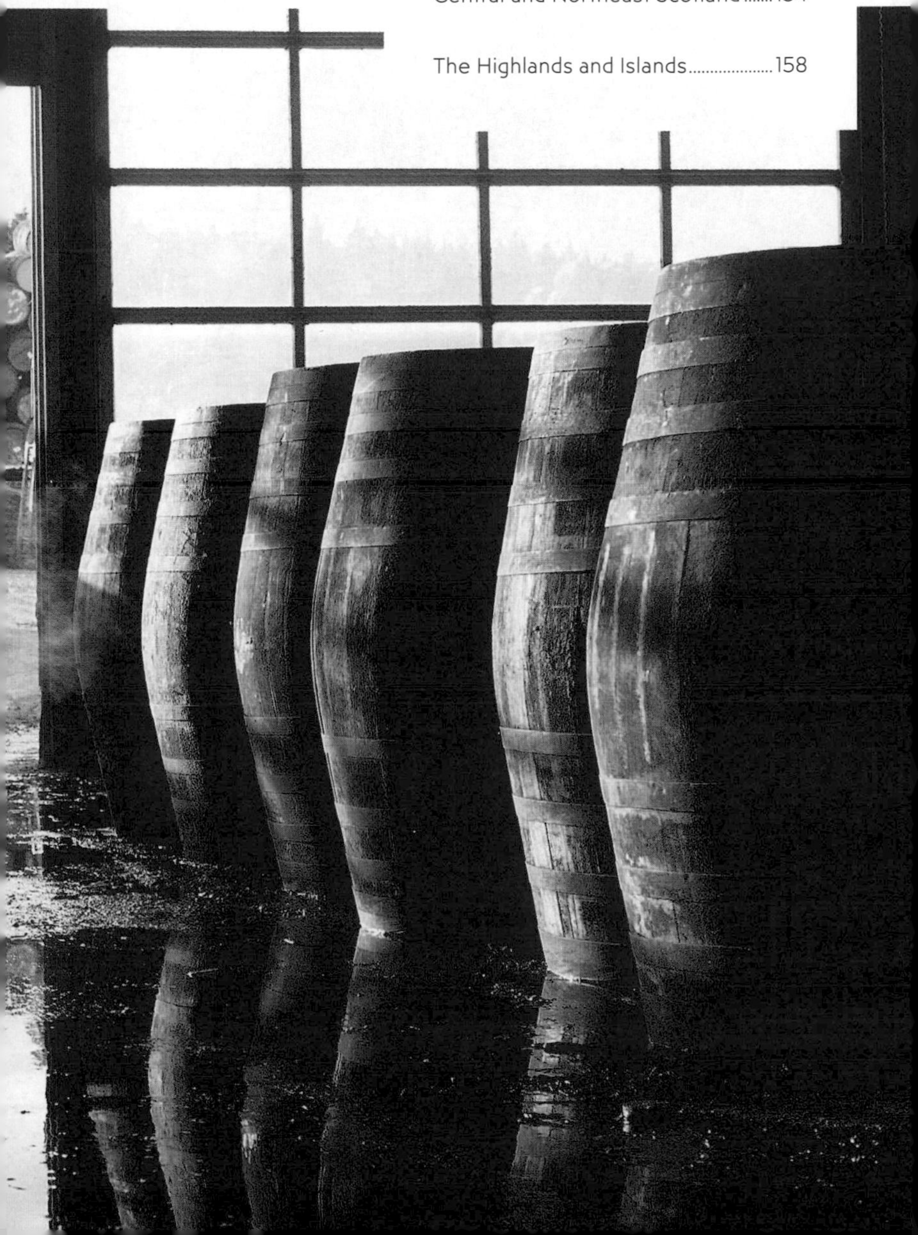

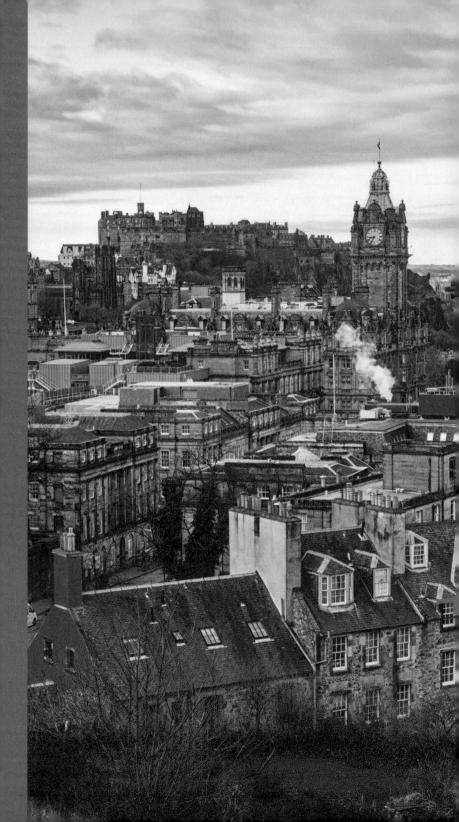

EDINBURGH

Edinburgh's uniquely intact medieval heritage makes it one of the world's most fascinating cities. The mighty Edinburgh Castle dominates the city from Castle Rock, a clifftop crag which has been occupied since the Bronze Age thanks to its strategic position overlooking the Firth of Forth. Below it the Royal Mile slopes through the Old Town to the Palace of Holyroodhouse, home of monarchs since the 15th century. However, it was not until the reign of James IV (1488–1513) that the city of Edinburgh gained the status of Scotland's capital in 1498.

Over the years, overcrowding made Edinburgh's Old Town a dirty and difficult place to live, and sickness and disease was rife. In 1645, the city was ravaged by the bubonic plague, killing almost half the population. In an attempt to prevent further infection, residents of vaults and closes were bricked into their homes and left to die, and new buildings were erected above this forgotten city. The construction of a Georgian New Town to the north in the late 1700s gave the wealthy an escape route, and the area is still viewed today as a world-class example of Georgian urban architecture, with its elegant façades and broad streets.

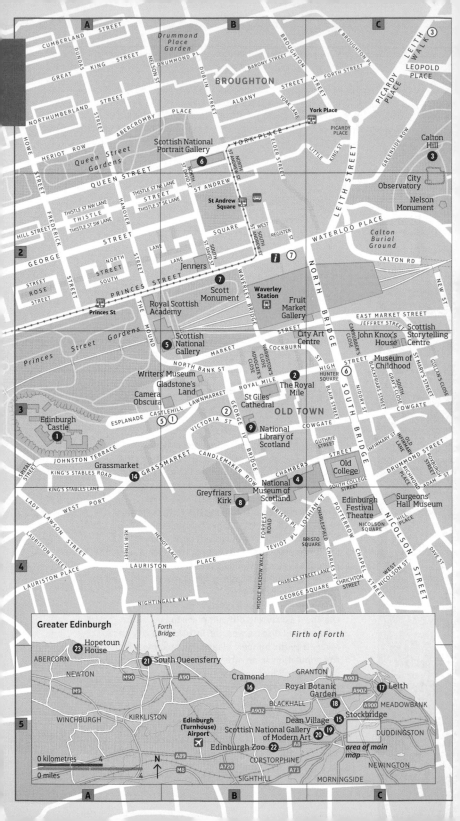

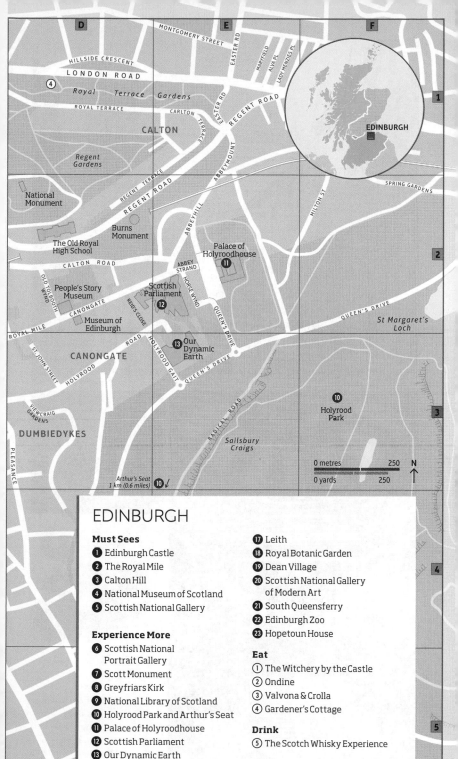

EDINBURGH

Must Sees

1. Edinburgh Castle
2. The Royal Mile
3. Calton Hill
4. National Museum of Scotland
5. Scottish National Gallery

Experience More

6. Scottish National Portrait Gallery
7. Scott Monument
8. Greyfriars Kirk
9. National Library of Scotland
10. Holyrood Park and Arthur's Seat
11. Palace of Holyroodhouse
12. Scottish Parliament
13. Our Dynamic Earth
14. Grassmarket
15. Stockbridge
16. Cramond
17. Leith
18. Royal Botanic Garden
19. Dean Village
20. Scottish National Gallery of Modern Art
21. South Queensferry
22. Edinburgh Zoo
23. Hopetoun House

Eat

1. The Witchery by the Castle
2. Ondine
3. Valvona & Crolla
4. Gardener's Cottage

Drink

5. The Scotch Whisky Experience

Stay

6. The Inn on the Mile
7. The Balmoral

1 St Stephen St, Stockbridge.

2 Intricate interior of
The Dome, George Street.

3 Visitors admire tapestry,
National Museum of Scotland.

4 Fine dining at 21212.

Edinburgh is marvellously compact, so in two leisurely days you can experience highlights such as the Royal Mile and Edinburgh Castle, then venture beyond the city centre to take in great galleries and enjoy the city's fresh air and greenery.

2 DAYS
in Edinburgh

Day 1

Morning Start exploring at Edinburgh Castle (*p68*), the city's central landmark. The Stone of Destiny and Scotland's crown jewels are displayed in the 15th-century palace. From the Argyle Battery there's a fine view of the city. A block south of the Royal Mile (*p70*), the treasures of the National Museum of Scotland (*p76*) include Highland silver, Iron Age jewellery, Pictish symbol stones, a Viking grave, a Roman treasure hoard and a huge Tyrannosaurus rex skeleton. The White Horse Oyster Bar, where the oldest inn on the Royal Mile stood, is a great spot for a lunch break.

Afternoon At the bottom of the Royal Mile, take a tour of the Palace of Holyroodhouse (*p82*) to discover royal treasures and portraits in the Throne Room, State Apartments and Queen's Gallery. A five-minute bus ride (hop off at St Andrew's House) takes you to Calton Hill (*p74*), where the view from Nelson Monument encompasses the Firth of Forth and Fife across the water.

Evening Enjoy a sunset view and admire the frivolous National Monument before descending the steps to Royal Terrace, where you can dine at Paul Kitchin's award-winning restaurant 21212. After dinner, head to The Stand comedy club on York Place for some late-night laughs. Choose your seats wisely – those in the front row are sure to be picked on.

Day 2

Morning St Giles' Cathedral (*p72*) is an unmistakable landmark from which to start a second day of discovery in Scotland's fine capital. It's downhill all the way to the Scottish National Gallery (*p78*), where keynotes include Landseer's *Monarch of the Glen* and Raeburn's *Reverend Robert Walker Skating on Duddingston Loch*. Hop on the Gallery Bus to the Scottish National Gallery of Modern Art (*p88*) where bronze sculptures adorn the grounds. Follow the Water of Leith Walkway to Stockbridge (*p86*), which offers up a plethora of pubs and eateries.

Afternoon It's a short walk to the Royal Botanic Garden (*p88*), a vast oasis of lawns, ponds, rhododendron walks and rock gardens. The palatial Victorian Palm Houses offer a refuge when weather is less than perfect.

Evening St Andrew Square, in the heart of the New Town, is home to Dishoom, which serves up superb, authentic Parsi Indian dishes alongside artisan Scottish ales. Its basement bar, the Permit Room, has a great cocktail list and stays open until late. Alternatively, take a stroll along George Street to The Dome. A favourite among Edinburgh's high-flyers, its Graeco-Roman façade and lavish interior make it a magnificent setting for after-dinner drinks. The street is lined by clubs and bars, should you wish to continue your evening into the wee hours.

Edinburgh Jazz and Blues Festival

See some of the hottest names in jazz, blues and funk in seriously intimate venues. Free events include open-air Mardi Gras performances in the Grassmarket *(p86)* and the spectacular Carnival in Princes Street Gardens.
When to go: *First two weeks in July*

Jazz and Blues musicians performing for Mardi Gras in the Grassmarket

EDINBURGH'S
SUMMER
FESTIVALS

First held in 1947, the Edinburgh International Festival has grown into the world's greatest celebration of art and culture. There really is something for everyone, with spin-off events of every genre including theatre, music, dance, cinema, comedy and street art taking place from June to September.

FREE FESTIVAL EXPERIENCES

There are more than 9,000 free shows held each year, all run by the Free Fringe, and the Royal Mile is packed with entertainers and musicians all summer long; they don't charge, but they do hope for a tip. Or why not head up Calton Hill *(p74)* and watch the dazzling pyrotechnics of the Festival's grand finale for free - and without being deafened.

Edinburgh International Festival

Combining performances by opera companies, ballet and contemporary dance ensembles, theatre groups and world premieres by the latest creative talents, this summer-long festival concludes with one of the world's biggest pyrotechnic displays, when more than 400,000 fireworks explode above Edinburgh Castle *(p68)*, accompanied by a live symphony orchestra.
When to go: *August*

→ Spectacular fireworks display above Edinburgh Castle

Edinburgh Festival Fringe

The Fringe celebrates both amateur and world-famous performers offering comedy, musicals, drama, dance and mind-bending performance art. The Pleasance Courtyard is a major hub of the Festival Fringe, with almost 30 venues hosting up to 250 shows each summer.

When to go: *August*

INSIDER TIP
Book Ahead!

Tickets for Edinburgh International Festival events go on sale at the beginning of the last week in March and they tend to sell out quickly. Buy online at eif.co.uk or call (0131) 473 2000.

↑ Street entertainer performing for a crowd of spectators on Edinburgh's Royal Mile

Edinburgh International Film Festival

Enjoy screenings of classic films, arthouse productions, world premieres and special events at artsy venues around the city. With stars and directors taking part, it's a great opportunity for celeb-spotting.

When to go: *Last two weeks in June*

←

Actor and director Stanley Tucci arrives at The Filmhouse for an EIFF event

Edinburgh Art Festival

The focus is on adventurous and challenging new work at this veritable feast for the eyes. Exhibitions take place at established galleries and at less conventional pop-ups in unexpected places, and most are free to visit.

When to go: *August*

→

Untitled, 2016, by Jonathan Owen at Edinburgh Art Festival

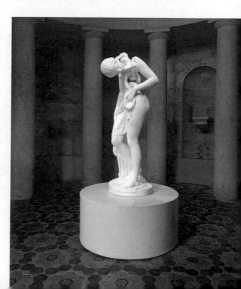

Royal Observatory of Edinburgh

A stargazer's haven, this observatory atop Edinburgh's Blackford Hill on the south side of the city hosts special events and public astronomy evenings throughout the year. These are always very popular so it is wise to book well in advance. Learn about the Royal Observatory of Edinburgh's research as you peer through a telescope at wonders of the night sky. You can also take a tour of the building and its Victorian telescopic dome.

Find out more: *www.roe.ac.uk*

→

Royal Observatory of Edinburgh overlooking the city from Blackford Hill

EDINBURGH'S
QUIET ESCAPES

Many visitors to Scotland's capital stay just long enough to visit Edinburgh Castle and stroll down the bustling Royal Mile, but there is so much more awaiting those who venture away from the city's well-trodden tourist trail.

Dalkeith Country Park

Only 5 miles (8 km) from the city centre, this estate has a lot to offer both adults and kids, including walking and cycling trails, picnic and play areas, a shop and café, plus special events, activities and more. Should you wish to extend your visit, there is also on-site accommodation.
Find out more: *www. dalkeithcountrypark.co.uk*

→

Tranquil forest trails in bloom, Dalkeith Country Park

Surgeons' Hall Museum

Not for the faint-hearted, but certainly appealing to the morbidly curious, this off-piste Edinburgh museum opened to the public in 1832. Originally intended as a teaching facility for medical students, the museum is home to one of the oldest and largest pathology collections in the United Kingdom. It contains an extensive collection of preserved organic tissue and bone, historic scientific instruments and an array of anatomic and medical artifacts, plus state-of-the-art interactive features.

Find out more: *www.museum.rcsed.ac.uk*

← Gory exhibits at Surgeons' Hall Museum

INSIDER TIP
Dunbar's Close

Numerous closes and secret alleyways veer off the main drag from the busy Royal Mile. Wander down Dunbar's Close and you will find a surprisingly tranquil 17th-century parterre garden sheltered beneath a leafy canopy. Entry to the garden is free of charge.

Craigmillar Castle

Craigmillar is Edinburgh's forgotten castle, but it's well worth making the short trip from the city centre to soak up some hidden history at this little-visited ruin. You're likely to be one of only a few people there, so you will have ample opportunity to pose for pictures beneath its massive 15th-century stone walls.

Find out more: *www.historicenvironment.scot*

→ Sunset at Craigmillar Castle, Edinburgh's forgotten fortress

❶ 🖉 🖍 🖳 🎒

EDINBURGH CASTLE

📍A3 🏠Castlehill 🕐9:30am-6pm daily (Oct-Mar: to 5pm); last admission: 45 mins before closing 🌐edinburghcastle.scot

Dominating the city's skyline since the 12th century, Edinburgh Castle is a national icon and is, deservedly, Scotland's most popular visitor attraction.

Standing upon the basalt core of an extinct volcano, Edinburgh Castle is an assemblage of buildings dating from the 12th to the 20th century, reflecting its changing role as fortress, royal palace, military garrison and state prison. Though there is evidence of Bronze Age occupation of the site, the original fortress was built by the 6th-century Northumbrian king, Edwin, from whom the city takes its name. The castle was a favourite royal residence until the Union of the Crowns (p53) in 1603, after which the king resided in England. After the Union of Parliaments in 1707, the Scottish regalia were walled up in the Palace for over a hundred years. The Palace is now the zealous possessor of the so-called Stone of Destiny, a relic of ancient Scottish kings which was seized by the English and not returned to Scotland until 1996.

> 💬 INSIDER TIP
> **Festival Fireworks**
>
> Every night during the Edinburgh Festival, the Castle hosts a fireworks display to mark the end of the Military Tattoo (p162). Climb to the top of Calton Hill (p74) to watch this pyrotechnic spectacle for free.

THE ONE O'CLOCK GUN

Resounding across the city at 1pm every day, Edinburgh's One O'Clock Gun has been startling visitors since 1861. It was originally intended to help ships moored in the Firth of Forth to synchronize their chronometers to Greenwich Mean Time, essential for accurate navigation, but it has now become a time-honoured tradition. The first guns were muzzle-loading cannons, but since 2001 a more modern 105mm artillery piece has served.

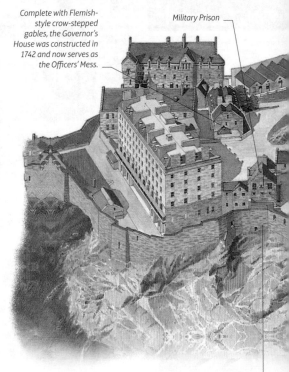

Complete with Flemish-style crow-stepped gables, the Governor's House was constructed in 1742 and now serves as the Officers' Mess.

Military Prison

↑ Illustration of Edinburgh Castle, an ancient fortress on top of Castle Rock

During the 18th and 19th centuries, the castle's prison vaults were used to hold French prisoners of war.

Edinburgh Castle dominates the city's skyline *(above)*; castle entrance gate *(inset)*. ↑

St Margaret's Chapel is the oldest surviving structure from the medieval castle. Built by David I (1124–1153) in honour of his sanctified mother, it is still used today.

Mons Meg, a giant six-tonne seige gun. Built in 1449, it was cutting-edge technology in the Middle Ages.

Argyle Battery offers a panoramic view north over Princes Street to the city's New Town, the Firth of Forth and Fife.

Mary Queen of Scots gave birth to James VI in this 15th-century Royal Palace, where the Stone of Destiny and Crown Jewels are now displayed.

Entrance

The Esplanade is the location of the Military Tattoo.

With its restored open-timber roof, the Great Hall dates from the 15th century and was the meeting place of the Scottish Parliament until 1639.

The Half Moon Battery was built in the 1570s as a platform for the artillery defending the eastern wing of the castle.

❷

THE ROYAL MILE

📍 B3 🏛 Castlehill to Canongate

Thronged with street entertainers and lined with shops, pubs and restaurants, the lively Royal Mile is for many the first taste of Edinburgh, and for good reason: most of the city's top attractions are dotted along this ancient thoroughfare.

Redolent of the city's history, the Royal Mile is a stretch of four ancient streets (from Castlehill to Canongate) which formed the main thoroughfare of medieval Edinburgh, linking the ancient castle to the Palace of Holyroodhouse (p82). Confined by the city wall, the "Old Town" grew upwards, with some tenements, or "lands", as they were known, rising 20 storeys above the dozens of dark, cobbled wynds and closes below.

↑ Visitors marveling at the 18th-century pinhole camera at Camera Obscura

Timeline

1124
▲ St Giles' Cathedral founded either by King Alexander I or by King David I

1688
Holyrood Abbey ransacked by anti-Jacobite protesters

1691
Canongate Kirk built

1745
▽ Bonnie Prince Charlie proclaims his exiled father king at the Mercat Cross

1856
▲ Burgh of Canongate, founded 1143, becomes part of the City of Edinburgh

2004
New Scottish Parliament opens at Holyrood

← Looking up Castlehill towards Edinburgh Castle at the top of the Royal Mile

life in the city centre as it happens. A marvel at the time, this feat of Victorian craftsmanship still astonishes visitors accustomed to 21st-century mobile devices, and it remains one of Edinburgh's most popular attractions.

②
Writers' Museum

🏠 Lady Stair's Close
🕐 10am-5pm daily
🌐 edinburghmuseums.org.uk

Celebrated Scottish authors Robert Burns (p112), Sir Walter Scott (p100) and Robert Louis Stevenson are the stars of this museum, which is crammed with intriguing memorabilia, including a cast of Burns's skull, journals, manuscripts and belongings such as Stevenson's riding boots. It occupies Lady Stair's House, a gracious 17th century building, constructed in 1622 on Makar's Court, where flagstones commemorate many more national treasures who lived by their pen.

EAT & DRINK

The Witchery by the Castle
Excels at dishes with a rural flavour, like pheasant and venison terrine. Ask for a seat in the Secret Garden.

🏠 352 Castlehill
🌐 thewitchery.com
£££

Ondine
Sleek and sophisticated seafood dishes, plus an oyster happy hour 5:30-6.30pm Mon-Sat.

🏠 2 George IV Bridge
🌐 ondinerestaurant.co.uk
£££

The Scotch Whisky Experience
Sample classic whiskies and new age malts at this centre for Scotland's national drink.

🏠 354 Castlehill
🌐 scotchwhiskyexperience.co.uk

Camera Obscura

🏠 Castlehill 🕐 Times vary, check website; 🌐 camera-obscura.co.uk

The lower floors of this building date from the early 17th century and were once the home of the Laird of Cockpen. In 1852, Maria Short added the upper floor, the viewing terrace and the Camera Obscura – a large pinhole camera that pictures

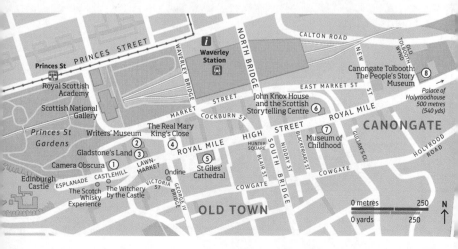

③

Gladstone's Land

⌂ 477B Lawnmarket
🕐 Apr-Oct: 10am-5pm daily
(Jul & Aug: to 6:30pm)
🌐 nts.org.uk

This restored 17th-century merchant's house provides a window on life in a typical Old Town house before overcrowding drove the rich inhabitants to the Georgian New Town. "Lands" were tall, narrow buildings on small plots of land. The six-storey Gladstone's Land was named after Thomas Gledstanes, the merchant who built it in 1617.

④

The Real Mary King's Close

⌂ 2 Warriston's Close
🕐 10am-9pm daily
🌐 therealmarykingsclose.com

Until the 18th century most residents of Edinburgh lived along and beneath the Royal Mile and the Cowgate. The old abandoned cellars and basements, which lacked any proper water supply, daylight or ventilation, were once centres of domestic life and industry. Under these conditions, cholera, typhus and smallpox were common. Mary King's Close, under the City Chambers, is one of the most famous of these areas – its inhabitants were all killed by the plague in around 1645. In 2003 many of these closes were opened up for the first time and visits are now possible through The Real Mary King's Close, a fascinating time capsule where costumed guides lead visitors in a walk back in time to learn about the Old Town's gruesome past.

⑤

St Giles' Cathedral

Properly known as the High Kirk (church) of Edinburgh, St Giles' is popularly known as a cathedral. Though it was twice

66

Alleys and closes lead off the Royal Mile, some to hidden courtyards.

the seat of a bishop in the 17th century, it was from here that John Knox directed the Scottish Reformation (p53), with its emphasis on individual worship freed from the authority of bishops. A tablet marks the place where Jenny Geddes, a local market stall-holder, scored a victory for the Covenanters in 1637 by hurling her stool at a preacher as he read from an English prayer book.

St Giles' Gothic exterior has a 15th-century tower, the only part to escape heavy renovation in the 1800s. Inside, the beautiful Thistle Chapel with its rib-vaulted ceiling and carved heraldic canopies, honours the knights

↓ Statue of philosopher David Hume opposite St Giles Cathedral

→ Street entertainers on the Royal Mile during Edinburgh's Festival season

of the Most Ancient and Most Noble Order of the Thistle. The royal pew in the Preston Aisle is reserved for Queen Elizabeth II during her visits to Edinburgh.

John Knox House and the Scottish Storytelling Centre

 43-45 High St ⏰ 10am-6pm Mon-Sat (Jul-Aug: also Sun) 🌐 tracscotland.org

This beautiful medieval building with its crow-step gables and overhanging upper storeys was home to the great patriarch of the Scottish Reformation only briefly, but as one of Edinburgh's oldest buildings it's well worth exploring for its many surviving decorative details. As a leader of the Protestant Reformation and minister at St Giles', John Knox (1513–72) was one of the most important figures in 16th-century Scotland. Ordained as a priest in 1536, Knox later became convinced of the need for religious change. He took part in the Protestant occupation of St Andrews Castle in 1547 and served two years as a galley slave in the French navy as punishment. On release, Knox went to London and Geneva to espouse the Protestant cause, returning to Edinburgh in 1559. This town house on the Royal Mile dates from 1470, and it was here that he spent the last few months of his life. Displays tell the story of Knox's life in the context of the political and religious upheavals of his time.

The building also incorporates the Scottish Storytelling Centre. This modern annex to the medieval John Knox House is a venue for local and visiting storytellers and other exponents of the spoken word, performing traditional tales and new work in English, dialect Scots and Gaelic.

Museum of Childhood

🏠 42 High Street ⏰ 10am-5pm Mon & Thu-Sat, noon-5pm Sun 🌐 edinburgh museums.org.uk

This is not merely a toy collection but an insight into childhood, with all its joys and trials. Founded in 1955, it was the world's first museum of childhood. The collection includes medicines, school books, clothing and uniforms, old-fashioned toys and a growing collection of computer games, action figures and game consoles.

Canongate Tolbooth: The People's Story Museum

🏠 163 Canongate ⏰ 10am-5pm Wed-Sat, noon-5pm Sun 🌐 edin burghmuseums.org.uk

Amid the Royal Mile's focus on monarchs and wealthy aristocrats, the People's Story Museum emphasizes the lives of ordinary city dwellers from the 18th century to the present day. Oral histories and historic documents tell their stories, while the collection, ranging from photos and tableaux to the protest banners and regalia of workers' organizations, brings them to life. The museum is housed in the 16th-century Tolbooth, which until the mid-19th century was the Edinburgh's courthouse, jail and council chamber.

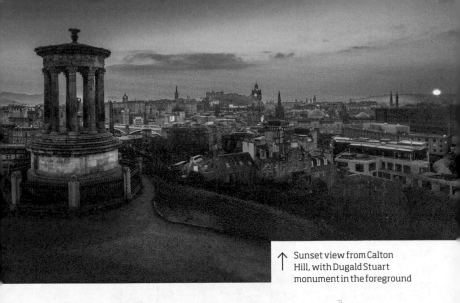

↑ Sunset view from Calton Hill, with Dugald Stuart monument in the foreground

 3

CALTON HILL

📍 C1 🏛 City centre east, via Waterloo Pl

Towering over the east end of Princes Street and crowned by an eclectic assortment of quirky Greek-style monuments, Calton Hill is the perfect place for a short stroll and summer picnic among sweet-scented gorse, complete with breathtaking views of the Old Town, Edinburgh Castle and the Firth of Forth.

 ①

National Monument

Calton Hill is home to one of Edinburgh's most memorable and baffling landmarks – a half-finished Greek-style Parthenon. Intended as a memorial to the Scottish soldiers and seamen of the French wars, construction of the National Monument began in 1822, only to run out of funding a few years later. The monument was never completed, and is now commonly referred to as "Edinburgh's Disgrace". A long-standing rumour has it that Glasgow City Council offered to pay for the monument's completion on the condition that it boldly display Glasgow City's official coat of arms. The offer was politely declined,

and over the years public shame over its condition has given way to affection, and even a certain degree of pride.

②

Nelson Monument

🕐 Apr-Sep: 10am-7pm Mon-Sat, noon-5pm Sun; Oct-Mar: 10am-4pm Mon-Sat 🌐 edinburgh museums.org.uk

For the ultimate view of Edinburgh, climb the breathtaking spiral stair to the battlements of this slender, multi-tiered tower, designed to resemble a telescope standing on its end. Built between 1807 and 1815, it is 32 metres (100 ft) high and commemorates Admiral Lord

Horatio Nelson's victory at the Battle of Trafalgar. The bronze cannon near its foot is a trophy of Britain's 19th-century conquest of Burma (Myanmar).

③

Collective Gallery

🏛 City Observatory & City Dome, 38 Calton Hill 🕐 Times vary, check website 🌐 collective gallery.net

A quirky hybrid of mock-Gothic and Greek temple architecture, this distinctive dome was originally an

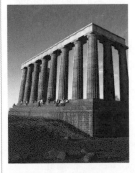

↑ Tourists climbing the half-finished National Monument

astronomical observatory. In 2018, it reopened as Collective, an art gallery and exhibition space, complete with a purpose-built restaurant.

Dugald Stewart Monument

This eight-columned Corinthian rotunda, designed by the ubiquitous William Henry Playfair as a homage to the Classical Monument of Lysicrates in Athens, is one of Edinburgh's most-photographed icons, appearing in innumerable snaps looking westward along Princes Street. Ironically, the philosopher Dugald Stewart (1753–1828) is far less well known than his memorial.

Burns Monument

It seems that every town and city in Scotland has its own memorial to the country's national bard. This modest mock-temple on the southern slope of Calton Hill, looking towards Arthur's Seat, is Edinburgh's. Begun in 1759, it was completed in 1796, the year of the poet's death. Originally it held a white marble bust of Robert Burns, which has since been removed and relocated to the Scottish National Portrait Gallery (p82).

The Old Royal High School

Also known as New Parliament House, The Royal High School was built during the 1820s on the Regent Road side of Calton Hill. Designed by Thomas Hamilton, it was based on the Temple of Theseus at Athens. Often cited as a possible home for a Scottish Parliament, the building was the focus for the

Vigil for Scottish Democracy, which campaigned from 1992 to 1997 for self government. A discreet cairn marking this effort stands a little way east of the National Monument on Calton Hill. The cairn contains several "gift" stones, including one from Auschwitz to commemorate a Scottish missionary who died there.

Calton Burial Ground

The obelisk of the Martyrs' Monument that towers over this ancient cemetery at the foot of Calton Hill was erected to honour members of the "Friends of the People", democracy campaigners convicted of sedition in 1793 and exiled to the Botany Bay penal colony in Australia. Tombs and monuments around its foot include the grave of philosopher David Hume (1711–1776), while a statue of Abraham Lincoln commemorates Scottish soldiers who gave their lives during the American Civil War.

EAT

Valvona & Crolla
The godfather of Italian delicatessens, this is the place to pick up the makings of a gourmet picnic. Its café-restaurant offers great risotto and pasta dishes.

🏠 19 Elm Row
🌐 valvonacrolla.co.uk

£ £ £

Gardener's Cottage
The seven-course taster menu at this cosy restaurant features fresh produce grown in the cottage's very own organic garden.

🏠 Royal Terrace Gdns, London Rd 🌐 the gardenerscottage.co.uk

£ £ £

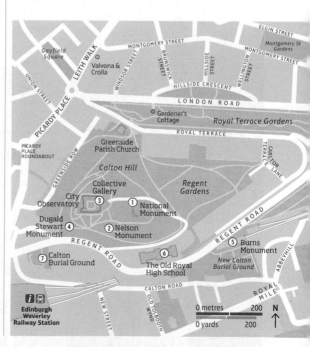

4 🖋️ Ⓜ️ 🍴 ☕ 🏛️

NATIONAL MUSEUM OF SCOTLAND

📍B3 🏛️Chambers St 🕐10am–5pm daily 🌐nms.ac.uk

Everything you ever wanted to know about Scotland can be discovered at this palace of wonders, housed within two radically different buildings that stand side by side. The grand 19th-century gallery is complemented by a contemporary new wing that has become one of Edinburgh's most striking modern buildings.

Old Wing

In the older of these two buildings, human, scientific and natural marvels are brought to life in zones that highlight world cultures, evolution and the natural world, design and fashion, technology and the remarkable exploits of Scottish inventors, engineers and scientists through the ages. Look out for grotesque masks, elaborate costumes and remarkable sculptures from Asia, Africa and South America on Level 3 and Level 4, and don't miss the late Dolly the Sheep, the world's first cloned mammal.

↑ Imagine Gallery, an inspiring and interactive space for children and families

Grand Gallery, designed by Captain Francis Fowke and completed in 1888 ↓

New Wing

The modern sandstone wing has been heralded as one of the most important constructs in postwar Scotland, and its exhibits are dedicated to the story of the country and its people .Begin your journey through the centuries with the prehistoric relics on the basement Level 0 and ascend floor by floor to the 21st century, on Level 6. Pause to admire exhibits including Pictish symbol stones with their mysterious carvings, the elaborately carved walrus-ivory Lewis Chessmen, carved by Viking craftsmen in the 12th century, Highland silver and weaponry, and the fearsome Maiden, a 16th-century ancestor of the guillotine.

↑ Entrance to the museum's contemporary wing

←

Dolly the Sheep, the first mammal cloned from an adult cell in 1996

UNMISSABLE EXHIBITS

Early People
These massive humanoid figures by sculptor Eduardo Paolozzi display delicate ornaments that demonstrate the skills of Iron Age Celtic goldsmiths.

Viking Grave
This stone tomb chamber from Orkney contains the skeleton of a Viking chief, buried with his most prized possessions.

Arthur's Seat Coffins
Found on Arthur's Seat in 1836, these tiny coffins and the individually dressed figures that they contain are the museum's most mysterious exhibit.

Tyrannosaurus Rex
The 12-metre skeleton of a Tyrannosaurus rex with its fang-filled gaping jaws dominates the grand multi-level atrium of the Animal World gallery, dwarfing the other animal exhibits.

Moby The Whale
This skull is from a 12-m (40-ft) sperm whale that swam up the River Forth in 1997. Efforts to send him back out to sea failed, and he died after beaching on the foreshore at Airth.

5 🚴 🍽 📷 🛍

SCOTTISH NATIONAL GALLERY

📍 B3 🏛 The Mound 🕐 10am–5pm daily (to 7pm Thu) 🌐 nationalgalleries.org

Home to one of the best collections of fine art in the world, this flagship gallery in the heart of the capital inspires and entrances with an international collection that spans over 500 years. It is also a place to see a uniquely rich concentration of works by Scottish masters from Ramsay and Raeburn to Wilkie and McTaggart.

Scottish society portraits by Allan Ramsay and Sir Henry Raeburn, including Raeburn's *Reverend Robert Walker Skating on Duddingston Loch*, and rural scenes and landscapes by David Wilkie and William McTaggart are among the highlights of the gallery's collections.

However, treasures are not limited to Scottish talents; the gallery is well worth visiting for its 15th- to 19th-century British and European paintings alone, though plenty more can be found to delight art lovers. An entire room is devoted to Nicholas Poussin's *The Seven Sacraments*, and Raphael's The *Bridgewater Madonna* appears alongside works by Titian, Tintoretto and Velazquez. Flemish and Dutch artists such as Rembrandt, Van Dyck and Rubens are also well represented. Paintings by Northern European Artists include Degas' *A Group of Dancers* and Van Gogh's *Olive Trees*, while Sir Edwin Landseer's iconic image of a red deer stag, *The Monarch of the Glen*, acquired in 2017, will have pride of place when refurbishment of gallery spaces devoted to Scottish art is completed in 2019.

↑ Van Gogh's *Olive Trees*, one of many works by 19th-century European masters

Treasures are not limited to Scottish talents; the gallery is well worth visiting for its 15th- to 19th- century British and European paintings alone.

↑ Neoclassical façade of the Scottish National Gallery, designed by William Henry Playfair

ROYAL SCOTTISH ACADEMY OF ART

This constantly growing treasury of almost 1,000 works by contemporary Scottish artists sits just next to the Scottish National Gallery, connected by an underground level. Don't miss the RSA's annual Open Exhibition in June and July each year. The event is a great opportunity for visitors to see and buy contemporary pieces by new Scottish talents at affordable prices.

Woman photographing the
iconic painting *The Monarch of
the Glen* by Sir Edwin Landseer

Rooftops of Edinburgh Waverley Station

The Scott Monument towering over Princes Street Gardens

images of contemporary Scottish movers and shakers such as Scotland's current makar (poet laureate) Jackie Kay, playwright and painter John Byrne, musician Annie Lennox, and home-grown film stars including Sean Connery, Ewan McGregor, Robert Carlyle, Karen Gillan, James McAvoy and Katie Leung.

Scott Monument

⑦ B2 ⏢ Princes St Gardens East ⏱ 10am-7pm daily (Oct-Mar: to 4pm) ⌨ edinburghmuseums.org.uk

Sir Walter Scott (p100) is one of the most important figures in Scottish literature. Born in Edinburgh, Scott initially pursued a legal career but turned to writing full time as his ballads and historical novels began to bring him success. His works looked back to a time of adventure, honour and chivalry, and did much to promote this image of Scotland abroad. In

EXPERIENCE MORE

Scottish National Portrait Gallery

⑥ B1 ⏢ 1 Queen St ⏱ 10am-5pm daily (to 7pm Thu) ⌨ nationalgalleries.org

This impressive sandstone gallery stands out from the austere Georgian façades of its New Town neighbours. Pause before entering to admire the statues that encrust its elaborate red sandstone exterior, including figures of philosopher David Hume and economist Adam Smith. A marble statue of Robert Burns presides over the atrium, surrounded by busts of such notables as Walter Scott, Robert Louis Stevenson and Scottish

Inventor James Watt. Upper galleries are dedicated to portraits of bewigged Stuart and Hanoverian grandees of the Enlightenment and the Victorian age. But it's not all about long-dead aristocrats and their literary figureheads. More vivid and engaging are the rooms dedicated to

> **⑥ INSIDER TIP**
> **Gallery Bus**
> The daily Gallery Bus circuit takes in the Scottish National Gallery, the National Portrait Gallery (drop-off only here) and the National Gallery of Modern Art, all for a reasonable £1 donation.

↑ Statue of the famous Greyfriars Bobby, a paragon of loyalty

addition to being a much celebrated novelist, Sir Walter was also a major public figure – he organized the visit of King George IV to Edinburgh in 1822. After Scott's death in 1832, the 61-m- (200-ft-) high Monument was constructed on the south side of Princes Street as a tribute to his life and work. This Gothic tower, designed by George Meikle Kemp, and completed in 1840, has a statue of Sir Walter at its base, sculpted by Sir John Steell. Inside the huge stone structure, 287 steps give access to the upper-most platform, which boasts impressive and far-reaching views across the Forth to Fife.

8

Greyfriars Kirk

📍B4 📍Greyfriars Place
🕐Times vary, check website 🌐greyfriars kirk.com

Greyfriars Kirk occupies a key role in the history of Scotland, as this is where the National Covenant was signed in 1638, marking the Protestant stand against the imposition of an episcopal church by King Charles I. Greyfriars was at that time a relatively new structure, having been completed in 1620 on the site of a Franciscan friary.

Throughout the 17th century the kirkyard was used as a mass grave for executed Covenanters. The kirk also served as a prison for Covenanter forces captured after the 1679 Battle of Bothwell Brig.

The original kirk building was severely damaged by fire in 1845 and was substantially rebuilt. Greyfriars is best known for its association with a little dog called Bobby, who, so the story goes, kept a vigil by his master's grave from 1858 until his own death in 1872. Bobby's well-loved statue stands outside Greyfriars Kirk.

9

National Library of Scotland

📍B3 📍George IV Bridge
🕐9:30am-7pm Mon, Tue, Thu; 10am-7pm Wed; 9:30am-5pm Fri-Sat
🌐nls.uk

This impressive library is not just about books and manuscripts, though it has thousands of each. Its collections also bring Scotland's past vividly to life through photography and film, postcards, newspapers, diaries, comics, posters and other ephemera on a variety of topics from football and politics to polar exploration. The John Murray Archive is a treasury of travel writing.

STAY

The Inn on The Mile
Built in 1923 as the British Linen Bank, this expertly preserved historic building is now a contemporary boutique inn with sleek, modern rooms that echo the hotel's unique history.

📍C3 📍82 High St, The Royal Mile 🌐theinn onthemile.co.uk

£££

The Balmoral
The graceful façade of this international five-star retreat is an iconic city landmark, home to palatial interiors, a fine-dining restaurant and brasserie, champagne bar and luxury spa.

📍B2 📍1 Princes Street 🌐roccofortehotels.com

£££

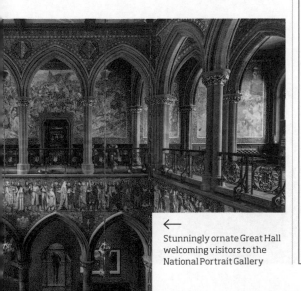

← Stunningly ornate Great Hall welcoming visitors to the National Portrait Gallery

10

Holyrood Park and Arthur's Seat

F3 **Main access via Holyrood Park Road, Holyrood Road and Meadowbank Terrace**

Holyrood Park, adjacent to the Palace of Holyroodhouse, covers over 2.6 sq km (1 sq mile) of varying terrain, topped by a rugged 250-m (820-ft) hill. Known as Arthur's Seat, the hill is actually a volcano that has been extinct for 350 million years. The area has been a royal hunting ground since at least the time of King David I, who died in 1153, and a royal park since the 16th century.

The name Holyrood, which means "holy cross", comes from an episode in the life of David I when, in 1128, he was knocked from his horse by a stag while out hunting.

Did You Know?

Some ancient traces of habitation in Holyrood Park date back as far as 10,000 years.

Legend has it that a cross appeared miraculously in his hands to ward off the animal and, in thanksgiving, the king founded the Abbey of the Holy Cross, Holyrood Abbey. The name Arthur's Seat is probably a corruption of Archer's Seat, a more prosaic explanation for the name than any link with the legendary King Arthur.

The park has three small lochs. St Margaret's near the Palace is the most romantic, positioned under the ruins of St Anthony's Chapel. Dunsapie Loch is the highest, sitting 112 m (367 ft) above sea level under Arthur's Seat. On the south side of the park, Duddingston Loch is home to a large number of swans, geese and wildfowl.

The Salisbury Crags are among the park's most striking features. Their dramatic profile, along with that of Arthur's Seat, can be seen from many kilometres away. The Crags form a parabola of red cliffs that sweep round and up from the Palace of Holyroodhouse, above a steep supporting hillside. A rough track, called the Radical Road, follows their base.

11

Palace of Holyroodhouse

E2 **East end of the Royal Mile** **9:30am–6pm daily (Nov-Mar: to 4:30pm)** **royalcollection.org.uk**

Known today as Queen Elizabeth II's official Scottish residence, the Palace of Holyroodhouse was built by James IV in the grounds of an abbey in 1498. It was later the home of James V and his wife, Mary of Guise, and was remodelled in the 1670s for Charles II. The Royal Apartments (including the Throne Room and Royal Dining Room) are used for investitures and for banquets whenever the Queen visits the palace. A chamber in the so-called James V tower is famously associated with the unhappy reign of Mary, Queen of Scots (p52). It was probably in this room, in 1566, that Mary saw the gruesome murder of her trusted Italian secretary, David Rizzio, authorized by her jealous husband, Lord Darnley. She was six months pregnant at the time.

↑ The Scottish Parliament building, designed by Enric Miralles

In the early stages of the Jacobite rising of 1745 (p54), the last of the pretenders to the British throne, Charles Edward Stuart (Bonnie Prince Charlie) held court here, dazzling Edinburgh society with his magnificent parties.

Tours are given daily from April to October, or take an audio tour; both are included in the ticket price. The Queen's Gallery has works from the Royal Collection.

Scottish Parliament

📍E2 🏠Holyrood ⏰10am-5pm Mon, Fri & Sat, 9am-6:30pm Tue-Thu ⓦparliament.scot

Following decades of Scottish calls for more political self-determination, a 1997 referendum on this issue resulted in a majority "yes" vote (p55). Designed by the late Enric Miralles, known for his work on buildings at the 1992 Barcelona Olympics, the Parliament building was opened in 2004 by Queen Elizabeth II. It's well worth taking one of the regular tours of this architecturally exciting public building.

Our Dynamic Earth

📍E3 🏠Holyrood Road ⏰Apr-Oct: 10am-5:30pm daily (Jul & Aug: to 6pm); Nov-Mar: 10am-5:30pm Wed-Sun ⓦdynamicearth.co.uk

In this permanent exhibition about the planet, visitors are taken on a journey from the earth's volcanic beginnings to the first appearance of life. Further displays cover the world's climatic zones and dramatic natural phenomena such as tidal waves and earthquakes. State-of-the-art lighting and interactive techniques provide 90 minutes of learning and entertainment.

The exhibition building is fronted by a 1,000-seat stone amphitheatre designed by Sir Michael Hopkins. Situated beneath Salisbury Crags, the modern lines of Our Dynamic Earth contrast sharply with the natural landscape.

↑ Holyrood Park and Arthur's Seat, overlooking the city

INSIDER TIP
Tide Times

Be sure to check the tide times when planning a trip across to Cramond Island. The causeway becomes submerged at high tide and walkers are often stranded. For information text CRAMOND to 81400.

Grassmarket

📍A3 🏠Old Town

A stroll down colourful Victoria Street from George IV Bridge will bring you to the bustling Grassmarket. Lined by restored medieval buildings, restaurants, busy pubs and funky boutiques, it is a hive of activity, particularly during the arts, crafts and street-food market on Saturday. Its pubs were favoured by Robert Burns (p112) and the notorious 19th-century "resurrection men" Burke and Hare. The Last Drop pub is opposite the site where public hangings took place until 1784.

Stockbridge

📍C5

Nowhere else in Edinburgh is quite like Stockbridge. Despite gentrification, this urban village straddling the Water of Leith retains its boho vibe, with gastropubs, lively café-bars, and distinctive architecture in the Colonies, built for 19th-century artisans and their families. Vintage stores and small galleries cluster on St Stephen Street, and the Royal Botanic Garden (p88) is a short walk from Raeburn Place, Stockbridge's main thoroughfare.

Mouthwatering street-food aromas drift from **Stockbridge Market** every Sunday, when you can sample snacks from all over the world and shop for artsy accessories and other unusual trinkets.

Stockbridge Market
🏠Saunders St ⏰10am–5pm Sun 🌐stockbridgemarket. co.uk

Cramond

📍B3 🏠Cramond Village

The Roman Empire once stretched as far as this pretty village of whitewashed houses on the east bank of the River Almond, and you can still see the foundations of a legionary fortress that dates from the 2nd century AD. At low tide you can cross the causeway to Cramond Island – an adventure involving a one-mile-walk to an uninhabited islet where cormorants and other waterfowl roost. From the island's shores there are views upriver to the three

Forth Bridges and across to Fife. World War II-era concrete bunkers are favourite targets for local graffiti artists.

Leith

📍C5 🏠Northeast of the city centre, linked by Leith Walk

Waterfront rejuvenation is the name of the game in Leith. Linked to the city centre by the broad thoroughfare of Leith Walk, often heralded as the next "up and coming" area, this former seaport has weathered hard times to gradually transform

EAT

The Roseleaf
This friendly, quirky pub-cum-brasserie has an imaginative comfort-food menu, with wild mushrooms on toast, cullen skink and a truly impressive full Scottish all-day breakfast.

⌖ C5 ⌂ 23-24 Sandport Place ⓦ roseleaf.co.uk.

ⓔⓔⓔ

The Scran and Scallie
Tom Kitchin, of the Michelin-starred eatery that bears his name, serves an outstanding gastro-pub menu here in trendy Stockbridge.

⌖ C5 ⌂ 1 Comely Bank Rd ⓦ scranandscallie. com

ⓔⓔⓔ

The Kitchin
To find out what makes this waterfront restaurant so special sample its modern British seasonal cuisine influenced by French cooking techniques

⌖ C5 ⌂ 78 Commercial St ⓦ thekitchin.com

ⓔⓔⓔ

↑ The Shore in Leith, an attractive and bustling port

Did You Know?

Leith did not become part of Edinburgh until 1920. Before that it was an independent borough.

itself into Edinburgh's most vibrant multi-ethnic community, one that is proud of its roots but looks to the future. Its lively Saturday farmers' market is a delight for foodies.

Leith is a historic port town that has traded for centuries with Scandinavia, the Baltic States and the Netherlands, and has always been the main trading port for Edinburgh. Although fiercely proud of its independence, it was eventually incorporated into the city in 1920, and now forms a charming north-eastern suburb. The medieval core of narrow streets and quays includes a number of

← World War II defences lining the Cramond causeway, visible at low tide

historic warehouses and merchants' houses dating from the 13th and 14th centuries. There was a great expansion of the docks in the 19th century, and many port buildings date from this period.

Shipbuilding and port activities have diminished, but there has been a renaissance in recent years in the form of conversions of warehouse buildings to offices, residences and, most notably, restaurants and bars. The Shore and Dock Place now has Edinburgh's most dense concentration of seafood bistros and varied restaurants.

The tourist attractions have been further boosted by the presence of the former **Royal Yacht Britannia**, the British royal family's vessel for more than 40 years. After sailing more than a million miles, it is now in Leith's Ocean Terminal.

Royal Yacht Britannia
⊛⊛⊛ ⌂ Ocean Terminal, Leith Docks ⌚ Daily
ⓦ royalyachtbritannia.co.uk

18 🛍 🎨 🍴 🖥 🛍

Royal Botanic Garden

📍 C5 🏠 Inverleith Row
🕐 10am–6pm daily (Feb &
Oct: to 5pm; Nov–Jan: to
4pm) 🌐 rbge.org.uk

This magnificent garden lies a
short way to the north of the
New Town, across the Water of
Leith river. The garden was
founded by two doctors in
1670 as a Physic Garden, near
Holyroodhouse and moved to
its present location in 1820, to
be progressively enlarged and
developed. Access from the
east is well served by buses;
from the west there's better
parking. From its hillside site,
there are views across the city.

There is a rock garden in
the southeast corner and an
indoor exhibition and
interpretation display in the
northeast corner. Extensive
greenhouses in traditional
and modern architectural
styles offer fascinating
hideaways on rainy days.
Don't miss the alpine display
to the northwest of the
greenhouses, or the beautiful,
fragrant rhododendron walk.

19

Dean Village

📍 C5 🏠 Northwest of the
city centre

This interesting, tranquil area
lies in the valley of the Water
of Leith, just a short walk
northwest of the city centre
down Bell's Brae from
Randolph Crescent. A series
of water mills along the river
has been replaced by attractive buildings of all periods.

A pretty riverside walk *(p92)*
threads its way between the
historic buildings, crossing
the river on a series of
footbridges. Downstream,
the riverside walkway passes
under Thomas Telford's
magnificent high level bridge,
via St Bernard's Well before
continuing towards the Royal
Botanic Garden.

↑ Antony Gormley
sculpture at Gallery of
Modern Art entrance

20 🛍 🎨 🖥 🛍

Scottish National Gallery of Modern Art

📍 C5 🏠 75 Belford Rd
🚌 Gallery bus (free, Mon–Fri
only) 🕐 10am–5pm daily
(Aug: to 6pm)

Since it opened its doors in
1960, the Scottish National
Gallery of Modern Art has
amassed some 5,000 pieces
dated from 1890 onwards.
Here you can find the work of
diverse figures such as Pablo
Picasso, Edvard Munch,
Charles Rennie Mackintosh

and the Pop Art trio of Richard
Hamilton, David Hockney and
Jake Tilson.

The gallery itself occupies
two buildings. Modern One is
housed in a Neo-Classical
building designed by William
Burn in 1825. The impressive
lawn and sculpture garden at
the entrance were designed
by Charles Jencks. The Pig
Rock Bothy was specially
commissioned by the Scottish
National Galleries as a
designated space for talks,
residences, performances and
special events. For exhibitions,
be sure to check out Modern
Two just opposite.

21

South Queensferry

📍 A5 🚆 Dalmeny, then taxi
🚌 43, 63

The vast red-painted
framework of the Forth Rail
Bridge looms over the pretty,
old-fashioned town of South
Queensferry like a steam-age
colossus. This spectacular rail
bridge, the first major steel-
built bridge in the world, was
opened in 1890 and remains
one of the greatest

Iconic Forth Rail Bridge,
named a UNESCO World
Heritage Site in 2015 ↑

achievements of the late Victorian era and was named as a UNESCO World Heritage Site in 2015.

You can see the rail bridge from the shore, or from the **Maid of the Forth**, which sails from South Queensferry to Inchcolm Island, with its ruined medieval abbey. Look out for seals and puffins on the way.

The quaint **Queensferry Museum** has a fascinating collection that highlights the building of the Forth Bridges, the ferries that carried traffic across the Firth before the opening of the first road bridge, and local history and traditions like the annual Queensferry Fair and the New Year's Day "Loony Dook" *(p48)* where locals plunge into the icy waters of the Forth.

Maid of the Forth

Hawes Pier, South Queensferry ◉ Scheduled sailings booked online ⓦ maidoftheforth.co.uk

Queensferry Museum

53 High St, South Queensferry ◉ 10am–5pm daily ⓦ edinburghmuseums.org.uk

22

Edinburgh Zoo

◉ B5 ◉ 134 Corstorphine Rd ◉ 12, 16, 26, 31 ◉ 9am–6pm daily (Mar & Oct: to 5pm; Nov–Feb: to 4pm) ⓦ edinburghzoo.org.uk

For a fun-filled family day out, you can visit Britain's only giant pandas, Tian Tian and Yang Guan. They are undoubtedly the stars of Edinburgh Zoo, but red pandas, meerkats, chimps, pelicans, penguins and hundreds of other mammal, bird and reptile species share the limelight.

Spreading across a vast hillside site south of the city centre, this non-profit zoo places a strong focus on conservation, education and research. Its range of spacious enclosures allow visitors to get close to animals in environments that imitate their natural habitat. Don't miss the Wee Beasties exhibition, where you can spot smaller reptiles, amphibians and insects, such as the tiny and brilliantly coloured poison dart frog.

23

Hopetoun House

◉ A5 ◉ West Lothian 🚂 Dalmeny ◉ Apr–Sep: 10:30am–5pm daily ⓦ hopetoun.co.uk

An extensive parkland designed in the style of Versailles is the setting for one of Scotland's finest stately homes. The original house was completed in 1707, and its dignified, horseshoe-shaped plan and lavish interior represent Neo-Classical 18th-century architecture at its best. A highlight of a visit here is the afternoon tea available in the stables tearoom, with the option of upgrading to a champagne tea.

📷 PICTURE PERFECT
Forth Rail Bridge

For that stunning upward shot of the vast framework of the Forth Rail Bridge, walk to Hawes Pier, and stand right under its massive supports at the east end of Edinburgh Road.

A SHORT WALK
NEW TOWN

Distance 2 km (1 mile) **Time** 20 minutes

The first phase of Edinburgh's "New Town" was built in the 18th century to relieve the congested and unsanitary conditions of the medieval Old Town. Charlotte Square, at the western end, formed the climax of this initial phase, and its new architectural concepts were to influence all subsequent phases. Of these, the most magnificent is the Moray Estate, where a linked series of very large houses forms a crescent, an oval and a twelve-sided circus. The walk shown here explores this area of monumental Georgian town planning and architecture.

The crowning glory of the Moray Estate, **Moray Place** consists of a series of immense houses and apartments, many of which are still inhabited.

Dean Bridge, built in 1829 to the design of Thomas Telford, offers views down to the Water of Leith and upstream to the weirs and old mills of Dean Village (p88).

At **Ainslie Place**, an oval pattern of town houses, forms the core of the Moray Estate, linking Randolph Crescent and Moray Place.

The Water of Leith is a small river running through a gorge below Dean Bridge. There is a riverside walkway (p92) to Stockbridge (p86).

MORAY PLACE

AINSLIE PLACE

GREAT STUART ST

DEAN BRIDGE

▶START

RANDOLPH CRESCENT

QUEENSFERRY STREET

FINISH ■

0 metres 100
0 yards 100

N ↑

No. 14 Charlotte Square was the residence of judge and diarist Lord Cockburn from 1813 to 1843.

←

The Water of Leith flowing through picturesque Dean Village

Locator Map
For more detail see p60

↑ The Georgian House and other grand period buildings on Charlotte Square

The Georgian House *at no. 7 Charlotte Sq is owned by the National Trust for Scotland and is open to the public. Repainted in its original colours and furnished with antiques, it is an insight into upperclass 18th-century Edinburgh.*

Bute House, *the official residence of the First Minister of the Scottish Parliament.*

No. 39 Castle Street *was the home of the writer Sir Walter Scott (p100).*

No. 9 *was the home of surgeon Joseph Lister from 1870 to 1877. He developed methods of preventing infection both during and after surgery.*

Charlotte Square *was built between 1792 and 1811 to provide a series of lavish town houses for the most successful city merchants. Most of the buildings are now used as offices.*

Princes Street *was part of the initial building phase of the New Town. The north side is lined with shops; Princes Street Gardens to the south lie below Edinburgh Castle.*

West Register House *was originally St George's Church, designed by Robert Adam.*

A LONG WALK
WATER OF LEITH WALKWAY

Distance 20.5 km (13 miles) **Walking Time** 4.5 hours
Terrain Well-maintained path, mostly paved with some
sections stony and unsurfaced. **Nearest Bus** Lothian
Bus number 44 from Shandwick Place to Balerno.

The tea-coloured Water of Leith rises in the Pentland Hills and
flows for 24 miles (40 km) through Edinburgh to meet the Firth
of Forth at Leith. On the way it passes through attractive urban
villages, parks and woodland. Old weirs and former watermills
hint at its history as a source of power for local industries. The
Water of Leith Walkway, following the river for around half its
length, forms part of the coast-to-coast John Muir Trail.

Locator Map
For more detail see p60

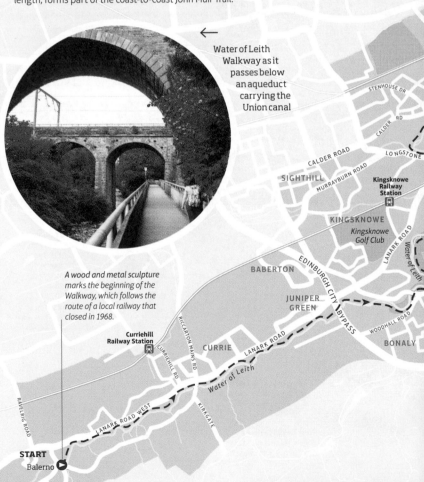

← Water of Leith
Walkway as it
passes below
an aqueduct
carrying the
Union canal

*A wood and metal sculpture
marks the beginning of the
Walkway, which follows the
route of a local railway that
closed in 1968.*

START
Balerno

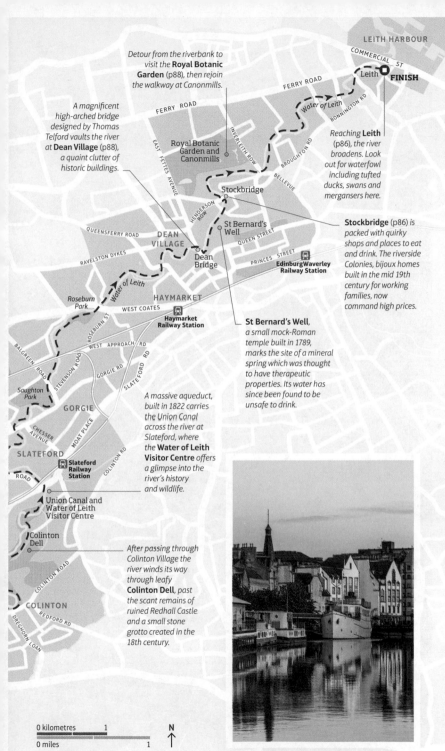

Detour from the riverbank to visit the **Royal Botanic Garden** (p88), then rejoin the walkway at Canonmills.

LEITH HARBOUR

Leith **FINISH**

A magnificent high-arched bridge designed by Thomas Telford vaults the river at **Dean Village** (p88), a quaint clutter of historic buildings.

Royal Botanic Garden and Canonmills

Reaching **Leith** *(p86), the river broadens. Look out for waterfowl including tufted ducks, swans and mergansers here.*

Stockbridge

St Bernard's Well

Dean Bridge

Edinburg Waverley Railway Station

Stockbridge *(p86) is packed with quirky shops and places to eat and drink. The riverside Colonies, bijoux homes built in the mid 19th century for working families, now command high prices.*

Roseburn Park

DEAN VILLAGE

Haymarket Railway Station

St Bernard's Well, *a small mock-Roman temple built in 1789, marks the site of a mineral spring which was thought to have therapeutic properties. Its water has since been found to be unsafe to drink.*

Saughton Park

GORGIE

SLATEFORD

Slateford Railway Station

Union Canal and Water of Leith Visitor Centre

Colinton Dell

COLINTON

A massive aqueduct, built in 1822 carries the Union Canal across the river at Slateford, where the **Water of Leith Visitor Centre** *offers a glimpse into the river's history and wildlife.*

After passing through Colinton Village the river winds its way through leafy **Colinton Dell**, *past the scant remains of ruined Redhall Castle and a small stone grotto created in the 18th century.*

0 kilometres   1
0 miles   1

N

↑ Boats moored on the still water of tranquil Leith Harbour

SOUTHERN SCOTLAND

In 1296 Scotland committed itself to the Wars of Independence against the English, and it was Southern Scotland that suffered the most. The strife caused by the many battles fought here lasted for three centuries, as first Scottish self-determination, and then alliances with France, led to strained relations between Scotland and its southern neighbour.

The virtual independence of the southern Borders district brought further conflict. Powerful families had operated under local laws set in place since the mid-12th century, and when Scottish kings were not fighting the English, they led raids into the Border country to try to bring it back under central control.

Over the years, some of the great dramas of Scottish history have been played out in Southern Scotland. Robert the Bruce's guerrilla army defeated an English force at Glen Trool in 1307, but Flodden, near Coldstream, was the scene of the country's worst military reverse in 1513, when King James IV of Scotland and thousands of his men fell in battle.Today, the quiet countryside around the Borders market towns, and the beautiful mountain scenery in Dumfries and Galloway, seem to belie such violent history. The area is now known for its manufacturing of textiles and for promoting its literary associations, as Sir Walter Scott lived at Abbotsford, near St Boswells. But it is the ruins of the great Border abbeys, castles and battlegrounds that serve as a reminder of Southern Scotland's turbulent past.

Rosyth
M90
Queensferry
EDINBURGH p58
Edinburgh

THE PENTLAND HILLS

A71
Carnwath
A70
A702
Melbourne
Biggar
A702

M74
Beattock
Moffat
A701
Parkgate
Lockerbie
A74(M)
Ecclefechan
Canonbie
Dumfries
A75
23
CAERLAVEROCK CASTLE
Kirkbean

Firth

LINLITHGOW PALACE **12**
M9

DIRLETON CASTLE **NORTH BERWICK**
6 **4** **5** **TANTALLON CASTLE**
EAST LOTHIAN COAST **3**
Dunbar
8 **NATIONAL MUSEUM OF FLIGHT**
7
HADDINGTON
Gifford
Grantshouse
A1
ST ABB'S HEAD **9**
Eyemouth

Pathhead
Lammermuir Hills
Cranshaws
Preston
A6438
Berwick-upon-Tweed

ROSSLYN CHAPEL **11**
Penicuik
10
A7
Lauder
Westruther
A697
Coldstream
Crookham
A697
Wooler

PEEBLES **14**
Galashiels
MELROSE ABBEY
19
KELSO **13**
A699
A698

TRAQUAIR HOUSE **16**
ABBOTSFORD **2**
18
EILDON HILLS

A708
Cappercleuch
Broad Law 840m
St Mary's Loch
Ashkirk
17 **JEDBURGH**
A7
A698
A68

Hart Fell 808m
Ettrick
Hawick

Teviothead

Newcastleton

Cheviot Hills

Harbottle

ENGLAND
Bewcastle
Longtown
Haltwhistle
Hexham
A68

Nith

North Sea

Grantshouse

SOUTHERN SCOTLAND

SOUTHERN SCOTLAND

Must Sees

1 Culzean Castle and Country Park
2 Abbotsford

Experience More

3 East Lothian Coast
4 North Berwick
5 Tantallon Castle
6 Direlton Castle
7 Haddington
8 National Museum of Flight
9 St Abb's Head
10 Pentland Hills
11 Rosslyn Chapel
12 Linlithgow Palace

13 Kelso
14 Peebles
15 Drumlanrig Castle
16 Traquair House
17 Jedburgh
18 Eildon Hills
19 Melrose Abbey
20 New Lanark
21 Dumfries House
22 Burns Heritage Trail
23 Caerlaverock Castle
24 Threave Castle
25 Whithorn
26 Firth of Clyde
27 Galloway Forest Park
28 The Rhinns of Galloway

❶ 🚲 Ⓜ 🖥 🛍 (NTS)

CULZEAN CASTLE AND COUNTRY PARK

🅰C6 🏠6 km (4 miles) west of Maybole, Ayrshire 🚆Ayr, then bus 🕐Castle: Apr-Oct: 10:30am-5pm (last entry 4pm); grounds: 9am-dusk daily year-round 🌐nts.org.uk

Standing on a cliff's edge in an extensive parkland estate, the late-16th-century keep of Culzean (pronounced Cullayn) is a masterpiece in a land full of magnificent castles, with a glorious estate to match.

Formerly a crumbling fortified tower house, Culzean Castle was transformed by the great Scots architect Robert Adam into a mansion of sumptuous proportions and elegance. Work began in 1777 and lasted almost 20 years, with no expense spared in the decoration and craftsmanship of this breathtaking clifftop fortress. Culzean was fully restored and gifted to the nation in the 1970s.

The Castle Grounds

The grounds became Scotland's first public country park in 1969 and, with farming flourishing alongside ornamental gardens, they reflect both the leisure and everyday activities of life on a great country estate. Free tours depart from the Home Farm visitor centre, or you can go it alone – the views across the water to the mountains of Arran are glorious from the clifftop and shoreline trails.

ORANGES AND LEMONS

Camellia House, Culzean's elegant stone-framed orangery, was restored in 2018 and replanted with clementine, lime, lemon and orange trees. Built in around 1840, it was designed by John Patterson, a disciple of Robert Adam. Orangeries in this style, built in emulation of those created for 17th-century monarchs like Louis XIV of France, were enviable status symbols for wealthy 19th-century notables.

The clock tower was originally the family coach house and stables.

Did You Know?

During the castle's prime, the caves below were used for smuggling contraband.

Illustration of Culzean Castle perched on its magnificent clifftop setting

Culzean Castle's iconic turrets
as seen from the beach below ↑

→

Culzean's oval
staircase, an
architectural triumph

The elegantly restored
18th-century Round
Drawing Room perches
on the cliff's edge
46 m (150 ft) above
the Firth of Clyde.

Illuminated by an overarching
skylight, the Oval staircase is
considered one of Adam's
finest design achievements.

The Armoury houses a
collection of 18th- and 19th-
century weaponry purchased
from the Tower of London.

State Bedroom
and Dressing
Rooms

Fountain Court
sunken garden
is a good place
to begin a tour
of the grounds
to the east.

The Eisenhower
Apartment was a gift to
the US president for his
support in World War II.
It is now a small hotel.

2 🗡️ 🚫 🖥️ 🛍️

ABBOTSFORD

E6 🏠 Tweedbank, Melrose 🚆 Tweedbank 🚌 X62, 72, Abbotsford Minibus from Tweedbank Station 🕐 Mar & Nov: 10am–4pm; Apr–Oct: 10am–5pm 🌐 scottsabbotsford.com

Few houses bear the stamp of their creator so intimately as Abbotsford House, the home of Georgian Scotland's greatest author, Sir Walter Scott, for the final 20 years of his life. The Place is adorned with arms and armour and Scott spared no expense in converting what was a humble farmhouse by the Tweed into this fabulous baronial home, complete with towers, turrets and grand halls.

Walter Scott bought a farm here in 1811, known as *Clarteyhole* ("dirty hole" in Borders Scots), though he soon renamed it Abbotsford, in memory of the monks of Melrose Abbey. He demolished the house to make way for the turreted building we see today, its construction funded by the sales of his novels.

Rob Roy's claymore is among the prized mementoes displayed in Scott's majestic home, where suits of armour and fearsome weaponry decorate the Great Hall. A treasury of rare books and memorabilia reflects his passion for a romanticized version of Scotland's history, showcasing relics of the Stuarts including a richly adorned crucifix owned by Mary, Queen of Scots, and a lock of Prince Charles Edward Stuart's hair. The study where Scott wrote many of his novels is a shrine to his prodigious literary output. Surrounding the house, the 120-acre Abbotsford Estate was laid out by Scott himself, and now boasts an award-winning visitor centre, beautiful formal gardens, extensive forest trails and family-friendly activity areas for all ages.

↑ Impressive interior of the celebrated Abbotsford Library

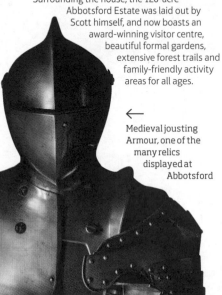

← Medieval jousting Armour, one of the many relics displayed at Abbotsford

SIR WALTER SCOTT

Sir Walter Scott (1771–1832) penned around 30 novels, 20 histories and biographies, and a dozen anthologies of verse, starting with *Waverley* in 1814. A heartfelt royalist, he stage-managed George IV's tour of Scotland in 1822 and was rewarded with a knighthood. His novels inspired other creative spirits, such as Donizetti, who turned one of Scott's tales into the opera *Lucia di Lammermoor*. Today, he's best remembered for *Rob Roy*, his swashbuckling saga of a Highland outlaw.

EXPERIENCE Southern Scotland

9,000

Rare books fill the shelves of Scott's impressive library at Abbotsford House.

↑ Abbotsford House surrounded by beautiful floral gardens

→

Sea Cliff's sandstone harbour with with Tantallon Castle in the distance

EXPERIENCE MORE

East Lothian Coast

⚑E5 ✇East Lothian
ⓘEdinburgh Lothians
(0845) 225 5121

Stretching east from Mussel-burgh for some 65 km (40 miles), the coast of East Lothian offers opportunities for beach activities, golf, windsurfing, viewing seabirds and coastal walks. It has a pleasant mixture of beaches, low cliffs, woodland, and some farmland. Although the A198 and A1 are adjacent to the coast for only short distances, they give easy access to a series of public car

---

💬 INSIDER TIP
East Lothian Coastal Walk

For a long scenic coast walk, take the coastal footpath from Gullane Bay to North Berwick, across grassy heath-land between sandy bays and low rocky headlands, with views of the coast of Fife to the north.

---

parks (a small charge is made in summer) close to the shore. Among these is Gullane, perhaps the best beach for seaside sports and activities. Yellowcraig, near Dirleton, is a lovely bay, lying about 400 m (440 yds) from the car park. Limetree Walk, near Tyning-hame, has the long, east-facing beach of Ravensheugh Sands (a ten-minute walk along a woodland track). Belhaven Bay, just west of Dunbar, is a large beach with walks along the Tyne estuary. Barns Ness, east of Dunbar, offers a geological nature trail and an impressive lighthouse. There is another delightful beach at Seacliff, reached by a private toll road that leaves the A198 about 3 km (2 miles) east of North Berwick.

North Berwick

⚑E5 ✇North Berwick
🚌X5, X24

A charming seaside town, North Berwick has plenty to keep visitors entertained, including boat trips, coastal walks, putting greens and golf

courses, plus quirky shops, coffee houses and ice-cream parlours. During the summer regular boat trips leave the picturesque harbour for a breezy tour of nearby islands and Bass Rock, home to Britain's largest gannet colony. Learn more about the area's birdlife at the **Scottish Seabird Centre**, where you can control cameras for live coverage of the birds without disturbing them. After a day of exploring, enjoy fish and chips on the beachfront. For golf, head to North Berwick, The Glen or Muirfield Links.

Scottish Seabird Centre
🅿🚫💬 ⏰Times vary, see website 🌐seabird.org

Tantallon Castle

⚑E5 ⌂ East Lothian
📞(01620) 892727 ✇North
Berwick 🚌120 ⏰Apr-Sep:
9:30am-5:30pm daily; Oct-Mar: 10am-4pm daily

For a magnificently snappable stop on a day trip from Edinburgh, Tantallon is hard to beat. Its 15-m (50-ft-) tall

and 4-m (12-ft-) thick battered red sandstone walls overlook the North Sea and the Bass Rock, and it's easy to see why the Red Douglases, among the mightiest families of medieval Scotland, chose it as their seat.

6 Dirleton Castle

🅰 E5 🏠 Dirleton 🚌 X5
🕐 Apr–Sept 9:30am–5:30pm daily (Jul: to 8:30pm); Oct–Mar: 10am–4pm daily; last entry half an hour before closing 🌐 historic environment.scot

A short bus ride from Edinburgh city centre, Dirleton Castle makes for a fun day out. It's De Vaux towers, built in the early 13th century, are among the oldest in Scotland and served a succession of aristocratic families, among them the Earl of Gowrie, executed in 1585 for plotting against James VI. Beneath the three-storey keep is a pit wherein languished prisoners of its noble owners. A huge

→

St Mary's Collegiate Church on the banks of the Tyne in Haddington

Did You Know?

The Firth of Forth is home to seals, dolphins, porpoises and several species of whale.

dovecot (pronounced *doocot* in the Scots vernacular) with space for 1,000 roosts stands in the impressive castle grounds, which are home to the world's longest herbaceous border.

7 Haddington

🅰 E6 🏠 East Lothian
ℹ Edinburgh & Lothians (0845) 225 5121

This attractive county town is about 24 km (15 miles) east of Edinburgh. It was destroyed during the Wars of Independence in the 13th–14th centuries, and again in the 16th century. The agricultural revolution brought prosperity, giving Haddington many historic houses, churches, and other public buildings, and a programme of restoration has helped to retain the town's character. The River Tyne encloses the town, and there are attractive riverside walks and parkland. ("A Walk Around Haddington" guide is available from most newsagents.)

The parish church of St Mary's, southeast of the town centre, dates back to 1462 and is one of the largest churches in the area. Parts of the church have been refurbished and rebuilt in later years, having been destroyed in the famous siege of Haddington in 1548.

EAT

The Lobster Shack
Delicious locally caught lobster freshly prepared with all the trimmings for market price.

🅰 E5 🏠 North Berwick Harbour 🕐 noon–6pm

£££

Marmion's
Borders produce meets Middle Eastern cuisine at this friendly place.

🅰 E6 🏠 5 Buccleuch St, Melrose 🕐 Sun

£££

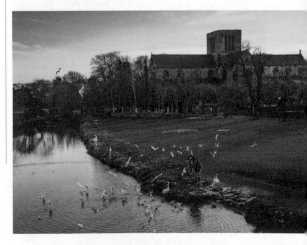

8

National Museum of Flight

⚑E6 ⚐East Fortune Airfield, EH39 5LF ⏱X5, change at Haddington for 121 to Museum of Flight, East Fortune ⚑Drem, change for 121 bus towards North Berwick ⏱Summer: 10am–5pm daily ⏱nms. ac.uk

Scotland's only Concorde is the star of the show at this former military airfield, with a supporting cast that includes civil aircraft and warbirds like the bizarre Weir W-2 auto-gyro, the iconic Spitfire, the supersonic English Electric

↑ Spitfire at National Museum of Flight

Lightning and the ominous nuclear bomber, the Avro Vulcan. The Concorde Experience reveals the history of supersonic aviation, and the free Airfield Explorer means that you can easily get around the hangars and outdoor exhibits.

9 (NTS)

St Abb's Head

⚑E6 ⚐The Scottish Borders ☎(01890) 771443 ⚑Berwick-upon-Tweed ⏱from Edinburgh ⏱Nature Centre: Mar–Oct: 10am–5pm daily

The jagged cliffs of St Abb's Head, rising 91 m (300 ft) from the North Sea, offer visitors a spectacular view of thousands of seabirds wheeling and div-ing below. During the May to June breeding season, St Abbs Head National Nature Reserve becomes an important site for more than 50,000 cliff-nesting seabirds, including fulmars, guillemots, kittiwakes and puffins. St Abb's village has one of the few unspoiled

> During the May to June breeding season, St Abbs Head National Nature Reserve becomes an important site for more than 50,000 cliff-nesting seabirds.

working harbours on Scotland's east coast. A cliff-top trail begins at the visitor centre, where displays include identification boards and a touch table for younger visitors to get to grips with wings and feathers.

10

Pentland Hills

⚑D6 ⚐The Lothians ⏱Edinburgh, then bus ⏱Regional Park Headquarters, Edinburgh: www.pentlandhills.org

The wilds of the Pentland Hills stretch for 26 km (16 miles) southwest of Edinburgh, and offer some of the best hill-walking country in Southern Scotland. Walkers can saunter along the many signposted footpaths, while the more adventurous can climb the 493-m (1,617-ft-) peak of Allermuir. More ambitious still is the classic scenic route along the ridge from Caerketton to West Kip. For those who would like a head start, you can take the

chairlift at **Midlothian Snowsports Centre**, where you'll find Britain's biggest artificial ski slope, to in order to reach the higher ground.

St Abbs, above, and a pair of resident guillemots (inset) ↑

Midlothian Snowsports Centre

⌂ Biggar Rd, Hillend, Midlothian ⊙ Mon-Fri 9:30am-9pm; Sat & Sun until 7pm ⌨ midlothian.gov.uk

Rosslyn Chapel

⌂ D6 ▤ 37, 140
▤ Eskbank ⊙ 9:30am-5pm daily (Jun-Aug: to 6pm); last admission 30 minutes before closing ⌨ rosslyn chapel.com

To the east of the A703, in the lee of the Pentland Hills, stands the exquisite and ornate 15th-century Rosslyn Chapel, which famously features in *The Da Vinci Code*, Dan Brown's bestselling novel, and the 2006 film adaptation of the same name starring Tom Hanks.

The building was originally intended as a church, but after the death of its founder, William Sinclair, it was used as a burial ground for his descendants. It has remained the property of the family since 1446, and the chapel continues to be used as a place of worship to this day.

The delicately wreathed Apprentice Pillar recalls the legend of the talented apprentice carver who was killed by the master stone mason in a fit of jealous rage when he discovered his pupil's superior skill. Photography and video recording are not permitted within the chapel.

DRINK

Glenkinchie Distillery

For a whisky experience that doesn't involve a long journey into the Highlands, head to Glenkinchie Distillery near the village of Pencaitland. It is one of only three remaining Lowland whisky distilleries. Informative tours end with single malt tastings.

⌂ E6 ⌂ Pencaitland, Tranent ⊙ 10am-5pm daily (Nov-Feb: to 4pm) ⌨ malts.com/en-row/distilleries/glenkinchie

← Rosslyn Chapel, still owned by descendants of its founder

12 Linlithgow Palace

D5 **Kirk Gate, Linlithgow** **Linlithgow** **From Edinburgh** **9:30am-5:30pm daily (Oct-Mar: 10am-4pm)** **historic-environment.scot**

Standing on the edge of Linlithgow Loch, amid lovely gardens, the former royal palace of Linlithgow is one of the country's most-visited ruins. It dates back largely to the building commissioned by James I in 1425, though some sections date from the 14th century. The vast scale of the building is best seen in the 28-m- (94-ft-) long Great Hall, with its huge fireplace and windows. The restored fountain in the courtyard, which can be seen in operation on Sundays in July and August, was a wedding present in 1538 from James V to his wife, Mary of Guise. His daughter, Mary, Queen of Scots (p52), was born at Linlithgow in 1542.

The adjacent Church of St Michael is Scotland's largest pre-Reformation church and a fine example of the Scottish Decorated style. Consecrated in the 13th century, the church was damaged by the fire of 1424 and largely rebuilt.

13 Kelso

E6 **The Scottish Borders** **From Edinburgh**

At the confluence of the rivers Teviot and Tweed, Kelso has a charming centre, with a cobbled square surrounded by Georgian and Victorian buildings. The focus of the town is the ruin of the 12th-century abbey. This was the oldest and wealthiest of the four Border Abbeys founded by David I, but it suffered from wars with England and was severely damaged in 1545. **Floors Castle** on the northern edge of Kelso was designed by William Adam in the 1720s, and reworked by William Playfair after 1837. A short drive away is **Mellerstain House**, a stunning stately home built by the Adam brothers. There are formal gardens, and the grounds include the Borders Sculpture Park which showcases the work of contemporary artists.

Floors Castle

Roxburghshire **May-Sep** **floorscastle.com**

Mellerstain House

Gordon **May-Sep: Fri-Mon** **mellerstain.com**

14 Peebles

D6 **The Scottish Borders** **From Edinburgh** **23 High St; (01721) 728095**

Set on the banks of the River Tweed, this charming Borders town is home to the **Tweeddale Museum and Gallery**, which houses full-scale plaster casts of part of the Parthenon Frieze, and casts of a frieze depicting the entry of Alexander the Great into Babylon. The walled **Kailzie Gardens** attract many day-trippers, while **Glentress Forest**, on the fringes of town, is popular with hikers and mountain bikers.

Tweeddale Museum and Gallery

Chambers Institution, High St **(01721) 724820** **10:30am-4pm Mon-Fri; 9:30am-12:30pm Sat**

Kailzie Gardens

Kailzie, Peebles **Times vary, check website;** **kailziegardens.com**

Glentress Forest

Daily **scotland.forestry.gov.uk**

↑ The River Tweed flowing through Peebles town centre

Kelso Abbey, a soaring medieval ruin

rebellions. Following a vow made by the fifth Earl, Traquair's Bear Gates (the "Steekit Yetts"), which closed after Bonnie Prince Charlie's visit in 1745, will not reopen until a Stuart reascends the throne. A secret stairway leads to the Priest's Room, which, with its clerical vestments that could be disguised as bedspreads, attests to the problems faced by Catholic families until Catholicism was legalized in 1829.

One wing of the house now contains the Traquair House Brewery, which dates back to the 18th century and still uses the original equipment and 200-year-old oak barrels. Its award-winning ales can be sampled in the 1745 Cottage Restaurant.

The grounds are home to the impressive Traquair Maze. Planted in 1981 with over 1,500 Leylandi Cyprus trees, it is now the largest hedged maze in Scotland. An annual Easter Egg hunt is held here on Easter Sunday.

15

Drumlanrig Castle

🅐D6 🏠Thornhill, Dumfries & Galloway 🚆🚌Dumfries, then bus 🕐Apr-Sep: 10am-5pm daily (castle: from 11am) 🌐drumlanrigcastle.co.uk

Rising squarely from a grassy platform, the massive fortress-palace of Drumlanrig Castle was built from pink sandstone between 1679 and 1691 on the site of a 15th-century Douglas stronghold. The castle's multi-turreted, formidable exterior conceals a priceless collection of art and Jacobite treasures.

Hanging on the walls of the oak-panelled rooms are paintings by Thomas Gainsborough, Sir Joshua Reynolds, Alan Ramsay and Rembrandt, whose *Old Lady*

Reading takes pride of place. The emblem of a crowned, winged heart recalls the famous Douglas ancestor "The Good Sir James". Legend has it he bore Robert the Bruce's heart on crusade against the Moors in Spain.

16

Traquair House

🅐D6 🏠Peebles, The Scottish Borders 🚌From Peebles 🕐Apr-Sep: 11am-5pm daily; Oct: 11am-4pm daily; Nov: 11am-3pm Sat & Sun 🌐traquair.co.uk

Scotland's oldest continuously inhabited house has deep roots in Scottish religious and political history stretching back over 900 years. Evolving from a fortified tower to a 17th-century mansion, the house was a Catholic Stuart stronghold for 500 years. Mary, Queen of Scots was among the many monarchs to have stayed here. Her crucifix is kept in the house and her bed is covered by a counterpane that she made herself. Family letters and engraved Jacobite drinking glasses are among the relics recalling the period of the Highland

STAY

Cringletie House
Set in beautiful private grounds, this grand house boasts traditional and deluxe rooms with modern amenities. Its award-winning restaurant offers a seasonal dinner menu and delightful afternoon teas.

🅐D6 🏠Edinburgh Rd, Peebles 🌐cringletie. com

£££

Winter view of Linlithgow Palace

⑰ Jedburgh

⒜ E6 ⌂ The Scottish Borders ▦ ⓘ Murray's Green; (01835) 863170

The town is home to the mock-medieval **Jedburgh Castle, Jail and Museum**. Built in the 1820s and once the local jail, it now serves as a museum, and has some good displays on the area's history and what life was like in a 19th-century prison.

Built around 1500, **Mary, Queen of Scots' House** is so called due to a visit by the queen in 1566. The house was converted into a museum in the 1930s, and in 1987 (on the 400th anniversary of Mary's execution) it became a centre dedicated to telling her life story. Exhibits include a copy of her death mask.

Jedburgh Abbey is one of the great quartet of 12th-century Border Abbeys, along with Dryburgh, Kelso and Melrose. The abbey church has some interesting features including a rose window.

Jedburgh Castle, Jail and Museum

⊗ ⓒ (01835) 864750
⌚ Mar-Oct: daily

Mary, Queen of Scots' House

⊗ ⓒ (01835) 863331
⌚ Mar-Nov: daily

Jedburgh Abbey

⊗ ⊕ ⓒ (01835) 863925
⌚ Daily

⑱ Eildon Hills

⒜ E6 ⌂ The Scottish Borders ▦ From Melrose

The three peaks of the Eildon Hills dominate the central Borders landscape. Mid Hill is the tallest at 422 m (1,385 ft), while North Hill once had a Bronze Age hill fort dating from before 500 BC, and later

Did You Know?

The town of New Lanark was once the UK's largest cotton-spinning mill complex.

it became home to a major Roman military complex strategically placed between Hadrian's Wall and the Antonine Wall (p153) to guard the crossing of the River Tweed at Newstead in the 2nd century AD. In summer guided walks through Melrose's medieval centre to key historic sights depart from the **Trimontium Museum of Roman Scotland**. The centre contains aerial photography of the Trimontium site, fascinating ancient artifacts and Roman treasures. The most celebrated name hereabouts is Sir Walter Scott (p100), who had a particular affection for these hills. A panorama of the Eildons Hills called Scott's View lies just east of Melrose, near Dryburgh Abbey. This is the best location to see the hills as they rise above the Tweed.

Trimontium Museum of Roman Scotland

⊗ ⌂ The Ormiston, Market Square, Melrose ⓒ Apr-Oct: 10:30am–4:30pm Mon-Sat
Ⓦ trimontium.co.uk

⑲   Melrose Abbey

⒜ E6 ⌂ Melrose, The Scottish Borders ⌚ 9:30am–5:30pm daily (Oct-Mar: to 4pm) Ⓦ historicenvironment. scot

The rose-pink ruins of this beautiful Border Abbey bear witness to the devastation of successive English invasions. Built by David I in 1136 for Cistercian monks, and also to replace a 7th-century monastery, Melrose was repeatedly ransacked by English armies, most notably in 1322 and 1385. The final blow came in 1545, when Henry VIII of England implemented his destructive Scottish policy known as the "Rough Wooing". This resulted from the failure of the Scots to ratify a marriage treaty between Henry VIII's son and the infant Mary, Queen of Scots. What remains of the

↑ Grand reception room welcomes visitors to Dumfries House

abbey are the outlines of cloisters, the kitchen, monastic buildings and the shell of the church. The south exterior wall includes a gargoyle shaped like a pig playing the bagpipes and several other animated figures.

An embalmed heart, found here in 1920, is probably that of Robert the Bruce, the abbey's chief benefactor, who had decreed that his heart be taken on a crusade to the Holy Land. It was returned here after its bearer, Sir James Douglas, was killed in Spain.

---

⑳
New Lanark

Ⓐ D6 Ⓐ Lanark, Clyde Valley 🚌🚉 Lanark
🌐 newlanark.org

By the beautiful Falls of Clyde, the village of New Lanark was founded in 1785 by the industrial entrepreneur David Dale. Ideally located for its water-driven mills, the village became the largest producer of cotton in Britain by 1800. Dale and his successor son-in-law, Robert Owen, were philanthropists whose reforms demonstrated that

commercial success need not undermine the wellbeing of the workforce. Cotton manufacturing continued here until the late 1960s.

The **New Lanark Visitor Centre** has exhibits illustrating the World Heritage Site's significance as a window on to the realities of working life in an industrial town during the early 19th century. A passport available here gives admission to many of the town's historical buildings.

24 km (15 miles) north, the town of Blantyre has a memorial to the Clyde Valley's most famous son, the explorer David Livingstone.

New Lanark Visitor Centre
🕐🚫♿ Ⓒ (01555) 661345
🕐 Daily

㉑
Dumfries House

Ⓐ C6 Ⓐ Cumnock, Ayrshire
🕐 Dawn to dusk daily (Nov–Mar: Sat & Sun only)
🌐 dumfries-house.org.uk

This wonderful Palladian villa is off the beaten track, but worth a detour. Sitting in sweeping parkland, the grand

↑ Autumnal colours at the three-tiered Falls of Clyde, New Lanark

symmetrical villa was built for the fifth Earl of Dumfries, William Crichton Dalrymple. Designed to lure a prospective wife, it was decorated in fashionable Rococo style between 1756 and 1760. Among the treasures is a priceless collection of Chippendale furniture.

> **DAVID LIVINGSTONE (1813-73)**
>
> Scotland's great missionary doctor began working life as a mill boy in Blantyre. From 1840 Livingstone made three epic journeys across Africa, promoting "commerce and Christianity". He became the first European to see Victoria Falls, and died in 1873 while searching for the source of the Nile. His body is buried in Westminster Abbey in London.

Burns Heritage Trail

🗺 C6 🏛 South Ayrshire, Dumfries & Galloway 🌐 visitscotland.com

Robert Burns (1759–96), Scotland's most beloved writer, left behind a remarkable body of work ranging from satirical poetry to tender love songs. His status as national bard remains unchallenged, and an official Burns Heritage Trail takes visitors on a tour of various sights in southwest Scotland where he lived.

In Dumfries, the **Robert Burns Centre** focuses on his years in the town, while **Burns House**, his home from 1793 to 1796, contains memorabilia. His Greek-style mausoleum is in St Michael's Churchyard.

> Alloway is the real centre of the Burns Trail. Here the Robert Burns Birthplace Museum is set in beautiful rolling countryside.

At **Ellisland Farm** there are further displays, with some of Burns's family possessions. Mauchline, some 18 km (11 miles) east of Ayr, has the **Burns House and Museum** in another former residence.

Alloway is the real centre of the Burns Trail. Here the **Robert Burns Birthplace Museum** is set in beautiful rolling countryside. Here, **Burns Cottage**, the poet's birthplace, houses a collection of memorabilia and manuscripts, while the ruins of Alloway Kirk and the 13th-century Brig o' Doon have the best period atmosphere.

CELEBRATING BURNS NIGHT

The birthday of Scotland's bard is celebrated with much pomp. A Burns Supper opens with the reading of Burns's Selkirk Grace, before the ceremonious piping in of the haggis, the event's main dish. The Address to the Haggis, the poet's homage to the "great chieftain o' the pudding-race", and other readings follow, along with the patronising Toast to the Lassies, traditionally met with a sarcastic riposte from a female guest. The event ends with Auld Lang Syne.

Robert Burns Centre

🅐 🅝 🏛 Mill Rd, Dumfries 🕐 Times vary, check website; 🌐 nts.org.uk

Burns House

🏛 Burns Street, Dumfries 📞 (01387) 255297 🕐 Apr-Sep: 10am–5pm Mon–Sat, 2–5pm Sun; Oct–Mar: 10am–1pm & 2–5pm Tue–Sat

Ellisland Farm

🅐 🅑 🏛 Holywood Rd, Auldgirth 🕐 Apr–Sep: 10am–1pm & 2–5pm Mon–Sat, 2–5pm Sun; Oct–Mar: 2–5pm Tue–Sat 🌐 ellislandfarm.co.uk

Modern wooden exterior of the Robert Burns Birthplace Museum in Alloway ↑

Burns House and Museum
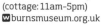 Castle St, Mauchline
(01290) 550045
10:30am–6pm Tue & Wed,
1:30–8pm Thu, 10:30am–4pm
Fri & Sat

Robert Burns Birthplace Museum
 Alloway
10am–5:30pm daily
(cottage: 11am–5pm)
burnsmuseum.org.uk

 23

Caerlaverock Castle

D7 Dumfries &
Galloway 9:30am–
5:30pm daily (Oct–Mar: to
4pm) historic-
environment.scot

This impressive, three-sided,
red stone structure, with its
distinctive moat, is southwest
Scotland's finest example of
a medieval castle. Built in
around 1270 some 14 km
(9 miles) south of Dumfries,
Caerlaverock came to prominence in 1300, during the
Wars of Independence, when
it was besieged by Edward I,
king of England, setting a
precedent for more than three

↑ Threave Castle sitting on
an island in the River Dee,
Kirkcudbrightshire

centuries of strife. Chronicles
of Edward's adventures de-
scribe the castle much as it
stands today, despite being
partially razed and rebuilt due
to clashes with the English
during the 14th and 16th
centuries. It remained the
stronghold of the Maxwell
family, and their crest and
motto remain over the door. It
was the struggle between
Robert Maxwell, a supporter
of Charles I, and a Covenanter
army that caused the castle's
ruin in 1640.

 24

Threave Castle

D7 Castle Douglas,
Dumfries & Galloway
Dumfries Apr–Sep:
10am–4:30pm daily (Oct:
to 3:30pm) historic-
environment.scot

A giant menacing tower, this
14th-century Black Douglas
stronghold on an island in the
River Dee commands the
most complete medieval
riverside harbour in Scotland.
Douglas's struggles against
the early Stuart kings led to

his surrender here after a
two-month siege in 1455.
Threave was dismantled
after Protestant Covenanters
defeated its Catholic
defenders in 1640. Only the
shell of the kitchen, great hall
and domestic levels remain.

 25

Whithorn

C7 Dumfries &
Galloway Stranraer
High St, Gatehouse of
Fleet dumfriesand-
galloway.co.uk

The earliest site of continuous
Christian worship in Scotland,
Whithorn (meaning white
house) takes its name from
the white chapel built by
St Ninian in 397. Though only
ruins remain, a guided tour of
the archaeological dig reveals
evidence of Northumbrian,
Viking and Scottish
settlements ranging from the
5th to the 19th centuries. **The
Whithorn Story** provides
audio-visual information on
the excavations, and contains
fascinating ancient carved
stone artifacts.

The Whithorn Story
45–47 George
St Easter–Oct: 10:30am–
5pm daily whithorn.com

26

Firth of Clyde

🅰 B7, C7 🕐 Numerous counties west of Glasgow 🚆 Helensburgh & Dumbarton in the north; Troon & Ayr in the south 🚢 from Largs to Great Cumbrae; from Gourock to Dunoon

As might be expected of a waterway that leads from Glasgow, a former economic powerhouse of the British Empire to the Irish Sea and the Atlantic, the Firth of Clyde has many reminders of its industrial past.

Greenock, some 40 km (25 miles) west of Glasgow, was once a shipbuilding centre. Few come here for the town's beauty, but the **McLean Museum and Art Gallery**, with its exhibits and information on the engineer James Watt, a native of Greenock, is worth a visit. Princes Pier is a departure point for cruises on the Clyde.

Dumbarton, 24 km (15 miles) from Glasgow on the northern bank, dates from the 5th century AD. Its ancient castle perches on a rock overlooking the rest of the town.

The Firth itself is L-shaped, heading northwest as it opens up beyond the Erskine Bridge.

Did You Know?

Ireland and the Isle of Man are visible from the Mull of Galloway, Scotland's most southerly point

On reaching Gourock, just west of Greenock, the Firth branches south to more open water. Kip Marina at nearby Inverkip is a major yachting centre, while many towns on the Ayrshire coast have served as holiday resorts for Glasgow since Victorian times.

Largs, site of the clash between Scots and Vikings in 1263, has a multimedia centre about Vikings in Scotland, as well as a modern monument to the 1263 battle. From here, a ferry service is offered to Great Cumbrae Island, which lies just off the coast. The main town on the island is Millport, which is built around a picturesque bay.

The western side of the Firth of Clyde is much less developed, and is bordered by the Cowal Peninsula with its hills and lochs. The only town of note in this wild country is Dunoon. Also once

a Victorian holiday resort, it still relies on tourism for its income. For many years there was a strong American influence in Dunoon due to the US nuclear submarine base at Holy Loch, but that is now closed.

McLean Museum and Art Gallery

🏠 15 Kelly St, Greenock 📞 (01475) 715624 🕐 Until May 2019 for renovation.

27

Galloway Forest Park

🅰 C7 🕐 Dumfries & Galloway 🚆 Stranraer 🅵 Clatteringshaws, Glen Trool, Kirroughtree 🌐 gallowayforestpark.com

This is the wildest stretch of country in Southern Scotland, with many points of historical interest as well as great beauty. The park extends to 670 sq km (260 sq miles) just north of Newton Stewart. The principal focal point is Loch Trool. By Caldons Wood, west of the loch, the Martyrs' Monument marks the spot where six Covenanters were killed at prayer in 1685. Bruce's Stone, above the north shore, commemorates

Clouds shadowing the Firth of Clyde, a historic sea route ↑

 Picturesque Loch Trool in Galloway Forest Park, Dumfries & Galloway

an occasion in 1307 when Robert the Bruce routed English forces. To the north of Loch Trool are several hills; Bennan stands at 562 m (1,844 ft) and Benyellary at 719 m (2,359 ft), while Merrick, at 843 m (2,766 ft), is the tallest mountain in Southern Scotland. The area is great for mountain biking and is home to the famous 7stanes route. It is also the UK's first Dark Sky park, with information panels mapping the night sky.

28

The Rhinns of Galloway

C7 Dumfries & Galloway Stranraer Stranraer; Portpatrick Cairnryan 28 Harbour St, Stranraer; (01776) 702595

In the extreme southwest, this peninsula is almost separated from the mainland by Loch Ryan and Luce Bay. At the **Logan Botanic Garden**, subtropical species thrive. Stranraer is 10 km (6 miles) from Cairnryan, the ferry port for Northern Ireland. Nearby

Portpatrick is prettier, with a ruined 17th-century church and the remains of 16th-century Dunskey Castle.

Logan Botanic Garden
Near Port Logan, Stranraer Mar-mid-Nov: 10am-5pm daily rbg.org.uk

---

EAT

The Waterside
This stunning restaurant and bar on the water's edge uses the freshest of local ingredients.

C6 Ardrossan Rd, West Kilbride waterside ayrshire.com

£££

Braidwoods
Ayrshire's only restaurant with a Michelin Star serves local produce with a multicultural twist.

C6 Drumcastle Mill Cottage, Dalry braidwoods.co.uk

£££

GLASGOW

Glasgow's city centre, on the north bank of the River Clyde, has been occupied since ancient times. The Romans already had a presence in the area some 2,000 years ago, and there was a religious community here from the 6th century. Records show Glasgow's growing importance as a merchant town from the 12th century onwards.

Historic buildings such as Provand's Lordship, a 15th-century town house, remind visitors of its pre-industrial roots, but modern Glasgow grew from the riches of the British Empire and the Industrial Revolution. In the 18th century Glasgow imported rum, sugar and tobacco from the colonies, while in the 19th century it reinvented itself as a cotton-manufacturing centre. It then became a hub for shipbuilding and heavy engineering works, attracting many incomers from poverty-stricken districts in the Scottish Highlands and islands, and Ireland, in the process.

Between the 1780s and the 1880s the population exploded from around 40,000 to over 500,000. The city boundaries expanded exponentially and, despite an economic slump between the two world wars, Glasgow clung to its status as an industrial giant until the 1970s, when its traditional skills were no longer needed. The city has since bounced back; it was named European Capital of Sport in 2003 and hosted the 2014 Commonwealth Games, while a £500 million project at Glasgow Harbour has transformed the city's old shipyards and dockland into a hub for commercial, residential and leisure usage.

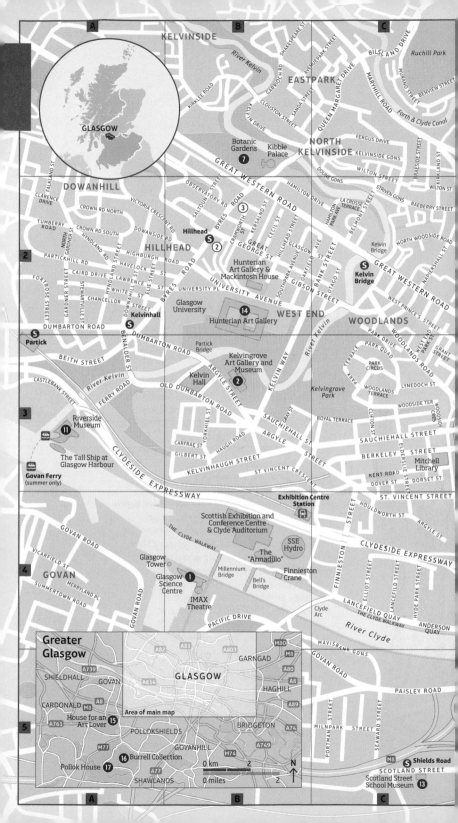

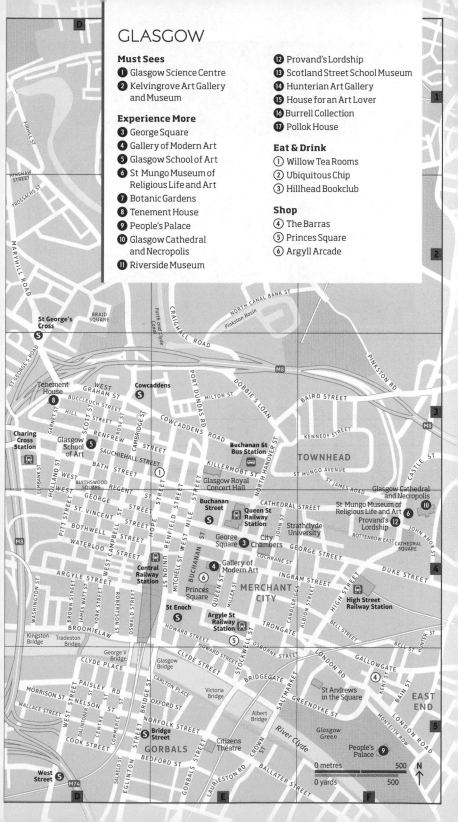

GLASGOW

Must Sees
1. Glasgow Science Centre
2. Kelvingrove Art Gallery and Museum

Experience More
3. George Square
4. Gallery of Modern Art
5. Glasgow School of Art
6. St Mungo Museum of Religious Life and Art
7. Botanic Gardens
8. Tenement House
9. People's Palace
10. Glasgow Cathedral and Necropolis
11. Riverside Museum
12. Provand's Lordship
13. Scotland Street School Museum
14. Hunterian Art Gallery
15. House for an Art Lover
16. Burrell Collection
17. Pollok House

Eat & Drink
1. Willow Tea Rooms
2. Ubiquitous Chip
3. Hillhead Bookclub

Shop
4. The Barras
5. Princes Square
6. Argyll Arcade

←

1 Ashton Lane.

2 Vintage clothing for sale at Glasgow Flea Market, The Barras.

3 Botanical Gardens.

4 Street art by Art Pistol and Rogue-One, Glasgow City Centre Mural Trail.

In just two experience-packed days in Glasgow you can travel in time from a 13th-century cathedral to a tenement time capsule, admire the ingenuity of Victorian engineers, and tip your hat to classical painters and 21st-century street artists.

2 DAYS
in Glasgow

Day 1

Morning Start the day by meandering through Glasgow's Botanic Gardens (p130), where palms and tropical blossoms flourish in vast, airy glasshouses. From there, stroll through the beautifully lush Kelvingrove Park to Kelvingrove Art Gallery and Museum (p126) where the work of the Scottish Colourists, Charles Rennie Mackintosh, and the "Glasgow Boys" take pride of place.

Afternoon Take your pick of pubs on nearby Argyle Street for lunch then walk to the Riverside Museum (p131) to spend a nostalgic afternoon admiring vintage vehicles and locomotives inside architect Zaha Hadid's impressive glass and metal building. The equally impressive Clyde-built sailing ship Glenlee is berthed alongside, and another historic vessel, the Clyde steamer Queen Mary II, is undergoing restoration nearby.

Evening Finish your day of exploration in style by boarding a speedboat for a high-speed evening cruise with a view of the Clyde and its bridges and brash new waterfront district from the river. Once back on dry land, choose from a stylish and eclectic range of dishes at Oran Mor's Brasserie Restaurant. The fun doesn't stop there; this legendary venue in a former church also hosts live music, comedy and club nights.

Day 2

Morning Start the day with a peek into everyday life in Glasgow's not-so-distant past at the Tenement House (p130). Find more insights into the lives of ordinary Glaswegians at the People's Palace (p130), then walk across Glasgow Green to stop for lunch at The Winged Ox Bar and Kitchen at St Luke's and browse vintage stalls at The Barras (p129).

Afternoon Pay your respects to St Mungo, the city's patron saint, at his tomb in the crypt of 13th-century Glasgow Cathedral (p130), then join a guided walk around the hilly Necropolis, which is filled with grandiose monuments to the city's great and wealthy. Back at street level, take in street art along the City Centre Mural Trail (p35) on your way to the Gallery of Modern Art (p128), an ever-growing collection of cutting-edge work by Glasgow-based artists.

Evening For a change of cultural pace, enjoy an evening at the Theatre Royal, home of Scottish Opera. For after-show dinner and drinks, book a table at late-night restaurant Ubiquitous Chip on buzzy Ashton Lane in Glasgow's West End. Don't be fooled by its seemingly casual vibe – its innovative menu features regional Scottish produce such as venison haggis, champit tatties and neep cream, and the wine list is a cut above the rest.

Clydebank Colossus

The towering giant steel structure of the Titan Crane is Glasgow's gritty answer to the Eiffel Tower. Built in 1906 to hoist massive loads on to ships for export worldwide, visitors can now enjoy awesome views from the top-level viewing platform, or swing, bungee-jump and abseil from its giant boom 50 m (164 ft) above the river.

Did You Know?

Glasgow was a hub for manufacturing ships and armaments during the first and second world wars.

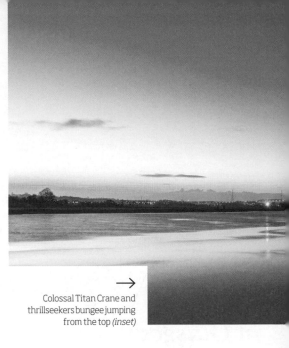

→

Colossal Titan Crane and thrillseekers bungee jumping from the top *(inset)*

GLASGOW'S
INDUSTRIAL HERITAGE

Coal, iron and steam turned Glasgow from a prosperous merchant city into the British Empire's greatest industrial centre. Although heavy industry declined in the 20th century, its legacy is still a source of pride.

All Aboard Glenlee

Glenlee is one of the last great Clyde-built sailing ships. Meet volunteers in period costume and imagine what life was like as a voyager aboard this three-masted seafaring vessel more than a century ago. Launched in 1896 she circumnavigated the globe four times before being rescued from dereliction in 1992. The ship is now moored next to the futuristic Riverside Museum *(p131)*.

←

Three masts of the Tall Ship *Glenlee* looming high above the Clyde

A Steam Cruise on the Clyde

Take a cruise aboard the Waverley paddle steamer to experience the age of steam first-hand. Built on the Clyde in 1947, the last seagoing paddle steamer in the world once carried Glasgow folk to ports like Ayr, Campbeltown, Rothesay and Helensburgh along the Firth of Clyde *(p112).*

SUGAR, SLAVES AND TOBACCO

Glasgow has only recently started to come to terms with the unsavoury sources of its early wealth. Much of the sugar and tobacco that enriched the city's 18th-century merchants came from slave plantations in America and the Caribbean. When slavery was finally abolished in 1833, plantation oweners reinvested their windfall in the new industrial economy.

→
Waverley paddle steamer moored at Pacific Quay on the River Clyde

Futuristic structures of Glasgow Science Centre reflected in the River Clyde ↑

❶ 🏄 🅜 🖥 🛍

GLASGOW SCIENCE CENTRE

📍B4 🏛50 Pacific Quay 🚇Cessnock 🚌X19, 90, 23, 26 🕐10am–6pm daily
(Sept & Oct: to 5pm; Nov–Mar: to 3pm) 🌐glasgowsciencecentre.org

Like a starship that has landed on the banks of the Clyde, the
gleaming tower and metallic dome of Glasgow Science Centre are
unmistakable landmarks on the city's skyline. Inside is a feast of
inspiring and interactice exhibits to fascinate visitors of all ages.

Opened by Queen Elizabeth II in 2001,
Glasgow Science Centre's titanium-clad
futuristic structures are designed to mimic
the hull of a ship, a homage to the Clyde's
maritime and industrial heritage. The
buildings are linked by a teflon fabric roof
and a "discovery" tunnel.

Inside, the three-storey Science Mall uses
interactive exhibits, laboratories and
multimedia tools to take visitors of all ages
on a journey through the inner workings of
cutting-edge applied science, from solar
power to artificial intelligence and the latest
advancements in quantum physics.

Next door, Scotland's only IMAX Theatre
projects breathtaking images
from the natural and scientific
world on to its 24-m (80-ft) by
18-m (60-ft) screen. Other
exhibits include a lab where
you can examine your hair
and skin, and a spectacular
planetarium featuring a state-
of-the-art full-dome digital
projection system.

↑ Children enjoying the many interactive
  exhibits in the busy Science Mall

↑ A Question of Perception,
  an exhibit where nothing
  is quite as it seems

UNMISSABLE EXHIBITS

Bodyworks
Research capsules in the Science Mall's Bodyworks
section showcase the latest developments in medical
science, while a giant hamster wheel, a virtual autopsy
and the "snot barrier" are perfect for curious kids.

Planetarium
State-of-the-art digital imagery takes audiences on a
virtual journey around our solar system, with live
narration by an expert team of astronomers, rocket
scientists and astronauts.

The Space Zone
The Space Zone lets visitors walk among the
planets of the solar system, from tiny Mercury
to the moons of Jupiter and beyond.

Quantum Technologies
Guaranteed to amaze, this interactive
exhibition aims to make the invisible visible,
untangling the weird and still unexplored
frontiers of quantum physics.

Powering the Future
This exhibit shows young visitors where the energy
that heats and lights their homes, schools and cities
comes from, with interactive features on climate change
and alternative energy sources.

Did You Know?

In 1996 a number of works were stolen from the collection and sold on the black market.

KELVINGROVE ART GALLERY AND MUSEUM

⊙B3 **⌂Argyle St, Kelvingrove** **⑤Partick** **🚌2, 3, 11** **⏱10am-5pm Mon-Thu & Sat, 11am-5pm Fri & Sun** **🌐glasgowlife.org.uk/museums**

Housed in a grand Spanish Baroque building in Glasgow's West End, the Kelvingrove Art Gallery and Museum is deservedly Scotland's most popular civic art collection.

Kelvingrove's 8,000-item-collection includes many pieces of international significance. Among these are 19th-century British artists including Turner and Constable, and French Impressionist and Dutch Renaissance painters. Scottish art and design is well represented with rooms dedicated to the Scottish Colourists and the Glasgow Style.

The museum offers insight into Glasgow's evolution from its medieval beginnings to its 19th- and 20th-century economic and cultural transformation, to the 2010 Commonwealth Games, which the city hosted.

↑ Kelvingrove Art Gallery and Museum, an imposing red sandstone building

↑ Spitfire hanging dramatically from the ceiling of the West Court

↑ Visitors exploring the Natural History Gallery

> Kelvingrove's collection is the world's leading portfolio of works by the dynamic "Glasgow Boys".

The Dutch Gallery

Rembrandt's *Man in Armour* sets the tone for Kelvingrove's collection of 17th-century Dutch and Flemish masters, which is recognized as one of the UK's finest. Other paintings worth seeking out include Benjamin Gerritszoon Cuyp's *The Quack Doctor*, and the supporting cast includes Nicolaes Pieterszoon Berchem, Daniel de Blieck, and Abraham van Beyeren.

The French Gallery

Van Gogh's portrait of the red-headed, red-bearded Alexander Reid makes the Glasgow-born art dealer, a friend of the artist, look almost like Vincent's twin brother. Raoul Dufy's *The Jetties of Trouville-Deauville* is another stand-out work in a stellar portfolio of paintings by 19th- and 20th-century greats including Braque, Gauguin, Monet, Pissarro and Renoir.

The Scottish Colourists

◄ Though they are more closely associated with Edinburgh than with Glasgow, the Scottish Colourists are well represented at Kelvingrove. Cadell's elegantly poised *A Lady in Black* and Peploe's *Roses* are outstanding examples of each artist's style. Hunter's *A Summer Day, Largo* and Fergusson's *On the Beach at Tangier* are variations on the classic maritime themes that both these painters loved.

The Glasgow Boys

James Guthrie's *Old Willie;The Village Worthy*, a sympathetic portrait of an elderly man, contrasts strongly here with the colourful, almost psychedelic mysticism of *The Druids: Bringing in the Mistletoe* by George Henry and E.A. Hornel, illustrating the breadth of vision of this celebrated group of painters. The Kelvingrove collection is the world's leading portfolio of works by the dynamic "Glasgow Boys".

Mackintosh and the Glasgow Style

Woodwork and gesso panels, stylish furniture, beautifully detailed light fittings and other decorative elements that are hallmarks of Charles Rennie Mackintosh's distinctive style have pride of place in the reconstructed Ingram Street Tearooms, designed by Mackintosh working together with his wife, Margaret MacDonald between 1900 and 1912. Tearooms were the first dining establishments to allow unaccompanied women, and the elegant Ladies Luncheon Room is the epitome of Edwardian elegance.

EXPERIENCE MORE

③ George Square

📍E4

George Square was laid out in the late 18th century as a residential area, but Victorian redevelopment conferred its enduring status as the city's focal point. The only building not to be affected by the later 19th-century makeover is the Millennium Hotel (1807) on the north side of the Square.

The 1870s saw a building boom, with the construction of the former Post Office (1876) at the southeast corner, and the Merchants House (1877) to the west side. The latter is home to Glasgow's Chamber of Commerce, founded in 1781 and the UK's oldest organization of its kind. The dominant structure, however, is the **City Chambers** on the east side. Designed by William Young in Italian Renaissance style, the imposing building was opened in 1888 by Queen Victoria. With its elegant interior, decorated in marble and mosaic, the opulence of this building makes it the most impressive of its type in Scotland.

City Chambers

🕸🕸 📍82 George St
🕐 Guided tours only:
10:30am & 2:30pm

④ Gallery of Modern Art

📍E4 📍Royal Exchange Sq
🕐10am–5pm Mon–Wed & Sat, 10am–8pm Thu, 11am–5pm Fri & Sun 🌐glasgow life.org.uk/museums

Once the home of Glasgow's Royal Exchange (the city's centre for trade), this building dates from 1829 and also incorporates a late-18th-century mansion that formerly occupied the site. The local authority took over the Exchange just after World War II, and for many years it served as a library. It finally opened its doors as the Gallery of Modern Art in 1996. One of the largest contemporary art galleries outside London, the GoMA is constantly building on its collection of work by Glasgow-based artists. Accordingly, most of the gallery is home to a lively and thought-provoking programme of temporary exhibitions featuring work by Scottish and international artists.

Many of these focus on contemporary and social issues, often featuring groups that are marginalized in today's society.

⑤ Glasgow School of Art

📍D3 📍167 Renfrew St 🕐For renovation 🌐gsa.ac.uk

Widely regarded as Charles Rennie Mackintosh's masterpiece, Glasgow School of Art is a well-loved Glasgow institution. Erected between 1897 and 1909, it was noted for the ground-breaking style of the exterior and high level of attention that Mackintosh devoted to every detail within, from decorative woodwork and windows to door handles and light switches. The interior was damaged by fire in 2014 and was due to reopen in 2019 after meticulous restoration. Tragically, a second and more severe fire in 2018 virtually destroyed the building, raising doubts over whether it could, or should, be rebuilt at all.

← Monument to Sir Walter Scott rising above the City Chambers on George Square

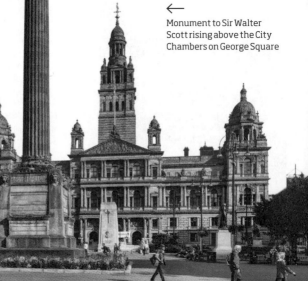

 Gallery of Modern Art, in the Royal Exchange building, surrounded by fairy lights

St Mungo Museum of Religious Life and Art

📍F4 🏠2 Castle St
🕐10am-5pm Tue-Thu & Sat, 11am-5pm Fri & Sun; tours by appointment only
🌐glasgowlife.org.uk/museums

Glasgow has strong religious roots, and the settlement that grew to become today's city started with a monastery founded in the 6th century AD by a priest called Mungo. He died in the early years of the 7th century, and his body lies buried underneath Glasgow Cathedral. The building itself dates from the 12th century, and stands on ground blessed by St Ninian as long ago as AD 397. The ever-growing numbers of visitors to the cathedral eventually prompted plans for an interpretive centre. Despite the efforts of the Society of Friends of Glasgow Cathedral, however, sufficient funds could not be raised. The local

authority decided to step in with money, and with the idea for a more extensive project – a museum of religious life and art. The site chosen was adjacent to the cathedral, where the 13th-century Castle of the Bishops of Glasgow once stood. The museum has the appearance of a centuries-old fortified house, despite the fact that it was completed in 1993. The top floor describes the story of the country's religion from a non-denominational perspective. Both Protestant and Catholic versions of Christianity are represented, as well as the other faiths of modern Scotland. The many, varied displays touch on the lives of communities as extensive as Glasgow's Muslims, who have had their own Mosque in the city since 1984, as well as local followers of the Baha'i faith. The other floors are given over to works of art – among them is Craigie Aitchison's *Crucifixion VII*, which sits alongside religious artifacts and artworks such as burial discs from Neolithic China (2000 BC), contemporary paintings by Aboriginal Australians, and some excellent Scottish stained glass from the early part of the 20th century. Further displays examine the issues that are of fundamental concern to people of all religions – war, persecution, death and the afterlife – and exhibits from

Did You Know?

Glasgow's name comes from the Gaelic phrase meaning green valley or dear green place.

SHOP

The Barras
This most Glaswegian of markets is a glorious mix of stalls selling everything under the sun. The Glasgow Vintage and Flea Market is a regular weekend fixture.

📍F5 🏠244 Gallowgate
🌐theglasgow barras.com

Princes Square
This five-storey atrium beneath a Victorian glass cupola is a paradise for fans of big-name fashion, with brands such as Vivienne Westwood, Kurt Geiger and Belstaff.

📍E4 🏠48 Buchanan St
🌐princessquare.co.uk

Argyll Arcade
Glasgow's glittering emporium of bling gleams with new and pre-loved goods, from luxury watches to diamond rings and vintage jewellery.

📍E4 🏠Argyll St
🌐argyll-arcade.com

cultures as far afield as West Africa and Mexico. In the grounds surrounding the building, there is a permanent Zen Garden, which was created by Japanese garden designer Yasutaro Tanaka. Such gardens have been a traditional aid to contemplation in Japanese Buddhist temples since the beginning of the 16th century.

↑ *Eve*, by Scipione Tadolini, in a glasshouse, Glasgow Botanic Gardens

7

Botanic Gardens

📍B1 🚪Great Western Rd 🚇Byres Road 🚌6, 6A 🕐7am–dusk; glasshouses: 10am–6pm 🌐glasgow botanicgardens.com

These gardens form a peaceful space in the heart of the city's West End, by the River Kelvin. Originally founded at another site in 1817, they were moved to the current location in 1839 and opened to the public three years later. Aside from the main range of greenhouses, with assorted displays including palm trees and an area of tropical crops, one of the most interesting features is the wrought-iron framed Kibble Palace. Built at Loch Long in the Highlands by John Kibble, the glass palace

GREAT VIEW
Glasgow Necropolis

Glasgow Cathedral's hauntingly beautiful necropolis boasts great views over the city's rooftops. Modelled on the Père Lachaise cemetery in Paris, it's a welcome escape from the busy streets below.

---

was moved to its present site in the early 1870s. It houses a collection of carnivorous plants and tropical orchids and the national collection of tree ferns.

8

Tenement House

📍D3 🚪145 Buccleuch St ☎(0141) 333 0183 🕐Apr–Sep: 1–5pm daily (Jul & Aug: from 11am Mon–Sat)

More a time capsule than a museum, the Tenement House is an almost undisturbed record of life as it was in a modest Glasgow flat on a tenement estate in the early 20th century. Glasgow owed much of its vitality and neighbourliness to tenement life, though in later years many of these Victorian and Edwardian apartments were to earn a bad name due to increased poverty and extreme overcrowding, which resulted in many of them having to be pulled down.

The Tenement House was the home of Miss Agnes Toward, who lived here from 1911 until 1965. It remained largely unaltered during that time and, since Agnes threw very little away, the house has become a treasure-trove of social history. In the parlour, which would have been used only on formal occas-ions, afternoon tea is laid out on a white lace cloth. The kitchen, with its coal-fired range and box bed, is filled with the tools of a vanished era, such as a goffering-iron for ironing lace, a washboard and a stone hot-water bottle.

Agnes's lavender water and medicines are still arranged in the bathroom as though she stepped out of the house 70 years ago and forgot to return.

→

Iconic jagged structure of the Riverside Museum on the Clyde waterfront

---

9

People's Palace

📍F5 🚪Glasgow Green 🕐10am–5pm Tue–Thu & Sat, 11am–5pm Fri & Sun 🌐glasgowlife.org.uk/museums

Built in 1898 as a cultural museum for the people of Glasgow's East End, this building houses everything from temperance tracts to trade-union banners, suffragette posters to comedian Billy Connolly's banana-shaped boots, providing a social history of the city from the 12th to the 20th century. A superb conservatory contains an exotic winter garden.

10

Glasgow Cathedral and Necropolis

📍F4 🚪Cathedral Square 🕐Apr–Sep: 9:30am–5:30pm Mon–Sat, 1–5pm Sun; Oct–Mar: 10am–4pm Mon–Sat, 1–4pm Sun; Necropolis: 24hrs daily 🌐glasgow-cathedral.org.uk

One of the few churches to survive the Reformation (*p53*) by adapting itself to Protestant worship, Glasgow Cathedral is a rare example of an original 13th-century church. It was built on the site of a chapel founded by the city's patron saint, St Mungo,

a 6th-century bishop. According to legend, Mungo placed the body of a holy man on a cart yoked to two wild bulls, telling them to take it to the place ordained by God. There he built his church.

The crypt contains the intricate tomb of St Mungo. The Blacader Aisle is reputed to have been built over an existing cemetery that was blessed by St Ninian.

Behind the cathedral, a likeness of John Knox *(p73)*, overlooks a necropolis filled with monuments to the dead of Glasgow's wealthy.

  11

Riverside Museum

📍A3 🏛100 Pointhouse Place 🚆Partick 🚌59 🕙10am–5pm Mon–Thu & Sat, 11am–5pm Fri & Sun 🌐glasgowlife.org.uk/museums

This landmark attraction sits on the Clyde in a dramatic zinc-panelled

building designed by architect Zaha Hadid. Focused on transport and its social impact on the city, the museum is crammed with locomotives and road vehicles of all styles and vintages. A tall ship, berthed alongside, is also open to the public.

12

Provand's Lordship

📍F4 🏛3 Castle St 🕙10am–5pm Tue–Thu & Sat, 11am–5pm Fri & Sun 🌐glasgow life.org.uk/museums

Built as a canon's house in 1471 Provand's Lordship is now Glasgow's oldest surviving house. Its low ceilings and wooden furniture create a vivid impression of life in a wealthy 15th-century household. Mary, Queen of Scots *(p53)* may have stayed here

when she visited Glasgow in 1566 to see her cousin, and husband, Lord Darnley.

 13

Scotland Street School Museum

📍C5 🏛225 Scotland St, 🚇Shields Road 🕙10am–5pm Tue–Thu & Sat, 11am–5pm Fri & Sun 🌐glasgow life.org.uk/museums

This museum housed in a former school, designed by Charles Rennie Mackintosh *(p132)*, contains audio-visual exhibits and reconstructed and restored classrooms to reflect developments in education from the Victorian era to the 1960s. You can read and hear recollections of former pupils covering topics such as classroom discipline, evacuation and World War II, school attire and playground games.

14

Hunterian Art Gallery

⚲ B2 🏠 82 Hillhead St
Ⓢ Hillhead 🚌 4, 4A
🕐 10am-5pm Tue-Sat,
11am-4pm Sun 🌐 gla.ac.
uk/hunterian

Built specifically to house
a number of paintings
bequeathed to Glasgow
University by an ex-student
and physician, Dr William
Hunter (1718–83), the
Hunterian contains Scotland's
largest print collection, with
works by many major
European artists, dating
from the 16th century.

A collection of work by
celebrated Glasgow designer
Charles Rennie Mackintosh,
often cited as the father of the
famous "Glasgow School",
known as the "Glasgow Boys",
a group of painters that came
to fame at the beginning of
the 20th century, is
supplemented by a recon-
struction of his home at No. 6
Florentine Terrace, where he
lived from 1906 to 1914.

The building also houses a
major collection of 19th- and
20th-century Scottish art, but
by far the most famous
collection is that containing
works by the Paris-trained
American painter James
McNeill Whistler (1834–1903),
who influenced so many of
the Glasgow School painters.

CHARLES RENNIE MACKINTOSH

Glasgow's most
celebrated designer
(1868-1928) entered
Glasgow School of Art at
the age of 16. After his
success with the Willow
Tea Room, he became a
leading figure in the Art
Nouveau movement.
His characteristic
straight lines and
flowing detail are the
hallmark of early 20th-
century style.

15

House for an Art Lover

⚲ A5 🏠 Bellahouston Park,
10 Dumbreck Rd Ⓢ Ibrox
🕐 10am- 5pm daily
🔒 Regularly for functions
🌐 houseforanartlover.
co.uk

Plans for the House for an Art
Lover were submitted by
Charles Rennie Mackintosh
and his partner Margaret
Macdonald in response to a
competition in a German
magazine in the summer of
1900. The competition brief
was to create a country retreat
for someone of elegance and
taste who loved the arts. As it
was a theoretical exercise, the
couple were unrestrained by
logistics or budget and won a
special prize for their efforts.
The plans lay unused for over
80 years until consulting
engineer Graham Roxburgh,
who had been involved in the
refurbishment of other
Mackintosh interiors in
Glasgow, decided to build the
House for an Art Lover.
Construction began in 1989
and was completed in 1996.
The House is host to a digital
design studio and post-
graduate study centre for
students at the Glasgow
School of Art. The rooms on
the main floor give a real
insight into the vision of
Mackintosh and the artistic
talent of Macdonald. The Oval
Room is a beautifully propor-
tioned space in a single light
colour, designed to be a
tranquil retreat for ladies,

Sun shining through
medieval stained glass
at the Burrell Collection ↓

while the Music Room and its centrepiece piano (enclosed within a four-poster bed) that is played to add to the atmosphere, is also bright and inspiring. The Main Hall leads into the Dining Room, which contains a long table, sideboard and relief stone fireplace. The great attention to detail demonstrated throughout the House, in the panelling, light fixtures and other elements, is enormously impressive. The exterior of the building is also an extraordinary achievement in art and design.

Grand exterior of Pollok House surrounded by lush parkland ↑

16

Burrell Collection

📍A5 🏛200 Pollokshaws Rd Ⓢ Pollokshaws West 🔒For refurbishment until 2020 🌐glasgowlife.org. uk/museums

Given to the city in 1944 by Sir William Burrell (1861–1958), a wealthy shipping owner, this internationally acclaimed collection is the gem in Glasgow's crown, however it is closed for renovations until 2020. The 9,000-piece collection features over 600 medieval stained-glass panels, 150 tapestries, a collection of ancient Middle Eastern, Greek and Roman treasures, Chinese ceramics and superb Oriental embroideries and carpets, and even celebrated works by Old Masters such as Rembrandt's *Self Portrait* (1632). Additional displays will be unveiled when the collection reopens.

> **The Hunterian contains Scotland's largest print collection, with works by many major European artists, dating from the 16th century.**

17

Pollok House

📍A5 🏛2060 Pollokshaws Rd Ⓢ Pollokshaws West 🕙10am–5pm daily 🌐nts. org.uk

Glasgow's finest 18th-century building boasts one of Britain's best collections of Spanish paintings. The Neo-Classical central block of Pollok House was finished in 1750, the sobriety of its exterior contrasting with the exuberant plasterwork within.

The Maxwells have lived at Pollok since the mid-13th century, but the male line ended with Sir John Maxwell, who added the entrance hall and designed the surrounding gardens and parkland.

Hanging above the family silver, porcelain, hand-painted Chinese wallpaper and Jacobean glass, are William Blake's *Sir Geoffrey Chaucer and the Nine and Twenty Pilgrims* (1745) as well as William Hogarth's portrait of James Thomson, who wrote the words to *Rule Britannia*. El Greco's *Lady in a Fur Wrap* (1541) and works by Francisco de Goya and Esteban Murillo adorn the library and drawing room.

In 1966 Anne Maxwell Macdonald gave the house and parkland, containing the Burrell Collection, to the City of Glasgow.

EAT & DRINK

Willow Tea Rooms
A famous and historic Glasgow institution, with a menu that includes gluten-free and vegetarian options.

📍E3 🏛217 Sauchiehall St 🌐willowtearooms. co.uk

£££

Hillhead Bookclub
This trendy bar and eatery has a dazzling portfolio of craft beers and cocktails.

📍B2 🏛17 Vinicombe St 🌐hillheadbookclub. co.uk

£££

Ubiquitous Chip
At this champion of Scottish produce and experimental cuisine, the casual vibe belies its fine-dining menu.

📍B2 🏛12 Ashton Lane 🌐ubiquitouschip.co.uk

£££

CENTRAL AND NORTHEAST SCOTLAND

Central and Northeast Scotland is a contrast of picturesque countryside and major urban centres, where a modern industrialized country meets an older and wilder landscape. Historically, it was here that the English-speaking Lowlands bordered the Gaelic Highlands, and there is still a strong sense of transition for anyone travelling north.

The Highland Boundary Fault runs through Central Scotland from Arran in the southwest to Stonehaven on the northeast coast. For hundreds of years this line was a border between two very different cultures. To the north and west was a Gaelic-speaking people, who felt loyalty to their local clan chiefs. This way of life was marginalized in the late 18th century, as the more Anglicized Lowlands established their dominance. Stirling Castle, parts of which date from the 16th century, was of great strategic importance during this time.

In the Lowlands, Scotland's industry developed, drawing on coal reserves in districts such as Lanarkshire and the Lothians, while the Highlands were depopulated and eventually set aside for sporting estates and sheep farming.

The country's first coal-run ironworks was built at Carron in 1759, very close to Falkirk, where Bonnie Prince Charlie had enjoyed one of his last military successes as claimant to the British throne 13 years earlier, while Perth and Dundee were important centres of commerce just a short distance from the relative wildness of the southern Highlands.

CENTRAL AND NORTHEAST SCOTLAND

Must Sees

1. Aberdeen
2. Scone Palace
3. Loch Lomond and the Trossachs National Park
4. Stirling Castle

Experience more

5. Stirling
6. Stonehaven
7. Dunnottar Castle
8. Pennan
9. Forvie National Nature Reserve
10. Duff House
11. Balmoral Castle and Royal Deeside
12. Castle Fraser Garden and Estate
13. Doune Castle
14. Elgin
15. The Malt Whisky Trail®
16. Loch Leven Castle and Heritage Trail
17. Perth
18. Glamis Castle
19. Dunkeld
20. Dunfermline
21. Culross
22. Falkirk Wheel
23. The Helix
24. Antonine Wall
25. Dundee
26. Falkland Palace
27. St Andrews
28. East Neuk

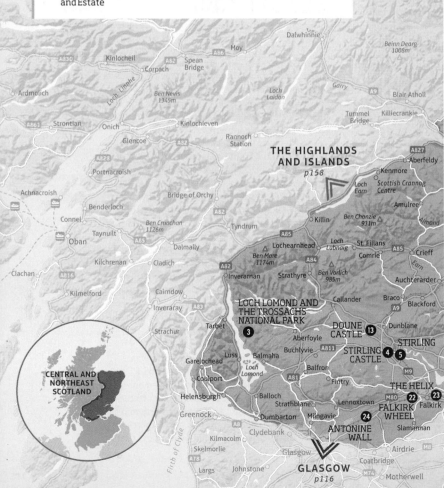

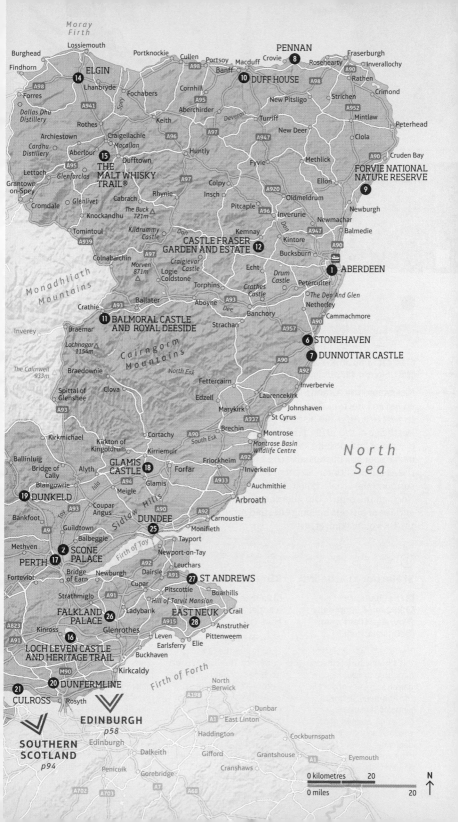

↑ Granite buildings of Union Street, Aberdeen's main thoroughfare

❶

ABERDEEN

🅰E4 🏠Grampian ✈13km (8 miles) NW of Aberdeen
🚉🚌Union Sq ℹ23 Union Street 🌐visitabdn.com

Nicknamed the "Granite City" for its distinctive, hard-edged architecture, Aberdeen is Scotland's third-largest city. After the discovery of oil beneath the North Sea in the 1970s, it became Europe's offshore oil capital and, despite some decline in recent years, its harbour still bustles with commercial shipping. At the east end of Union Street modern redevelopments surround the ornate granite walls of Marischal College. North of the centre, Old Aberdeen is a late medieval enclave of historic buildings nestled around one of the UK's oldest universites.

①
St Machar's Cathedral

🏠The Chanonry
🕐9:30am-4:30pm daily
(Nov-Mar: 10am-4pm)
🌐stmachar.com

The twin granite towers of this 15th-century cathedral, dedicated to Aberdeen's patron saint, rise above the Old Aberdeen skyline to pinpoint St Machar's Cathedral. Stained-glass windows light the interior, depicting the 6th-century saint and the cathedral's earliest bishops.

②
King's College

🏠College Bounds 🕐Daily
(chapel: 10am-3:30pm
Mon-Fri)

Founded in 1495, King's College was the city's first university. The visitor centre gives background on its long history. The chapel has a distinctive lantern tower, rebuilt in 1633. Douglas Strachan's stained-glass windows add a modern touch to the interior, where a 1540 pulpit is carved with heads of Stuart monarchs.

③
St Andrew's Cathedral

🏠King St 🕐Times vary, check website
🌐standrewscathedral aberdeen.org.uk

The Mother Church of the Episcopal Church in the United States, St Andrew's has a memorial to Samuel Seabury, the first Episcopalian bishop in the US, who was consecrated in Aberdeen in 1784. Coats of arms representing the American states and Jacobite families contrast with the white interior.

④
Maritime Museum

🏠Shiprow 🕐10am-5pm
Mon-Sat; noon-3pm Sun
🌐aagm.co.uk

Overlooking the harbour is Provost (Mayor) Ross's house, which dates back to 1593. It now houses the Maritime Museum, which traces the history of Aberdeen's seafaring tradition from medieval times to the offshore oil boom during the 1970s. The exhibitions cover numerous topics from shipbuilding, shipwrecks, rescues and oil excavation.

St Nicholas Kirk

🅰 Union Street 🕐 Jun–Sep: noon–4pm Mon–Fri; 9:30am–1pm Sun 🌐 kirk-of-st-nicholas-org.uk

Founded in the 12th century and rebuilt in 1752, St Nicholas Kirk is Scotland's largest parish church. Many ancient relics can be seen inside, including iron rings which were used to secure women accused of witchcraft in the 17th century.

Aberdeen Art Gallery

🅰 Schoolhill 🕐 For renovation 🌐 aagm.co.uk

This landmark art gallery's collection of works by British artists including Raeburn, Reynolds, Hogarth, Paul Nash, Stanley Spencer and Francis Bacon, and by Monet, Renoir, Degas and Toulouse-Lautrec, may once again be viewed when a long-delayed redevelopment is completed.

Provost Skene's House

🅰 Guestrow 🕐 For renovations 🌐 aagm.co.uk

This 16th-century house is one of the city's most historic buildings. It is temporarily closed due to the Marischal Square redevelopment.

Marischal College

🅰 Broad St

The world's second-largest granite building (narrowly loosing out to the Escorial in Spain for the top spot),

↑ Student cycling along cobbled lanes of Kings College campus

Marischal College was founded in 1593 by the fifth Earl Marischal of Scotland as a Protestant alternative to King's College. It's austere façade, a symbol of the "Granite City", now houses Aberdeenshire Council's headquarters.

EAT

Musa
Contemporary art and live music complement the menu at this lively bar-restaurant. Choose from vegan, veggie and thoroughly carniverous options.

🅰 33 Exchange St 🌐 musaaberdeen.com

£ £ £

Moonfish
Imaginative bites precede delightful mains at this hideaway restaurant off Union Street.

🅰 9 Connection Wynd 🌐 moonfishcafe.co.uk 🕐 Sun & Mon

£ £ £

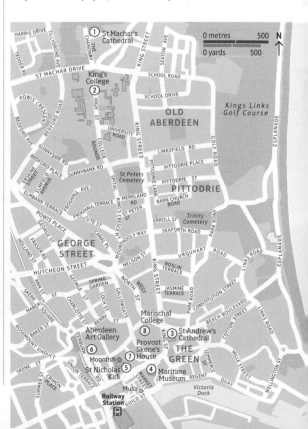

2

SCONE PALACE

A D5 **A** Scone, Perthshire **B** From Perth **C** Apr-Oct: 9:30am-4pm daily
W scone-palace.co.uk

The historic home of the Stone of Destiny, this ornate slice of Gothic grandeur was once the crowning place of Scottish Kings. Its opulent interior and annual events, such as the Perth Highland Games and medieval combat re-enactments, are a spectacle to behold.

Pronounced "scoon", this magnificent palace in the heart of Perthshire dates back to the 12th century. The site was once a Pictish gathering place, and since then has been a Christian church, an Augustinian priory and the seat and the crowning place of Scottish Kings. The last coronation in Scotland took place here in 1651, when King Charles II was crowned atop Moot Hill. Today the palace is one of the UK's finest examples of the late Georgian Gothic style, having been rebuilt in the early 19th century for William Murray, first Earl of Mansfield. It is now a breathtaking treasury of fabulous *objets d'art*. Portraits of the Murray family gaze down from the walls of the Long Gallery, while beautifully inlaid furnishings, marble busts, ornate sculptures from mythology and elaborately crafted 18th- and 19th-century timepieces are displayed in every room.

Scone's huge wooded gardens are home to red squirrels, roe deer and the rare Hawfinch, as well as peacocks who patrol the palace grounds. Stroll along the serene Laburnum Walkway, or climb to the top of Moot Hill, where famed Scottish kings, such as Macbeth and Robert The Bruce, were crowned.

THE STONE OF DESTINY

Scottish Kings were crowned on the rough-hewn Stone of Destiny from the dawn of the Scots kingdom until 1296, when Edward I took it to Westminster Abbey. In 1996 it was returned to Scotland, and it is now held at Edinburgh Castle *(p68)*. A replica sits atop Moot Hill, marking the site of the original.

① In the palace grounds, 2,000 trees and 800 m (2620 ft) of paths make up the famous Murray Star Maze, a labyrinth leading to a central statue of the water nymph Arethusa.

② A piping ceremony at the unveiling of Scone Palace's restored 16th-century historic archway.

③ The ornate interior of the Long Gallery, adorned with paintings of the Murray family.

← Red sandstone exterior and castellated roof of Scone Palace

LOCH LOMOND AND THE TROSSACHS NATIONAL PARK

🅰C5 🏠West Dunbartonshire, Argyll & Bute, Trossachs
🚆Balloch; Arrochar and Tarbet 🚌Callander; Balloch;
Balmaha 🅵Ancaster Sq, Callander; (01877) 330342;
National Park Visitor Centre, Balmaha; (01389) 722100
🇼lochlomond-trossachs.org

Combining the ruggedness of the Grampians with the pastoral tranquillity of the Borders, this beautiful region of craggy hills and sparkling lochs is the meeting place of the Lowlands and Highlands.

Loch Lomond

Of Scotland's many lochs, Loch Lomond is perhaps the most popular and best loved. Lying just 30 km (19 miles) northwest of Glasgow, its accessibility has helped its rise to prominence. Duncryne, a small hill some 5 km (3 miles) northeast of Balloch on the southern shore, gives an excellent view of the loch, while the western shore is the more developed, with villages such as Luss and Tarbet attracting many visitors.

Walkers pass by Loch Lomond's shores on the West Highland Way, Scotland's most popular long-distance footpath running from Glasgow to Fort William, and the 30-mile (50 km) Great Trossachs Path which runs between Callander and Inversnaid skirts its banks. Boat trips operate from Balloch Pier and can be rented from various points around the loch.

GREAT VIEW
Ben Lomond

The 12-km (7.5-mile) hike to the summit of Ben Lomond, 990m (3,217 ft) above the lochside starting point at Rowardennan, calls for good boots and reasonable fitness. The path leads through oak and birch woods, then up to the summit for a breathtaking panoramic view.

↓ Walker overlooking Loch Katrine from the summit of Ben A'an, Trossachs

Inversnaid Hotel Harbour *(above)* and Loch Lomond *(right)* as viewed from Beinn Dubh ↑

The Trossachs

In 2002, 1,865 sq km (720 sq miles) of the Trossachs area was designated Scotland's first national park. Home to a variety of wildlife, including the golden eagle, peregrine falcon, red deer and the wildcat, the Trossachs have inspired many writers, including Sir Walter Scott *(p100)*. Loch Katrine, just north of Loch Lomond, was the setting of Sir Walter Scott's *Lady of the Lake* (1810). The Victorian steamer *Sir Walter Scott* cruises from Trossachs Pier. Callander is the most popular town from which to explore the Trossachs, while Queen Elizabeth Forest Park between Loch Lomond and Aberfoyle offers spectacular woodland walks through this vast tract of Scottish countryside.

Did You Know?

At 45 sq km (27.5 sq miles), Loch Lomond is the largest stretch of fresh water in Britain by surface area.

④ ⓂⒹⒶ

STIRLING CASTLE

🅐 D5 🏠 Castle Esplanade, Stirling 🚆🚌 ⏱ Apr-Sep: 09:30am-6pm daily; Oct-Mar: 09:30am-5pm daily 🌐 stirlingcastle.gov.uk

Rising high on a rocky crag, this magnificent castle, which dominated Scottish history for centuries, now remains one of the finest examples of Renaissance architecture in Scotland.

Overlooking the plains where some of Scotland's most decisive battles took place, Stirling Castle was one of the nation's greatest strongholds. Legend says that King Arthur wrested the original castle from the Saxons; however, the first written evidence of a castle is from 1100. The present building dates from the 15th and 16th centuries. From 1881 to 1964 it was used as a depot for recruits into the Argyll and Sutherland Highlanders.

Today you can explore the palace vaults, try your hand at some medieval crafts and rub shoulders with costumed characters as they bring the castle's fascinating history to life.

↑ Highland cattle grazing on pastures overlooked by Stirling Castle

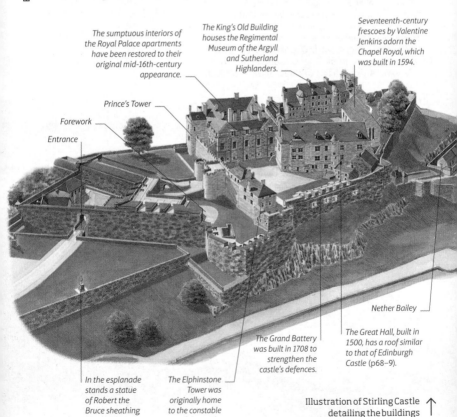

The sumptuous interiors of the Royal Palace apartments have been restored to their original mid-16th-century appearance.

The King's Old Building houses the Regimental Museum of the Argyll and Sutherland Highlanders.

Seventeenth-century frescoes by Valentine Jenkins adorn the Chapel Royal, which was built in 1594.

Prince's Tower

Forework

Entrance

Nether Bailey

The Grand Battery was built in 1708 to strengthen the castle's defences.

The Great Hall, built in 1500, has a roof similar to that of Edinburgh Castle (p68–9).

In the esplanade stands a statue of Robert the Bruce sheathing his sword.

The Elphinstone Tower was originally home to the constable of the castle.

↑ Illustration of Stirling Castle detailing the buildings within its fortified walls

EXPERIENCE MORE

STIRLING BATTLES

Standing at the highest navigable point of the Forth and holding the pass to the Highlands, Stirling occupied a key position in Scotland's many struggles for independence. Seven battlefields can be seen from the Stirling Castle; the 67-m (220-ft) Wallace Monument at Abbey Craig recalls William Wallace's defeat of the English army at Stirling Bridge in 1297, foreshadowing Robert the Bruce's victory in 1314.

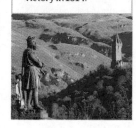

5

Stirling

Ⓐ D5 ⓐ Stirlingshire 🚋🚌
ⓘ Old Town Jail, St John St;
Ⓦ destinationstirling.com

Between the Ochil Hills and the Campsie Fells, the city of Stirling grew up around its castle, historically one of Scotland's most important fortresses. Below the castle the Old Town is still protected by the original walls, built in the 16th century to keep Mary, Queen of Scots safe from Henry VIII. The medieval Church of the Holy Rude, on Castle Wynd, where the infant James VI was crowned in 1567, has one of Scotland's few surviving hammerbeam oak roofs. In front of the church, the ornate façade of Mar's Wark is all that remains of a grand palace, destroyed by the Jacobites in 1746.

Just 3 km (2 miles) south of Stirling, the **Battle of Bannockburn Experience** stands by the field where Robert the Bruce defeated the English in 1314 (*p52*), after which he

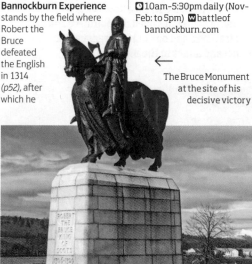

← The Bruce Monument at the site of his decisive victory

dismantled the small castle that once stood there to prevent it from falling into English hands. A statue commemorates the man who became an icon of Scottish independence.

Battle of Bannockburn Experience

♿ 🅿 🚻 Ⓐ Glasgow Rd ⏰ 10am–5:30pm daily (Nov–Feb: to 5pm) Ⓦ battleof bannockburn.com

EAT

Birds and The Bees
This family-friendly gastropub serves brasserie favourites.
Ⓐ D5
Ⓐ Easter Cornton Rd
Ⓦ thebirdsandthebees-stirling.com
Ⓔ Ⓔ Ⓔ

1745

The year of the last military assault on Stirling Castle, lead by the Jacobite army.

Stonehaven

⚑E4 ⚑Aberdeenshire
≋Stonehaven

Situated on a long crescent of sandy beach, this small town is known for its annual Hogmanay Fireball Festival (*p49*) and its heated seawater **open-air swimming pool**. It is also infamous as the birthplace of the deep-fried Mars Bar. The **Stonehaven Tolbooth Museum** is housed in a 16th-century building on the quayside and once served as the town's courthouse and jail. It now displays a large collection of oddball, punishment-related artifacts such as the stocks and the crank, a distinctly horrible torture device.

Stonehaven Tolbooth Museum

⚑Old Pier, Stonehaven Harbour ⏱1:30–4:30pm Wed-Mon ⓦstonehaven tolbooth.co.uk

Open-air swimming pool

⚑Queen Elizabeth Park ⏱Times vary, check website; ⓦstonehavenopenairpool.co.uk

Dunnottar Castle

⚑E4 ≋X7, 107 from Stonehaven ⏱Apr-Sep: 9am-5:30pm daily; Oct-May: times vary, check website; may also close in bad weather ⓦdunnottar castle.co.uk

Perched on its sea-girt crag just 3 km (2 miles) south of Stonehaven, Dunnottar is the northeast's most spectacular castle. It featured in *Victor Frankenstein*, the 2015 sci-fi film adaptation of Mary Shelley's 1818 novel, starring Daniel Radcliffe. It also featured as Elsinore in Franco Zeffirelli's *Hamlet*. The castle sits on a superb natural stronghold, with steep cliffs on three sides and a narrow neck of rock connecting it to the land. The Scottish crown jewels were famously hidden from Oliver Cromwell's invading army here in the 17th century. Originally constructed for the Earl of Marischal in the 12th century, the surviving parts, mostly in ruins, date from the 15th and 16th centuries, and the 14th-century tower house is still in relatively good shape, though roofless. The castle is accessible by car, or via a steep well-marked clifftop path from Stonehaven.

Did You Know?

Dunnottar's Gaelic name is *Dùn Fhoithear*, meaning "fort on the shelving slope".

Pennan

⚑E3 ⚑Aberdeenshire
≋From Aberdeen

Tiny Pennan is a picturesque fishing hamlet sandwiched between towering sandstone

> **Forvie National Nature Reserve is one of Scotland's most dramatic coastal stretches, and one of the largest areas of sand dunes in the UK.**

→ Dramatic ruins of Dunnottar Castle, poised on its iconic clifftop precipice at sunrise

cliffs and the choppy waters of the North Sea. This single row of pretty, whitewashed stone houses achieved fame as a location for the 1983 film *Local Hero* in which it doubled as the fictional village of Ferness. Look out for the iconic red phone box on the seafront; originally installed just for the movie, it is now a local landmark.

Forvie National Nature Reserve

E4 **Forvie, Colliestoun, Ellon** **61 or 63 from Aberdeen** **Visitor Centre: Apr–Oct: daily** **nature.scot**

A bleak and beautiful expanse of windswept coast near Balmedie, a somnolent suburb of Aberdeen, Forvie National Nature Reserve is one of Scotland's most dramatic coastal stretches, and one of the largest areas of sand dunes in the UK. This unique environment, where stark empty sand dunes meet the mudflats of the Ythan Estuary, is home to some spectacular wildlife including eider ducks, wading oystercatchers and seals. Just 2.5 km (4 miles) south of Forvie, the opening of Trump International Golf Links in 2012 sparked controversy within the local community, as the previously protected Menie Estate was bulldozed to make way for the development. Donald Trump's grandiose promises of a $1.25 billion investment creating 6,000 jobs persuaded the Scottish government to ignore environmental considerations and approve the scheme. The local economy has not benefited as promised. The resort comprises one course

↑ Opulent Duff House, home to a priceless collection of artwork

(open only seven months of the year) and a 16-room hotel that employs fewer than 100 people.

Duff House

E3 **Banff** **Banff** **35, 300** **11am–5pm daily (Nov–Mar: to 4pm)** **historicenvironment. scot**

This grand mansion, well off the tourist trail, but its spectacular collection of artworks and renowned masterpieces by Scottish and European masters is a revelation. El Greco's *St Jerome in Penitence* is a highlight, and there are also works by Allan Ramsay, Sir Henry Raeburn and Dutch, German and Italian Renaissance painters. Surrounded by immaculate gardens, the house was designed by famed architect William Adam for William Duff, Earl of Fife, in 1735, but the two allegedly fell out over a structural flaw in the building, which led to a long-drawn-out court case, and Duff never actually moved into the finished house.

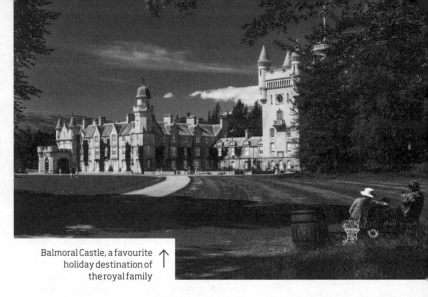

Balmoral Castle, a favourite holiday destination of the royal family ↑

Balmoral Castle and Royal Deeside

🅰D3 🏰Balmoral Estate, Ballater 🚌201, 203 from Aberdeen ⏰Times vary, check website 🌐balmoral castle.com

Balmoral Castle is a kitsch Victorian vision that is the high point of any visit to leafy Royal Deeside. Queen Victoria bought the estate for 30,000 guineas in 1852, after its owner choked to death on a fishbone. Her Prince Consort,

VICTORIA AND ALBERT'S BALMORAL

It was the riverside setting that Queen Victoria fell for in 1848 when she first visited Balmoral, and it was her husband, Prince Albert, who worked with Aberdeen-born architect William Smith to create the white granite palace that replaced the old castle. It stands here still, a medley of fantastical turrets typical of the Baronial style.

Albert, had a hand in the design and it reflects his Teutonic tastes. The grand ballroom is the only part of the castle open to the public, but splendid walking trails allow visitors to explore the gardens and grounds.

Castle Fraser Garden and Estate

🅰D3 🏰Inverurie, Aberdeenshire ⏰Times vary, check website 🌐nts.org.uk

Castle Fraser, within beautifully kept landscaped grounds, is an architectural riot of towers, turrets and crow-step gables. Most of these were added in the late 18th century, but the original castle, which is more than 400 years old, is one of the oldest and largest "z-plan" tower houses in Scotland. Inside, grand medieval halls and Regency salons house Fraser family portraits and exquisite Regency furniture.

→

Cardhu Distillery in Speyside, founded in 1811 in this remote spot

Doune Castle

🅰D5 🏰Doune 🚂Doune, 🚌From Stirling ⏰Apr-Sep: 9:30am-5:30pm daily; Oct-Mar: 10am-4pm daily 🌐historicenvironment. scot

Built as the residence of Robert, Duke of Albany, in the late 1300s, Doune Castle was a Stuart stronghold until it fell into ruin in the 18th century. Now fully restored, it offers a unique view into the life of the medieval royal household.

The Gatehouse leads to the central courtyard, then into the Great Hall. With its open-timber roof, minstrels' gallery and central fireplace, the Hall adjoins the Lord's Hall and

Private Room, and retains its original privy and well-hatch. A number of private stairs and narrow passages illustrate the ingenious means by which the royal family protected itself. The film *Monty Python and the Holy Grail* was shot here, and it has also featured in *Game of Thrones* and *Outlander*.

Elgin

D3 ⌂Moray
🚌🚂 *ℹ️* Elgin Library, Cooper Park; (01343) 562608

With its cobbled marketplace and crooked lanes, Elgin retains much of its medieval layout. The 13th- century cathedral ruins are all that remain of one of Scotland's architectural triumphs. Once known as the Lantern of the North, it was damaged in 1390 by the Wolf of Badenoch (son of Robert II) in revenge for his excommunication by the Bishop of Moray. Further damage came in 1576 when the Regent Moray had the lead roofing stripped. Among the remains is a Pictish cross-slab in the nave and a basin where one of the town benefactors, Andrew Anderson, was kept as a baby by his homeless mother. The **Elgin Museum** has anthropological and geological displays, and the **Moray Motor Museum** has vehicles dating back to 1904.

Elgin Museum
🕐 ⌂1 High St 🕐 Apr-Oct: 10am-5pm Mon-Fri, 11am-4pm Sat 🌐 elginmuseum. org.uk

Moray Motor Museum
🕐🕐 ⌂Bridge St 🕐 Easter-Oct: 11am-5pm daily 🌐 moraymotormuseum.org

The Malt Whisky Trail®

D3 ⌂Speyside, Moray
🌐 maltwhiskytrail.com

Due to its climate and geology, Speyside is home to half of Scotland's whisky distilleries. The signposted trail includes eight distilleries though one (Dallas Dhu) no longer makes whisky, and a cooperage, where barrels to store whisky are made.

There is no secret to whisky distilling *(p41)*: barley is steeped in water and allowed to grow, a process called "malting"; the grains are then dried with peat smoke, milled, mixed with water and allowed to ferment in a double process of distillation. The final result is a raw, rough whisky that is then stored in old oak sherry casks for three to 16 years, during which time it mellows. Worldwide, an average of 30 bottles of Scotch whisky are sold every second.

The visitor centres at each of The Malt Whisky Trail® distilleries provide similar, and equally good, guided tours and informative audio-visual displays. Their entry charges can usually be redeemed against the purchase of a bottle of their whisky.

TOP 5 SPEYSIDE DISTILLERIES

Cardhu
⌂Knockando, Aberlour
🌐 malts.com
Founded in 1811, Cardhu is the first distillery to be pioneered by a woman.

Macallan
⌂Easter Elchies Estate, Aberlour 🕐 Mon-Fri 9:30am-6pm; Sun 12-6pm
🌐 themacallan.com
The state-of-the-art Macallan visitor experience is the perfect place to sample the the "Rolls Royce of single malts".

Glenlivet
⌂Castleton Of Blairfindy
🌐 theglenlivet.com
Enjoy multi-sensory tours and tastings in this remote setting.

Glenfiddich
⌂Dufftown
🌐 glenfiddich.com
Traditional craftmanship and innovation come together at this family-run distillery.

Speyside Cooperage
D3 ⌂Craigellachie
🌐 speysidecooperage.co.uk
Here visitors can learn about the making of the wooden casks that are used to store and age the whisky.

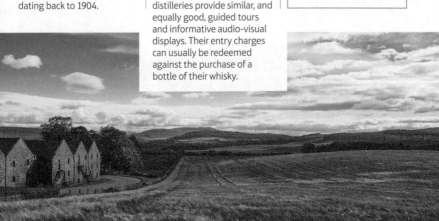

16

Loch Leven Castle and Heritage Trail

D5 Kinross Pier
From Kinross
Times vary, check
website lochleven
heritagetrail.co.uk

Sitting proudly atop a tiny island in the middle of Loch Leven, this eerie tower-house castle, often shrouded in mist, is one of Scotland's oldest, dating back to the 14th century. Mary, Queen of Scots was held captive here between 1567 and 1568, when she suffered a miscarriage and was subsequently forced to abdicate the throne to her infant son James VI. She escaped and was exiled to England, never to return. Other notable visitors include Robert the Bruce and Robert II, who was King of Scots from 1371 to his death in 1390. Boats depart regularly from the mainland pier; the crossing takes around 10 minutes. Tickets must be bought from the ticket office. The Loch Leven Heritage Trail is a 22-km (14-mile) gravel path that circles the loch – perfect for a scenic cycle or walk. Cycle hire is available at Kinross Pier.

> It was while on holiday in the countryside around Dunkeld that the children's author Beatrix Potter found inspiration for her Peter Rabbit stories.

17

Perth

D5 Perthshire
45 High St perthcity.
co.uk

The capital of medieval Scotland, Perth's rich heritage is reflected in many of its buildings. In the Church of St John, founded in 1126, John Knox delivered fiery sermons that led to the destruction of many local monasteries. On North Port, the Victorianized Fair Maid's House (c. 1600) is one of the city's oldest, and the fictional home of the heroine of Sir Walter Scott's *The Fair Maid of Perth* (1828).

In **Balhousie Castle**, the Museum of the Black Watch commemorates the first ever Highland regiment, while the **Museum and Art Gallery** has local industry displays and Scottish art exhibitions.

Three km (2 miles) north of Perth, Gothic Scone Palace *(p140)* stands on the site of an abbey destroyed by John Knox's followers in 1559.

Between the 9th and 13th centuries, Scone guarded the sacred Stone of Destiny, now in Edinburgh Castle *(p140)*.

Balhousie Castle

RHQ Black Watch,
Hay St (01738) 638152
9:30am–4:30pm daily
(Nov–Mar: 10am–4pm)

Museum and Art Gallery

78 George St (01738)
632488 10am–5pm Tue–
Sat (Apr–Oct: also Sun)

18

Glamis Castle

D5 Glamis, outside
Forfar, Tayside Dundee
then bus Apr–Oct: 10am–
5:30pm glamis-castle.
co.uk

With the pinnacled outline of a Loire chateau, the imposing medieval tower house of Glamis Castle began as a royal hunting lodge in the 11th century, but later underwent a thorough

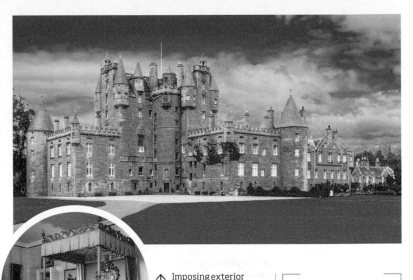

↑ Imposing exterior of Glamis Castle and one of the opulent bedrooms *(inset)*

reconstruction in the 17th century. It was the childhood home of the late Queen Elizabeth the Queen Mother, and her former bedroom can be viewed, including a youthful portrait by Henri de Laszlo (1878–1956). Her daughter, the late Princess Margaret, was born here.

Many rooms are open to the public, including Duncan's Hall, the oldest room in the castle and Shakespeare's setting for the king's murder in *Macbeth*. The castle's opulent rooms present china, paintings, tapestries and furniture spanning 500 years. In the extensive grounds stands a pair of wrought-iron gates made for the Queen Mother on her 80th birthday in 1980. In summer the spectacular gardens are in full bloom.

←

Loch Leven, at the heart of a national nature reserve

 19

Dunkeld

🅰 D5 🏠 Tayside
🚉 Dunkeld & Birnam
🚌 From Perth & Kinross

By the River Tay, crossed here by an elegant Thomas Telford bridge, this ancient and charming village was all but destroyed in the Battle of Dunkeld in 1689. The Little Houses lining Cathedral Street were the first to be rebuilt, and remain fine examples of an imaginative restoration.

The partly ruined 14th-century cathedral enjoys an idyllic setting on shady lawns beside the Tay, against a backdrop of steep and wooded hills. The choir is used as the parish church, and its north wall contains a leper's squint (a little hole through which lepers could see the altar during mass).

It was while on holiday in the countryside around Dunkeld that the children's author Beatrix Potter found inspiration for her Peter Rabbit stories.

 Pretty Culross, preserved by the National Trust for Scotland

⑳ Dunfermline

🅐D5 🄰Fife 🚆🚌

Scotland's capital until 1603, Dunfermline is dominated by the ruins of the 12th-century abbey and palace, which recall its royal past. The town first came to prominence in the 11th century as the seat of King Malcolm III, who founded a priory on the present site of **Dunfermline Abbey and Palace**. With its Norman nave and 19th-century choir, the abbey church contains the tombs of 22 Scottish kings and queens, including that of the renowned Robert the Bruce. The ruins of the palace soar over the gardens of Pittencrieff Park. Dunfermline's most famous son, the philanthropist Andrew Carnegie (1835–1919), had been forbidden entrance to the park as a boy. After making his fortune, he bought the entire Pittencrieff estate and gave it to the people of Dunfermline. Carnegie emigrated to Pennsylvania in his teens and, through iron and steel, became one of the wealthiest men in the world. He donated some $350 million for the benefit of mankind. The **Carnegie Birthplace Museum** tells his fascinating story.

Dunfermline Abbey and Palace

⏱ 🄰St Margaret St 🕐Apr–Oct: daily (Sun pm only) 🅆dunfermline abbey.co.uk

Carnegie Birthplace Museum

🄰Moodie St 🕐Mar–Nov: daily (Sun pm only) 🅆carnegiebirthplace.com

㉑ (NTS) Culross

🅐D5 🄰Fife 🚆🚌From Dunfermline & Perth 🅆nts.org.uk

An important religious centre in the 6th century, Culross is reputed to have been the birthplace of St Mungo in 514. Now a beautifully preserved 16th- and 17th-century village, Culross prospered in the 16th century due to the growth of its coal and salt industries, most notably under the genius of Sir George Bruce. Descended from the family of Robert the Bruce, Sir George took charge of the colliery in 1575 and created a drainage system called the "Egyptian Wheel" which cleared a mine 1.5 km (1 mile) long, running underneath the River Forth. The National Trust for Scotland began restoring the

town in 1932 and provides a guided tour from the visitor centre in the former prison.

Built in 1577, Bruce's palace has the crow-stepped gables, decorated windows and red pantiles typical of the period. Inside, its original painted ceilings are among the finest in Scotland. Crossing the square past Oldest House (1577), head for the Town House to the west. Behind it, a cobbled street known as the Back Causeway leads to the turreted Study, built in 1610 as a house for the Bishop of Dunblane. The main room, with a Norwegian ceiling, is open to visitors. If you continue north to the ruined abbey, fine church and Abbey House, don't miss the Dutch-gabled House with the Evil Eyes.

Palace, Town House and Study

 🕐Apr–Oct: 11am–4pm daily (July & Aug: to 5pm daily)

㉒ Falkirk Wheel

🅐D5 🄰Lime Rd, Tamfourhill, Falkirk 🚆Falkirk 🕐10am–5:30pm daily for boat trips 🅆scottishcanals.co.uk

This impressive, elegant boat lift is the first ever to revolve and the centrepiece of Scotland's ambitious canal regeneration scheme. Once important for commercial transport, the Union and the Forth and Clyde canals were blocked by numerous roads during the 1960s. Now the Falkirk Wheel gently swings boats between the two waterways for an uninterrupted link between Glasgow and Edinburgh. This huge, moving sculpture constantly rotates, lifting boats 35 m (115 ft), equivalent to 11 traditional locks, in just 15 minutes. Visitors can ride the wheel on boats that leave the visitor centre every 40 minutes.

The Helix

⚑D5 ⌂Falkirk ⏰9:30am-5pm daily 🌐thehelix.co.uk

Two amazing, glittering equine heads tower above the Forth and Clyde and Union canals. The Kelpies, 30-m- (98-ft-) tall metal sculptures created by sculptor Andy Scott, are the keynote landmark of The Helix, an expansive new canalside park with miles of walking and cycling trails. The visitor centre explains the history and renewal of the canals.

24 Antonine Wall

⚑D5 ⌂Falkirk 🚆Falkirk ⏰Mon-Sat ℹFalkirk Wheel, Lime Road; (01324) 620244 🌐antoninewall.org

The Romans invaded Scotland for a second time around AD 140, during the reign of Emperor Antonius, and built a 60-km (37-mile) earth rampart that stretched across Central Scotland from the Firth of Clyde to the Firth of Forth, further defended by ditches and forts at strategic points. One of the best-preserved sections of the wall can be seen at Rough Castle, west of Falkirk.

DRINK

Red Lion Inn
Hearty pub grub served in a quintessentially quaint setting.

⚑D5 ⌂Low Causeway, Culross 🌐redlion culross.co.uk

£££

The Wine Library
Family-owned wine bar serving all manner of independent and unusual wines.

⚑D5 ⌂1 Princes St, Falkirk 🌐 thewine libraryscotland.com

£££

↑ The Falikirk Wheel connecting the Union, Forth and Clyde Canals

Sun setting over Andy Scott's *Kelpies,* Falkirk

25 Dundee

D5 Tayside
16 City Sq; www.
dundeecity.gov.uk

Dundee was a major ship-building centre in the 18th and 19th centuries. In Victoria Docks stands **HMS *Unicorn***: built in 1824, it is the oldest British-built warship still afloat. Berthed at Riverside is the royal research ship *Discovery*, built here in 1901 for the first of Captain Scott's voyages to the Antarctic. Housed in a Victorian Gothic building, the **McManus Galleries** give a glimpse of Dundee's industrial heritage, with archaeology exhibitions and Victorian art.

A more recent gem in Dundee's crown is the stunning **V&A Museum of Design** by architect Kengo Kuma, which opened in 2018 and shows the best of Scottish and international design in a monumental modern building with curving concrete walls.

Along the coast, Arbroath Abbey contains a copy of *The Declaration of Arbroath*, which attested Scotland's independence in 1320.

HMS *Unicorn*

Victoria Docks,
Times vary, check website
frigateunicorn.org

Discovery

Discovery Point
10am-6pm Mon-Sat (from 11am Sun); tours by appt only
rrsdiscovery.com

McManus Galleries

Albert Institute, Albert Sq
Daily mcmanus.co.uk

V&A Museum of Design

 1 Riverside Esplanade 10am-5pm daily vam.ac.uk/dundee

26 Falkland Palace

D5 Falkland, Fife
Ladybank, then bus Times vary, check website nts.org.uk

This stunning Renaissance palace was designed as a hunting lodge for the Stuart kings. Begun by James IV in 1500, most of the work was carried out by his son, James V, in the 1530s. He ordered the redecoration of the façade with dormers, buttresses and medallions. The palace fell into ruin during the years of the Commonwealth and was occupied briefly by the infamous Rob Roy, Scotland's very own Robin Hood, in 1715.

After buying the estates in 1887, the third Marquess of Bute became the Palace Keeper and subsequently restored the building. The richly panelled interiors are filled with superb furniture and contemporary portraits of the Stuart monarchs. The royal tennis court, built in 1539 for King James V, is the oldest in Britain.

27 St Andrews

E5 Fife Leuchars
Station Road 70
Market St; www.visitst
andrews.com

Scotland's oldest university town and one-time eccle-siastical capital, St Andrews is now a shrine to golfers from all over the world. Its main

Did You Know?

Dundee is undergoing a £1 billion transformation, centred on the new V&A museum.

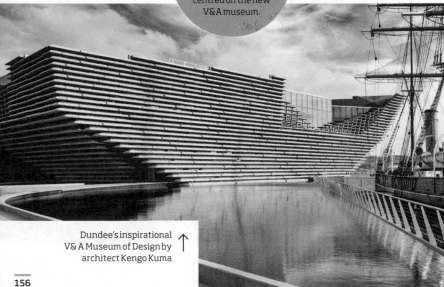

Dundee's inspirational V&A Museum of Design by architect Kengo Kuma

St Andrews Royal and
Ancient golf clubhouse

streets and cobbled alleys, full of crooked housefronts, university buildings and medieval churches, converge on the venerable ruins of the 12th-century cathedral. Once the largest cathedral in Scotland, it was later pillaged for its stones, which were used to build the town. **St Andrews Castle** was built for the town's bishops in 1200 and the dungeon can still be seen. The St Andrews golf courses are to the west of the town, and each is open for a modest fee.

The **British Golf Museum**, which tells how the city's Royal and Ancient Golf Club became the ruling arbiter of the game, will delight golf enthusiasts. One of the chief pleasures here is a walk along the sands.

St Andrews Castle

 ⓐ The Scores
📞 (01334) 477196
🕐 9.30am–5.30pm daily

British Golf Museum

Ⓐ Bruce Embankment
🕐 Daily 🅆 britishgolf
museum.co.uk

㉘
East Neuk

🅰 E5 ⓐ Fife 🚆 Leuchars
🚌 Glenrothes & Leuchars
🅹 St Andrews
🅦 eastneukwide.co.uk

A string of pretty fishing villages peppers the shoreline of the East Neuk of Fife stretching from Earlsferry to Fife Ness. Much of Scotland's medieval trade with Europe passed through here, reflected in the towns' Flemish-inspired architecture. The herring industry has declined, but the sea still dominates village life.

The harbour is the heart of charming St Monans, while Pittenweem is the base for the East Neuk fishing fleet. The town is also known for St Fillan's Cave, retreat of the 9th-century hermit.

A church stands among the cobbled lanes and colourful cottages of Crail; the stone by its gate is said to have been hurled from the Isle of May by the Devil himself.

Anstruther is home to the **Scottish Fisheries Museum**, with boats, cottage interiors, and displays on whaling. From here you can visit the nature reserve on the Isle of May.

A statue of Alexander Selkirk in Lower Largo recalls his seafaring adventures that inspired Daniel Defoe's novel *Robinson Crusoe* (1719). After disagreeing with his captain, he was put ashore on a deserted island for four years.

Scottish Fisheries Museum

Ⓐ St Ayles, Harbour Head, Anstruther
🕐 Daily 🅦 scotfish
museum.org

EAT

The Playwright
This pioneer of fine dining in the heart of Dundee's arts quarter is perfect for pre- or post-theatre dining.

🅰 E5 ⓐ 11 Tay Sq, Dundee 🅦 theplay
wright.co.uk

£ £ £

East Pier
This unassuming former boat shed serves home-smoked shellfish.

🅰 E5 ⓐ East Shore, St Monans 🕐 Jun–Aug: daily; May & Sep: Wed–Sun; Apr–Oct: weekends
🅦 eastpier.co.uk

£ £ £

THE HIGHLANDS AND ISLANDS

Most of the stock images of Scottishness – clans and tartans, whisky and porridge, bagpipes and heather – originate in the Highlands, and enrich the popular picture of Scotland as a whole. But for many centuries the Gaelic-speaking, cattle-raising Highlanders had little in common with their southern neighbours.

Clues to the non-Celtic ancestors of the Highlanders lie scattered across the Highlands and islands in the form of stone circles, brochs and cairns spanning over 5,000 years. By the end of the 6th century, the Gaelic-speaking Celts had arrived from Ireland, as had St Columba, who taught Christianity to the monastic community he established on the island of Iona.

For over 1,000 years, Celtic Highland society was founded on a clan system, built on family ties to create loyal groups dependent on a feudal chief. However, the clans were systematically broken up by England after 1746, following the defeat of the Jacobite attempt on the British crown led by Bonnie Prince Charlie.

A more romantic vision of the Highlands began to emerge in the early 19th century, due largely to Sir Walter Scott's novels and poetry depicting the majesty and grandeur of a country previously considered merely poverty-stricken and barbaric. Another great popularizer was Queen Victoria, whose passion for Balmoral Castle helped establish the trend for acquiring Highland sporting estates. But behind the sentimentality lay harsh economic realities that drove generations of Highland farmers to seek a new life overseas.

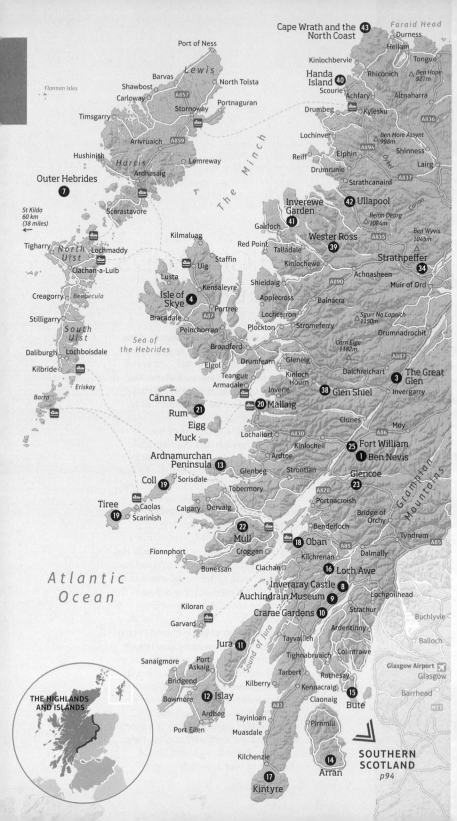

Northern Isles

Shetland Islands ⑥
Yell   Unst
Brae
Walls
Foula
Tingwall Airport
Lerwick
Mainland

Orkney Islands
Westray   ⑤
Sanday
Mainland
Stronsay
Stromness
Kirkwall   Aberdeen
Hoy   St Margaret's Hope
Fair Isle

area of main map
Thurso   John O'Groats
A897   A9
Wick

0 km   50
0 miles   50
N

Strathy
Thurso   Dunnet   John O'Groats
Bowertower
Halkirk   Reiss
Dalhalvaig   Wick
A897
Forsinard   Achavanich   Thrumster
A9   A99
Kinbrace   △ Morven   Dunbeath
705m
Kildonan   Berriedale
Lothmore   ㊲ Helmsdale
A9
Golspie
㊱ Dornoch
Tain
㉚   Moray
Firth
Black   ㉛
Isle
A9   Cromarty
㉜ Fort George
㉟ Cawdor Castle
㉙ ㉝ Culloden
Inverness
Lossiemouth
Elgin
A941
Aberlour   Huntly
Peterhead
A939   A95
Grantown-on-Spey
Elion
Tomatin   N9
Carrbridge
Inverurie
Aberdeen
Cairngorms
National Park
②
North
Sea
Insh
Braemar
Beinn Dearg   Inverey
1008m
△
㉖ Blair Castle
㉘ Killecrankie
㉗ Pitlochry
㉔
Rannoch Moor
Fortingall   Alyth
A93
**CENTRAL AND
NORTHEAST
SCOTLAND**
p134
A9
Bridge
of Earn
M90
Rosyth
Denny   M9
Lennoxtown   Edinburgh
Coatbridge
A702
A721   A703
M74

0 kilometres   30
0 miles   30
N

THE HIGHLANDS AND ISLANDS

Must Sees
❶ Ben Nevis
❷ Cairngorms National Park
❸ The Great Glen
❹ Isle of Skye
❺ Orkney Islands
❻ Shetland Islands
❼ Outer Hebrides

Experience More
❽ Inveraray Castle
❾ Auchindrain Museum
❿ Crarae Gardens
⓫ Jura
⓬ Islay
⓭ Ardnamurchan Peninsula
⓮ Arran
⓯ Bute
⓰ Loch Awe
⓱ Kintyre
⓲ Oban
⓳ Coll and Tiree
⓴ Mallaig
㉑ Rum, Eigg, Muck and Canna
㉒ Mull
㉓ Glencoe
㉔ Rannoch Moor
㉕ Fort William
㉖ Blair Castle
㉗ Pitlochry
㉘ Killiecrankie
㉙ Inverness
㉚ Black Isle
㉛ Moray Firth
㉜ Fort George
㉝ Culloden
㉞ Strathpeffer
㉟ Cawdor Castle
㊱ Dornoch
㊲ Helmsdale
㊳ Glen Shiel
㊴ Wester Ross
㊵ Handa Island
㊶ Inverewe Garden
㊷ Ullapool
㊸ Cape Wrath and the North Coast

Fast and Furious Highland Sport

Camanachd (shinty), the fast and fearsome sport of the Highlands, plays out much like a ferocious clan battle. Players raise their sticks to hit the ball in the air and physical contact is allowed. Men's and Women's finals for the Camanachd and Valerie Fraser cups take place in September. Check www.shinty.com for local fixtures.

$\longrightarrow$

Players engaged in the traditional Highland sport of Camanachd, or shinty

HIGHLAND
TRADITIONS
AND CULTURE

After the Battle of Culloden in 1706, the British government set out to destroy Highland culture. Some say this only strengthened Highlanders' resolve to celebrate their heritage, which continues to this day in the form of clan gatherings, spectacular sporting tournaments, and Highland Games.

Traditional Highland Games

Kilted muscle-men (and women) are a high point of any Highland Games, where athletes toss mighty cabers, hurl massive hammers and throw mammoth weights. Over 80 events take place in villages, castle grounds and Highland estates across the country every weekend from May to September.

$\longleftarrow$

Competitor in a Highland Games hammer-tossing competition

Royal Edinburgh Military Tattoo

After the defeat of the Jacobites, clans who fought for Bonnie Prince Charlie *(p54)* were recruited to fight for King George. The Black Watch is the oldest of these kilted regiments, which in 2006 were merged to create the Royal Regiment of Scotland. They can be seen (and heard) in their full tartan glory at the Edinburgh Military Tattoo *(p48)*, held at Edinburgh Castle during the month of August.

Soldiers from the 5th Battalion of the Royal Regiment of Scotland

BEHIND THE KILT

In the 16th century, the kilt was a full-length garment, with the upper half worn as a cloak. An elaborate code lays down who can wear what tartan. Most clans have at least two tartans – a bold pattern for formal dress and a second more muted version for everyday wear. Up to 20 new tartans are created every year and kilts in stripes or polka dots, accessorized with fake-fur sporrans in rainbow colours, are a fun alternative to the traditional plaid.

INSIDER TIP
The Royal National Mòd

Listen to traditional pipe and clarsach (harp) music and melancholy Gaelic song and verse at the Royal National Mòd, which is held in a different location in the Scottish Highlands every year.

Braemar Gathering, Ballater

Held annually in Ballater, the Braemar Gathering hosts one of the most prestigious and renowned Highland clan gatherings in the country. Thousands attend to enjoy the spectacle. Watch Highland dancers compete for style points as hundreds of pipers and drummers march in unison, and sample all manner of traditional Scottish food and drink.

→

Kilted dancers perform a traditional Highland Fling at a Highland Gathering

The Summer Isles

For solitude, magnificent sunsets and stupendous views, look no further than this cluster of 17 tiny islets peppered along the mouth of Loch Broom, just off the Coigach Peninsula in the northwest Highlands. These remote islands are far removed from the frenetic pace of modern life, and the largest island of the archepelago, Tanera Mòr, is accessed by boat from Old Dornie Harbour in Achiltibuie, 45 minutes from Ullapool (p203). Bookings must be made in advance.

$\rightarrow$

A crisp winter view across the Wester Ross coast looking towards the Summer Isles

REMOTE ISLAND
GETAWAYS

A visit to one of Scotland's tiniest and most remote islands is a once-in-a-lifetime experience. Each island, however small, has its own unique character, close-knit community, and even microclimate. Embark on your own island adventure and find out why the inhabitants of these tiny isles are said to be among the happiest people in the world.

Torsa Island

If total seclusion is what you're after, why not rent an entire island? Well, the only house on the island, to be more precise. Sheltered between the island of Luing and Degnish Point on the mainland, Torsa is only one mile long and half a mile wide. Accessible from Luing, a short crossing from Oban, Torsa House is the island's only property. You'll have freedom to roam, so long as you don't mind sharing the space with sheep and Luing cattle.

$\leftarrow$

Beautifully remote Torsa Island, as viewed from Arduaine Gardens, Oban

INSIDER TIP
Sleep Under the Stars

Places to stay are in short supply in summer, and accommodation gets snapped up fast. Alternatively, take your own tent. Camping is allowed almost anywhere in Scotland, as long as you are respectful of the nearby community and leave the site as you found it. If you're planning a wild camping trip, be sure to familiarize yourself with the Scottish Outdoor Access Code *(p209)* before you set off on your adventure.

Handa Island Wildlife Reserve

Handa Island has 100,000 inhabitants, but none are human. Here, puffins, kittiwakes, skuas and the largest colony of guillemots in Britain rule the roost. Accessible by boat from Tarbet, there is an easygoing 6-km (4-mile) circular route, and a 4-km (3-mile) cliff walk, from which you can spot dolphins, minke whales and basking sharks.

←

Pair of guillemots at Handa Island Wildlife Reserve

Go off-grid on the Isle of Muck

Home to more wildlife than people, the tiny island of Muck *(p194)* is an excellent choice for those looking to escape the daily grind. Accommodation options include a bunkhouse, holiday cottages, a catered lodge and a Mongolian-style yurt with views over the Cuillins of Skye, a landscape that (legend has it) inspired J R R Tolkein's *Lord of the Rings*. Wake to the dulcet tones of waves lapping the island's north shore and forget about those pesky emails.

←

Wild camper taking in the view on the tiny island of Muck

Did You Know?

Ben Nevis was once an active volcano which erupted and collapsed in on itself millions of years ago.

Snow-capped Ben Nevis reflecting on the calm surface of Loch Linnhe ↑

❶

BEN NEVIS

🅐 C4 🏠 Lochaber 🚆 Fort William 🚌 Glen Nevis ℹ️ Glen Nevis Visitor Centre, Fort William: open summer: 8:30am–6pm daily; spring and autumn: 9am–5:30pm daily; winter: 9am–3pm daily

In a land where spectacular mountains and mist-shrouded peaks abound, Ben Nevis reigns king. Standing at a whopping 1,344 m (4,408 ft), Britain's highest peak offers walking routes to suit all abilities, and the breathtaking views from the summit reward hikers handsomely for their efforts.

With its summit in cloud for about nine days out of ten, and capable of developing blizzard conditions at any time of the year, Ben Nevis is a mishmash of metamorphic and volcanic rocks. The sheer northeastern face poses a technical challenge to experienced rock climbers, while thousands of visitors each year make their way to the peak via a western trail known as the Old Bridle Path. This can be joined from the visitor centre, Achintee House, or 400 m (440 yds) beyond the campsite.

←

Dappled sunlight on the verdant slopes of Glen Nevis, near Fort William

→ Hikers walking through Glen Nevis towards the summit of Ben Nevis

On rare fine days, visitors who make their way to the summit will be rewarded with breathtaking views. On a cloudy day, a walk through Glen Nevis may be more rewarding than making an ascent, which will reveal little more at the summit than a ruined observatory and memorials testifying to the tragic deaths of walkers and climbers. For a more leisurely pace, head to the Nevis Range Gondola in Torlundy just north of Ben Nevis, which climbs 650 m (2,130 ft) to the mountain ski centre and restaurant on the north face of Aonach Mor.

Climbing Ben Nevis

In Gaelic *Beinn Nibheis* means "the terrible mountain", but don't be put off. Almost anyone can add Ben Nevis to their list of exploits. In 2016, seven-year-old Steven Brown became the youngest person to reach the summit, and the oldest was reportedly 82.

The main footpath is relatively gentle, but the nine-hour walk to the summit and back is no easy stroll. Weather quickly changes from fine to foul (check www.bennevisweather.co. uk). Walking boots and warm, weatherproof outerwear are essential. Bring plenty of food and water, a compass and a map as mobile reception is patchy.

> In Gaelic *Beinn Nibheis* means "the terrible mountain", but don't be put off. Almost anyone can add Ben Nevis to their list of exploits.

THE BEN NEVIS RACE

Held on the first Saturday in September, the Ben Nevis Race brings a whole new energy to Glen Nevis, as experienced hill runners and lycra-clad adrenaline junkies prepare to conquer this formidable mountain. The first event was run by local barber William Swan in 1865. The current record for men and women was set in 1984 by Kenny and Pauline Stuart: 1 hr 25 mins 34 secs and 1 hr 43 mins 25 secs respectively.

2

CAIRNGORMS NATIONAL PARK

⚠D4 **⌂ The Highlands** **🚌🚊 Aviemore** **ℹ 7 The Parade, Grampian Rd, Aviemore; (01479) 810930** **Ⓦ visitcairngorms.com**

There is no better place in Scotland to get away from it all than this rolling, near-Arctic massif of moors and lochs dotted with impressive mountain peaks. A range of activities are offered year-round.

This vast wilderness, home to reindeer, red deer, golden eagles and mountain hare, is within easy reach of all Scotland's major cities. The Cairngorm plateau is dominated by Ben Macdhui, which is Britain's second-highest mountain at 1,309 m (4,296 ft) and can be ascended from both Speyside and Deeside. It is said to be haunted by a resident spectre, the Old Grey Man. However, the brooding peak of Lochnagar, with its magnificent northern corrie, is perhaps the most coveted munro of the lot. It was immortalised in verse by Lord Byron, who lauded its wild crags and the "steep frowning glories of dark Lochnagar".

Activities for all Seasons

Aviemore, commonly considered the gateway to the Cairngorms, is a purpose-built resort town with a wide choice of places to stay, eat and be entertained throughout the year. In winter, this is Scotland's snow sports paradise, with good snow cover for skiing as late as April or even May. Chairlifts and tows provide access to almost 30 ski runs on the flanks of 1,245-m (4,084-ft) Cairn Gorm during the ski season. Visitors can also head up the mountain on Scotland's only funicular railway, which operates all year. In summer, the **Rothiemurchus Centre** offers outdoor activities including river kayaking,

Did You Know?

The Cairngorms is home to Scotland's two highest villages: Tomintoul and Dalwhinnie.

→

A mountain biker riding across bleakly beautiful moorland in the Cairngorms white-water rafting, quad biking, off-road safaris and pony trekking on the Rothiemurchus Estate near Aviemore. Treetop-level zip wires and swings add to the excitement for families. On rainy days, the **Highland Folk Museum**, where actors in authentic period costume bring history to life on a working croft, is well worth a visit.

Rothiemurchus Centre
⊛⊛⊜⊕ 🏠Rothiemurchus, by Aviemore, Inverness-shire ⏰Times vary, check website 🌐rothiemurchus.net

Highland Folk Museum
🏠Newtonmore ⏰Apr-Aug: 10:30am-5:30pm; Sep & Oct: 11am-4:30pm 🌐highlandfolk.com

> **The brooding peak of Lochnagar, with its magnificent northern corrie, is perhaps the most coveted munro of the lot.**

Wildlife Encounters
Driving through the **Highland Wildlife Park** visitors can see bison alongside bears, wolves and wild boar, all of which were once common in the wilds of the Highlands. Britain's only herd of wild reindeer roam free at the **Cairngorm Reindeer Centre**, where they were introduced in 1952.

Highland Wildlife Park
⊛ 🏠Kincraig, Kingussie ⏰Times vary, check website 🌐highlandwildlifepark.org.uk

Cairngorm Reindeer Centre
⊛⊛ 🏠Glenmore, Aviemore ⏰Times vary 🌐cairngormreindeer.co.uk

Reindeer ploughing through deep snow in the Cairngorms National Park

TOP 4 WALKS IN THE CAIRNGORMS

Loch Brandy
An easy half-day walk from Clova village to a mirror-calm loch.

Glen Doll
A two- to three-hour stroll on a well-surfaced path from Glen Doll to Corrie Fee, a dramatic natural amphitheatre.

Lairig Ghru
This age-old mountain trail runs from Spey waide to Deeside and climbs to 835 m (2,740 ft). A tough but rewarding full-day hike with amazing views.

Jock's Road
This iconic long-distance trail traverses three Munro summits. Allow a full day to complete the walk.

THE GREAT GLEN

🅰C4 🏠The Highlands ✈Inverness 🚌🚆Inverness, Fort William
ℹ36 High St, Inverness; (01463) 252401 🌐visitscotland.com

Cleaving through Scotland, the four lochs of the Great Glen offer exciting activities on both land and water. Explore on foot, by bike or kayak, on a canal cruiser or by steam train to discover fabulous scenery and evocative ruined castles of this iconic glen.

Following the path of a huge geological fault that slices the landscape in two, the Great Glen, also known as Glen More or Glen Albyn, forms a scenic route from Inverness on the east coast to Fort William on the west. The glacial rift valley was created when the landmass split and moved 400 million years ago, and now comprises four lochs, the famous Loch Ness, home of the elusive monster, Loch Dochfour, Loch Lochy and Loch Linnhe. The Caledonian Canal links the lochs, and has been a shipping channel as well as a popular tourist route since 1822. Hiring a boat or taking a leisurely drive are ideal ways to see the Glen.

Loch Ness

Deep, dark and forbidding, Loch Ness stretches for 23 miles (37 km). Learn about Loch Ness's history and legends at the **Loch Ness Centre and Exhibition**, or visit ruined **Urquhart Castle**, which offers a fine view for photographers and monster spotters.

Loch Ness Centre and Exhibition
🎫🎫🎫🎫
🏠Drumnadrochit, Loch Ness
🕐Daily 🌐lochness.com

Urquhart Castle
🎫🎫🎫
🏠Drumnadrochit, Loch Ness
🕐Apr–Jul & Sept: daily
🌐historicenvironment.scot

↑ Falls of Foyers thundering down the hillside to Loch Ness

←
The *Jacobite Queen* taking visitors on a tour of Loch Ness

THE LOCH NESS MONSTER

First sighted by St Columba in the 6th century, "Nessie" has attracted attention since photographs – later revealed to be faked – were taken in the 1930s. Though serious investigation is often undermined by hoaxers, sonar techniques continue to yield enigmatic results: plesiosaurs, giant eels and too much whisky are the most popular explanations. The Loch Ness Centre presents the photographic evidence and a wide variety of scientific explanations.

Did You Know?

It is said that after the Battle of Culloden Bonnie Prince Charlie hid in the caves near Loch Lochy.

↑ Autumnal view of Loch Lochy from Laggan Locks on the Caledonian Canal

↑ Lone walker exploring other-worldly rock formations at The Storr

④

ISLE OF SKYE

 B3,B4 ⬥ Inner Hebrides ⬥ Kyle of Lochalsh ⬥ Portree
🚢 From Mallaig or Glenelg ⬥ isleofskye.com

The largest of the Inner Hebrides, Skye boasts some of Britain's most dramatic scenery. From rugged volcanic plateaus to ice-sculpted peaks, the island is divided by numerous sea lochs. Limestone grasslands dominate in the south, where hills are scattered with ruined crofts abandoned during the Clearances (*p198*).

①

Portree

 Bayfield House, Portree; (01478) 612992

With its harbour lined with colourful houses, Portree (meaning "port of the king") is Skye's mini-metropolis. It received its name after a visit made by James V in 1540 in a bid to bring peace to local warring clans. With beautiful views of the surrounding mountains, and its fair share of cosy pubs, restaurants and B&Bs, Portree is an excellent base from which to explore this rugged island.

②

Dunvegan Castle

⬥ Dunvegan ⬥ Apr–mid-Oct: daily ⬥ dunvegan castle.com

For over eight centuries, Dunvegan Castle has been the seat of the chiefs of the Clan MacLeod. The castle's architecture is a unique mix of building styles due to numerous structural additions and renovations that took place from the 13th to mid-19th centuries. Seal-spotting adventures, a favourite with kids, and fishing trips on the loch depart from the castle.

③

The Storr

Erosion of a basalt plateau on the Trotternish ridge has resulted in the Storr's other-worldy rock formations. The Old Man of Storr, a monolith rising to 49m (160 ft), is the highest of these curious structures. Hike the 2.6-mile (3.8-km) Storr Ascent, accessed from the main road from Portree to Staffin, and head to the north side for spectacular views of these rocky pinnacles. North of the Storr, Quiraing's terrain of

↑ Boats moored in the still waters of Portree harbour at sunset

spikes and towers is a fantastic area to explore on foot, and is easily acessed off the Uig to Staffin road.

Talisker Distillery

🏠 Carbost 📞 (01478) 614 308 🕐 Jun–Sep: daily; Oct & Apr–May: Mon–Sat; Nov–Mar: Mon–Fri

Overlooking the Cuillins from the banks of Loch Harport at Carbost, this is the oldest working distillery on the island, famed for its sweet, full-bodied Highland malts which are often described as "the lava of the Cuillins".

The Skye Museum of Island Life

🏠 Kilmuir, Portree 🕐 Apr–Sep: 9:30am–5pm Mon–Sat 🌐 skyemuseum. co.uk

This award-winning museum, takes visitors back in time to an old Highland village, comprising a community of well-preserved thatched cottages and crofts, where they can discover what island life was like 100 years ago.

Cuillin Mountains

Britain's finest mountain range is within walking distance of Sligachan, and in summer a boat sails from Elgol to the desolate inner sanctuary of Loch Coruisk. As he fled across the surrounding moorland, Bonnie Prince Charlie is said to have claimed: "even the Devil shall not follow me here!"

A particular highlight of the area, at the foot of Skye's Black Cuillins on the River Brittle, are the Fairy Pools. Here, white water cascades into deep stone cauldrons filled with clear pale turquoise water. The pools are also a favourite with wild swimmers daring enough to plunge into their chilly waters. Allow around an hour to follow the riverside trail that leads to the most spectacular upper pools, with breathtaking views of the Cuillins along the way.

Armadale Castle Gardens and Museum of the Isles

🏠 Armadale, Sleat 🕐 Mar–Oct: daily 🌐 armadale castle.com

Once the seat of Clan Donald, who reigned over the area as Lords of the Isles, this ruined castle and its impressive grounds make for a fascinating day out. The gardens date back to the 1790s, and are home to many remarkable specimens of trees and rare plants. Beyond the gardens there are numerous woodland trails.

At the award-winning Museum of the Isles, visitors can discover the story of Scotland's most powerful clan, while its six galleries cover the 1,500 years of history and culture of the Kingdom of the Isles. An additional gallery hosts visiting exhibitions.

5

ORKNEY ISLANDS

ⓐD1, E1 ⓐOrkney ⓣto Kirkwall ⛴from Scrabster or Gill's Bay (Caithness), Aberdeen, Lerwick (Shetland), and John O'Groats (May–Sept only)
ⓘKirkwall ⓦvisitorkney.com

Beyond the Pentland Firth, less than 10 km (6 miles) off the Scottish mainland, the Orkney archipelago consists of some 70 islands and rocky skerries boasting the densest concentration of archaeological sites in Britain. Today, only about 16 of these islands are permanently inhabited. Orkney's way of life is predominantly agricultural – it's said that, whereas the Shetlanders are fishermen with crofts, the Orcadians are farmers with boats.

The Mainland is the archipelago's main island, home to Orkney's two largest towns, Kirkwall and Stromness. Almost 5,000 years ago, rings of colossal stone walls enclosed a complex of temples at Ness of Brodgar, the most recently rediscovered of Orkney's Neolithic relics. In 1999, sites including the chambered tomb at Maeshowe and the Standing Stones of Stenness and the Ring of Brodgar were granted UNESCO World Heritage status, and archaeologists continue to unearth exciting finds that tell of a sophisticated ancient culture that flourished here long ago.

Hoy, Orkney's second-largest island, takes its name from the Norse word for "high island", which refers to its spectacular cliff-lined terrain. Hoy is very different from the rest of the archipelago, and its northern hills make excellent walking and bird-watching country.

Orkney's outlying islands are sparsely populated and mostly the preserve of seals and seabirds. Rousay is known as the "Egypt of the North" for its many archaeological sites, and Egilsay was the scene of St Magnus's grisly murder in 1115. The 12th-century round-towered church dedicated to his memory is a rare example of Irish-Viking design. Sanday is the largest of the Northern Isles, its fertile farmland fringed by sandy beaches, while North Ronaldsay, the northern most of the Orkney Islands, is noted for its hardy, seaweed-eating sheep and rare migrant birds.

↑ Ancient stone monoliths form the Ring of Brodgar Neolithic henge, Orkney

① Kirkwall

Orkney's capital is lined with period houses. Opposite **St Magnus Cathedral**, an 870-year-old masterpiece of red and yellow stone, lie the ruins of the **Bishop's Palace**, dating from the 16th century. The **Orkney Museum** tells the history of the islands, while the **Highland Park Distillery** dispenses a fine dram at the end of its guided tours.

St Magnus Cathedral
⊘ 🅰 Broad St 🅾 Mon-Fri
🅆 stmagnus.org

Bishop's Palace
⊘ 🅰 Watergate
🅾 Apr-Sep: daily 🅆 historic environment.scot

Orkney Museum
🅰 Broad St 🅾 Mon-Sat
🅆 orkney.gov.uk

Highland Park Distillery
⊘🅾🕒 🅰 Holme Rd
🅾 Times vary, check website
🅆 highlandparkwhisky.com

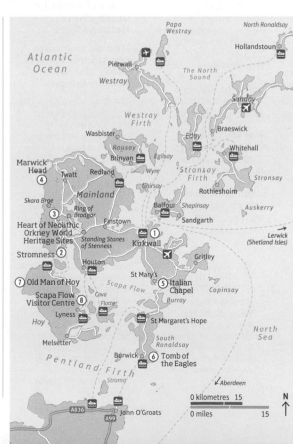

Orcadian town of Stromness with the hills of Hoy in the background

Did You Know?

Captain Cook's famous ships *Discovery* and *Resolution* moored in Stromness harbour in 1780.

②

Stromness

Many of the waterfront buildings in Stromness date from the 18th and 19th centuries. Among them, the **Pier Arts Centre** contains a fine collection of 20th-century works. **The Stromness Museum** traces Orkney's history as a trading port.

Pier Arts Centre

28-36 Victoria St
10:30am-5pm Tue-Sat
pierartscentre.com

Stromness Museum

52 Alfred St Daily (Nov-Mar: Mon-Sat) orkney communities.co.uk

INSIDER TIP
Day Trips to Remote Islands

There are flights from Kirkwall to a dozen outlying islands several times a week, as well as daily ferries. Inter-island transport is weather-dependent.

③

Heart of Neolithic Orkney World Heritage Sites

Various locations on Central & West Mainland
Daily historic environment.scot

Almost 5,000 years ago, rings of colossal stone walls more than 100 metres long enclosed the complex of temples at Ness of Brodgar, the most recently discovered of Orkney's Neolithic relics. Said to date from around 2750 BC, Maeshowe is a chambered tomb aligned with the winter solstice. Vikings plundered it around 1150, leaving a fascinating legacy of runic graffiti on the walls. Nearby are the huge Standing Stones of Stenness and the Ring of Brodgar, a megalithic henge of 36 stones. The Neolithic village of Skara Brae was discovered when a storm stripped dunes from the site in 1850 to reveal relics of everyday Stone Age life. In 1999 these ancient sites were granted UNESCO World Heritage status.

④

Marwick Head

The cliffs of Marwick Head, overlooking Birsay Bay, are one of several RSPB reserves on West Mainland, home to thousands of nesting seabirds in early summer. A memorial Commemorates Lord Kitchener and the crew of HMS *Hampshire*, which was sunk off this headland by a German mine in 1916.

⑤

Italian Chapel

Lambholm, Hoy
Daily (Mass: 1st Sun of month, Apr-Sep)

East of Kirkwall, the road runs through quiet agricultural land over a series of causeways linking the southernmost islands to Mainland. The Churchill Barriers were built by Italian prisoners of war in the 1940s to protect the British fleet stationed in Scapa Flow. In their spare time, these POWs constructed the Italian Chapel, containing beautiful frescoes.

Tomb of the Eagles

 South Ronaldsay Mar–Oct: daily tombofthe eagles.co.uk

On South Ronaldsay, the 5,000-year-old Tomb of the Eagles, or Isbister Chambered Cairn, was discovered by a local farmer. Some 340 burial sites were later unearthed, along with stone tools and the talons of many sea eagles. The mile-long walk from the visitor centre to the tomb through a Bronze Age excavation site teems with birdlife and wild flowers.

Old Man of Hoy

The Old Man of Hoy, a 137-m (450-ft) vertical stack off the western coast, is the island's best-known landmark, a popular challenge to keen rock climbers. Near Rackwick, the 5,000-year-old Dwarfie Stane is a unique chambered cairn cut from a single block of stone.

Scapa Flow Visitor Centre

 Lyness, Hoy For renovation until 2020 orkney.gov.uk

On the eastern side of Hoy, the Scapa Flow Visitor Centre contains a fascinating exhibition on this deep-water

 Must See

STAY

Merkister Hotel
Only 15 minutes from Stromness and close to the Neolithic Orkney World Heritage Sites, this family-run hotel offers cosy rooms, exquisite home cooking set against fabulous sunset views.

D1 Harray merkister.com

£££

The Creel
Multi-award-winning seafront B&B and restaurant in a timeless stone village. Quaint rooms and imaginative cooking – try the wolf-fish broth.

E1 St Margaret's Hope thecreel.co.uk

£££

naval haven. Temporarily rehoused in Hoy Hotel, the exhibition recounts events of 16 June 1919, when the captured German fleet was scuttled on the orders of its commanding officer to prevent handover: 74 ships were sunk. Many have been salvaged; others provide one of the world's great wreck-diving sites. Tours from Houton Pier, using a remote-controlled vehicle fitted with an underwater camera, give a glimpse of this sub-aquatic graveyard. Guided tours of the former Royal Naval Base depart at 11am every Tuesday and Thursday from the Ferry Waiting Room.

←

Orkney's iconic sea stack, the Old Man of Hoy is a popular rock climbing spot

St Ninian's Isle, separated from Mainland by a thin isthmus of white sand →

6

SHETLAND ISLANDS

🄰F1, F2 🄰Shetland 🚌🚢From Aberdeen and Stromness, Orkney
🅘Lerwick; (01595) 693434 🅦shetland.org

With the North Sea to the east, and the Atlantic Ocean ravishing its western shores, this windswept archipelago is where Scotland meets Scandinavia, and the sense of transition here tangible. Shetland's rugged coastline, oceanic climate and fascinating geology will delight all who venture to this most northerly enclave.

More than 100 rugged, cliff-hemmed islands form Scotland's most northerly domain. Nowhere in Shetland is further than 5 km (3 miles) from the sea, and fishing and salmon farming are mainstays of the economy, boosted in recent decades by North Sea oil. Severe storms are common in winter, but in summer, the sun may shine for as long as 19 hours, and a twilight known as the "simmer dim" persists throughout the night.

Mainland is home to Shetland's main town, Lerwick, and the quiet port of Scalloway. North of Lerwick, Shetland rises to its highest point at Ronas Hill (454 m/1,475 ft) amid tracts of bleak, empty moorland. The west coast has spectacular natural scenery, notably the red granite cliffs and blow-holes at Esha Ness, from where you can see the wave-gnawed stacks of The Drongs and a huge rock arch called Dore Holm.

The northern isles of Yell, Fetlar and Unst have regular, though weather-dependent, boat connections to Mainland. Beyond the lighthouse of Muckle Flugga is Out Stack, Britain's most northerly point.

West of Mainland, Foula has dramatic sea cliffs, while Fair Isle, midway between Orkney and Shetland, is owned by the National Trust for Scotland. There are regular internal flights to Fair Isle, Foula and Papa Stour, as well as inter-island ferries. Most routes depart from Tingwall, on Central Mainland.

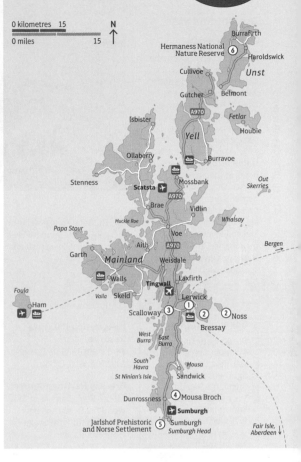

FAIR ISLE KNITWEAR

Fair Isle sweaters have been knitted by hand from hand-spun wool by the island's womenfolk for more than 200 years. Each garment takes up to 100 hours to create and is a unique work of art, using traditional patterns in muted shades of grey, blue, brown and yellow, reflecting the tones of the Shetland Isles' flora, fauna and natural landscapes. Skills are passed on from mothers to daughters, and learning them takes up to four years. Prices are high and would-be buyers may have to wait several years for their garment to be completed.

①

Lerwick

Shetland's chief town is a pretty place of grey stone buildings and narrow, flag-stoned lanes. First established by Dutch fishermen in the 1600s, it grew to become wealthy from the whaling trade. The increase in North Sea oil traffic has made the harbour area very busy. At the heart of the town is Commercial Street, its northern end guarded by Fort Charlotte, which affords fine views from its battlements. At the **Shetland Museum and Archive**, on Hay's Dock, you can admire a fine collection of historic boats, archaeological finds and Shetland textiles tracing the islands' unique and fascinating history.

On Lerwick's outskirts lie the Clickminin Broch, a prehistoric fort dating from around 700 BC, and the 18th-century **Böd of Gremista**, birthplace of Arthur Anderson, co-founder of the P&O shipping company, which now houses a textile museum.

Shetland Museum and Archive

⏹️⏹️ ⏹️Daily ⬛shetland museumandarchives.org.uk

Böd of Gremista

⏹️ ⏹️May–Sep: Tue–Sat ⬛shetlandtextilemuseum. com

②

Bressay and Noss

🚌 From Lerwick

Sheltering Lerwick from the winter gales is Bressay, an island with fine walks and views. The Bressay ferry departs from Lerwick every hour, weather-dependent, and boats run a regular service from Lerwick to Noss, off Bressay's east coast. **Noss National Nature Reserve** is home to thousands of breeding seabirds, including gannets and great skuas (or bonxies), while both islands are outstandingly beautiful and abundant in bird and mammal life. **The Bressay Heritage Centre** holds seasonal exhibitions on the island's culture, history and

↑ Shetland Pony grazing on gentle grasslands of West Burra, Scalloway Islands

natural heritage, and is open to the public part time from May to September.

Noss National Nature Reserve

☎ (01595) 693345 🕐 May-Aug: Tue, Wed, Fri-Sun

Bressay Heritage Centre

🕐 May-Sep: 10am-4pm Tue, Wed, Fri & Sat; 11am-5pm Sun 🌐 shetlandheritage association.com

---

🔺 GREAT VIEW
Sumburgh Head

For dramatic clifftop vistas and a spectacular sea view, the cliffs and lighthouse atop Sumburgh Head, at the very southern tip of the South Mainland, are well worth a visit. Keep your eyes peeled when looking out to sea; you may spot a white-sided dolphin, harbour porpoise or minke whale. Closer to shore, grey seals bask and play on the rocks below.

---

③

Scalloway

West of Lerwick is the quiet fishing port of Scalloway, Shetland's second town and the islands' former capital. Scalloway Castle is a fortified tower dating from 1600, while the **Scalloway Museum** contains an exhibition on the "Shetland Bus", a wartime resistance operation that used fishing boats to bring refugees from German-occupied Norway. North of Scalloway, near Weisdale, the fertile region of Tingwall is a well-known angling centre.

Connected by bridges to Central Mainland's west coast are the islands of Burra and Trondra, with lovely beaches and walks.

Scalloway Museum
🏛 Castle St 🕐 Times vary, check website 🌐 scalloway museum.org

Mousa Broch

🏛 Mousa 🕐 Apr-Sep: daily 🌐 mousa.co.uk

The ornate Mousa Broch, on an easterly islet reached by a summer ferry from Sandwick, is the best example of this type of ancient fortified tower in Britain. These drystone roundhouses, which are unique to Scotland, consist of two concentric walls, between which is a narrow passage containing a stone stairway to the top. Thought to have been constructed in around 300 BC, Mousa is the tallest of all the remaining brochs in Scotland. Its 13-m- (42-ft-) tall towering walls are clearly visible from the main road, and make ideal nestboxes for a colony of storm petrels.

SHETLAND'S BIRDLIFE

Millions of migrant and local birds can be admired on these islands. Over 20 species of seabirds regularly breed here, and over 340 different species have been recorded passing through Fair Isle, one of the world's great staging posts. Inaccessible cliffs provide excellent security at vulnerable nesting times for huge colonies of gannets, guillemots, puffins, kittiwakes, fulmars and razorbills. Species found here but in very few other UK locations include great skuas and storm petrels.

Jarlshof Prehistoric and Norse Settlement

🏛 Sumburgh 🚌 Jarlshof 🕐 Apr-Sept: 9.30am-5.30pm daily 🌐 historic environment.scot

Jarlshof, in the far south, spans over 3,000 years of occupation from Neolithic to Viking times. Preserved under layers of sand and grit for thousands of years, this ancient site was discovered in the 1890s thanks to powerful storms that ravished the land to reveal ancient treasures hidden underneath the ground. Explore ancient Bronze Age dwellings, Iron Age wheelhouses and Viking longhouses and outbuildings, and evidence of the island's

Clifftop lighthouse at Sumburgh Head on the southern tip of Mainland

Norse occupation, all set against the dramatic backdrop of the beautiful West Voe of Sumburgh.

Hermaness National Nature Reserve

🏛 Muckle Flugga Shorestation 🚌 Unst 🚌 from Lerwick to Haroldswick 🕐 Daily (Visitor Centre: Apr-Sep only) 🌐 nnr.scot

Of all Shetland's islands, Unst has the most varied scenery and the richest flora and fauna, plus an excellent visitor centre at the Hermaness National Nature Reserve, home to thousands of seabirds. Here visitors can learn about the local birdlife, and stroll along the clifftop paths and grassy moorland. Beyond the lighthouse of Muckle Flugga is Out Stack, Britain's most northerly point.

Cliffs and sea stacks near Mangersta, on the west coast of Lewis ↑

7

OUTER HEBRIDES

🅰 A3, B2 🏠 Western Isles, Outer Hebrides ⛴ from Uig (Skye), Oban, Mallaig, Kyle of Lochalsh & Ullapool ✈ Stornoway, Benbecula, Barra ℹ 26 Cromwell St, Stornoway, Lewis 🌐 visitouterhebrides.co.uk

Western Scotland ends with this remote chain of islands, made of some of the oldest rock on earth. Barren landscapes are divided by countless waterways, while the western, windward coasts are edged by white sandy beaches.

Hundreds of windswept and beautiful islands lie scattered off Scotland's northwest coast. Some are tiny rocky skerries inhabited only by seabirds, while others are home to bustling farming and fishing communities. White sandy bays fringe these rugged coasts, bordered by sweet-smelling natural wild-flower meadows known as machair that pepper the land with splashes of yellow, white, blue and pink.

In the low-lying hinterlands, vast peat bogs provide many homes with fuel, and the rich tang of peat smoke is the signature scent of the isles. These are some of the longest-inhabited parts of Scotland, with ancient standing stones attesting to over 6,000 years of human settlement, though abandoned dwellings and monuments attest to the difficulties in commercializing traditional local skills. Home to Scotland's largest Gaelic-speaking community, many islanders use the ancient Celtic tongue as their first language.

↑ Sheep in wild-flower meadows on rugged and remote Harris

Butt of Lewis
Port of Ness
North Tolsta
Barvas
Shawbost
A857
Carloway
Portnaguran
Timsgarry
Breasclete
Newmarket
Standing Stones of Callanais
Lewis
Stornoway
Scarp
Arivruaich
Balallan
Ullapool
St Kilda
50 miles
(80 km)
Hushinish
Loch Langavat
A859
Loch Seaforth
Lemreway
Lewis and Harris ①
Ardhasaig
Taransay
Tarbert
Shiant Islands
Scarastavore
Harris
Scalpay
Pabbay
Leverburgh
Fladda Chuain
Boreray
Berneray
Rodel
Valley
The Little Minch
Newtonferry
Tigharry
Lochmaddy
North Uist
Uig
Monach Islands
Baleshare
Clachan-a-Luib
Lusta
Gramsdale
Ronay
Milovaig
Carbost
Creagorry
Benbecula
Wiay
Dunvegan
Portree
Stilligarry
② The Uists and Benbecula
South Uist
Sea of the Hebrides
Isle of Skye
Daliburgh
Lochboisdale
Kilbride
Canna
Barra ④
Fuday
③ Eriskay
Castlebay
Gighay
Rhum
Vatersay
Muldoanich
Eigg
Pabbay
Sandray
Mingulay
Berneray
Muck
Oban
Atlantic Ocean

①
Lewis and Harris

Forming the largest landmass of the Western Isles, Lewis and Harris are a single island, though Gaelic dialects differ between the two areas. The administrative centre of Stornoway is a bustling harbour town with colourful house fronts. The **Museum nan Eilean** offers a fascinating insight into the culture, language and traditions of the people of the Outer Hebrides. From here, the ancient Standing Stones of Callanais are only 26 km (16 miles) to the west. Just off the road on the way to Callanish are the cone-shaped ruins of Carloway Broch, a Pictish tower over 2,000 years old. The more recent past can be explored at **The Blackhouse** in Arnol – a showcase of rural crofting life as it was until 50 years ago.

South of the rolling peat moors of Lewis, a range of mountains marks the border with Harris, which is entered via the head of Loch Seaforth. The mountains of Harris are a paradise for hill walkers, offering views of the distant islands of St Kilda 80 km (50 miles) to the west.

The ferry port of Tarbert stands on a slim isthmus separating North and South Harris. The tourist office provides addresses for local weavers of the tough Harris Tweed. Some weavers still use indigenous plants to create the dyes. From Leverburgh a ferry sails to North Uist, linked by a causeway to Berneray.

Museum nan Eilean
🎨🖼️📷 🏛️Lews Castle grounds, Stornoway 🌐lews-castle.co.uk

The Blackhouse
🎨🖼️ 🏛️Arnol 📞(01851) 710 395 🕐Apr–Sep: Mon–Sat; Oct–Mar: Mon, Tue & Thu–Sat 🌐historicenvironment.scot

> **White sandy bays fringe these rugged coasts, bordered by sweet-smelling natural wild-flower meadows known as *machair*.**

EAT

Crown Inn

This cosy inn doubles as a lively bar-restaurant that hosts occasional live performances by local musicians.

🅰 B2 🏠 Castle St, Stornoway, Lewis
📞 (01851 703734

ⓔⓔⓔ

Langass Lodge

Locally caught seafood and produce from Langass's own garden feature on the menu at this small restaurant with rooms.

🅰 A3 🏠 Locheport, North Uist
🔤 langasslodge.co.uk

ⓔⓔⓔ

The Uists and Benbecula

After the dramatic scenery of Harris, the lower-lying, largely waterlogged southern isles may seem an anticlimax, though they nurture secrets well worth discovering. Long, white, sandy beaches fringe the Atlantic coast, edged with one of Scotland's natural treasures: the lime-rich soil known as machair. During the summer months, the soil is covered with wild flowers, the unique fragrance of which can be detected far out to sea.

From Lochmaddy, North Uist's main village, the A867 crosses 5 km (3 miles) of causeway to Benbecula, the isle from which the brave Flora MacDonald smuggled Bonnie Prince Charlie to Skye (p172). Benbecula is a flat island covered by a mosaic of small lochs. Like its neighbours, it is known for good trout fishing. Here, and to the north, the Protestant religion holds sway, while Catholicism prevails in the southern islands. Benbecula's chief source of employment is the Army Rocket Range, which has its headquarters in the main village of Bailivanich. Another causeway leads to South Uist, which has golden beaches that are renowned as a National Scenic Area.

Eriskay

One of the smallest and most enchanting of the Western Isles, Eriskay epitomizes their peace and beauty. The island is best known for the wrecking of the SS *Politician* in 1941, which inspired the book and film *Whisky Galore*. A bottle from its cargo and other relics can be seen in Eriskay's only bar. It was at the beautiful beach of Coilleag A'Phrionnsa (Prince's beach) that Bonnie Prince Charlie first set foot on Scotland at the start of his 1745 campaign. As a result, a

↑ The quaint village of Gearrannan Blackhouse, Carloway, Lewis

→ Village bay and abandoned settlement of the Island of Hirta, St Kilda

rare convolvulus flower that grows here has become associated with him.

 ④

Barra

The dramatic way to arrive on the pretty island of Barra is by plane *(p45)* – the airstrip is a beach and the timetable depends on the tide. The island has a central core of hills and circular road, with beaches on the western coast.

The view over Castlebay from the Madonna and Child statue on top of Heaval hill is particularly fine. The romantic **Kisimul Castle**, set on a tiny island, is the fifteenth seat of the Clan MacNeil. It is currently being restored. Other attractions are the **Barra Heritage Centre** and a golf course.

Kisimul Castle
⊛ 🅲 (01871) 810313
🅦 historicenvironment.scot

Barra Heritage Centre
🅲 (01871) 810413
🅞 May–Sep: Mon–Sat
🅦 barraheritage.com

⑤

St Kilda

These "Islands on the Edge of the World" were the most isolated habitation in Scotland until the ageing population requested to be evacuated in 1930. The largest gannetry in the world (40,000 pairs) is now found here. There are three islands and three sea stacks of awesome beauty, each with sheer, soaring cliffs rising as high as 425 m (1,400 ft). Such is the

islands' isolation that separate subspecies of mouse and wren have evolved here.

Tours are run by **Westernedge Charters** and **Island Cruising**. Volunteers can occasionally pay to join summer work parties on the islands, organised by the National Trust for Scotland, owners of the **St Kilda World Heritage Site**.

Island Cruising
⊛⊛ 🏠 1 Erista, Uig, Lewis
🅞 May–Sep 🅦 islandcruising.com

Westernedge Charters
⊛⊛ 🏠 Berneray, North Uist
🅞 May–Sep 🅦 westernedge.co.uk

St Kilda World Heritage Site
⊛ 🅦 kilda.org.uk

CROFTING

Crofts are small parcels of agricultural land. They originated in the early 1800s when landlords decided to lease out poor-quality land on the coast in an effort to clear the people from more fertile areas. Crofters became dependent on wages from either fishing or collecting kelp, which was used to make commercial alkali. When these sources of income diminished, they endured extreme hardship through famine, high rents and lack of security. In 1886 an Act was passed to allow crofting families the right to inherit (but not own) the land. Today there are 17,000 registered crofts, almost all in the Highlands and islands. Most crofters raise sheep, but recent trends include tree planting and providing habitats for rare birds.

Windswept Nisabost Beach, Harris

EXPERIENCE MORE

8

Inveraray Castle

▲C5 ⬛Inveraray, Argyll & Bute 🚂Dalmally, then bus 🚌From Glasgow ⏰Apr-Oct: 10am-5:45pm daily (last admission 5pm) 🌐inveraray-castle.com

This multi-turreted mock Gothic palace is the family home of the powerful Clan Campbell, the Dukes of Argyll since 1701. Building started in 1746 by architects Roger Morris and William Adam on ruins of a 15th-century castle. The conical towers were added after a fire in 1877.

The magnificent interiors, designed by Robert Mylne in the 1770s, form a backdrop to such treasures as Regency furniture, a huge collection of Oriental and European porcelain and portraits by Ramsay, Gainsborough and Raeburn. The Armoury Hall contains early weaponry collected by the Campbells to fight the Jacobite rebels. The Combined Operations Museum commemorates the 250,000 Allied troops who trained at Inveraray during World War II.

9

Auchindrain Museum

▲C5 ⬛Inveraray, Argyll & Bute 🚌Inveraray, then bus ⏰Apr-Oct: 10am-5pm daily 🌐auchindrain org.uk

The first open-air museum in Scotland, Auchindrain illuminates the working lives of the kind of farming community typical of the Highlands until the late 19th century. Constituting a township of some 20 thatched cottages, the site was communally farmed by its tenants until the last one retired in 1962. Visitors can wander through the houses, most of which combine living space, kitchen and a cattle shed all under one roof. They are furnished with box beds

Did You Know?

The final scenes of the 1963 James Bond film *From Russia With Love* were filmed around Argyll and Bute.

and rush lamps, and edged by herb gardens. Auchindrain is a fascinating memorial to a time before the Highland farmers made the transition from subsistence to commercial farming.

10

Crarae Gardens

▲C5 ⬛Crarae, Argyll & Bute 🚌Inveraray, then bus ⏰Apr-Oct: 9:30am-sunset daily; tours by appointment 🌐nts.org.uk

Considered to be the most beguiling of all the gardens of the West Highlands, the Crarae Gardens were created in 1912 by Lady Grace Campbell. She was the aunt of explorer Reginald Farrer, whose specimens from Tibet were the beginnings of a collection of exotic plants. The gardens now resemble a Himalayan ravine, nourished by the warmth of the Gulf Stream and the high rainfall of the region. Although unusual Himalayan rhododendrons flourish here, the gardens are also home to exotic plants from Tasmania, New Zealand and the US. Great plant collectors still contribute to the gardens, which thrive in late spring.

11

Jura

▲B5, B6 ⬛Argyll & Bute 🚢From Kennacraig to Islay, Islay to Jura

Barren, mountainous and overrun by red deer, Jura has only one road connecting the single village of Craighouse, home to the **Jura Distillery**, to the Islay ferry. Though hiking is restricted from July to the end of October during the deer-stalking season, Jura

↑ Romantic Inveraray Castle, with its Gothic and Baroque features

Copper stills used to make single malt whisky at Laphroaig Distillery *(inset)*, on Islay

offers superb hill walking, especially on the slopes of the three main peaks known as the Paps of Jura. The tallest of these is Beinn An Oir at 784 m (2,572 ft). Beyond the northern tip of the isle are the notorious whirlpools of Corryvreckan. The author George Orwell, who came to the island to write his final novel, *1984*, nearly lost his life here in 1946 when he fell into the water. Legend tells of Prince Breackan who drowned in his attempt to win the hand of a princess. He tried to keep his boat anchored in the whirlpool for three days, held by ropes made of hemp, wool and maidens' hair, until one rope, containing the hair of an unfaithful girl, finally broke.

Jura Distillery

🌐🕐📷 ◪Craighouse
🕐10am–4:30pm Mon-Sat (Nov–Mar: 10am–4pm Mon-Fri) ⓦjurawhisky.com

> **Barren, mountainous and overrun by red deer, Jura has only one road connecting the single village of Craighouse, home to the Jura Distillery, to the Islay ferry.**

Islay

◪B6 ◪Argyll & Bute
🚢From Kennacraig
ⓘBowmore ⓦislay
jura.com

The most southerly of the Western Isles, Islay (pronounced "Eyeluh") is home to such Highland single malt whiskies *(p40)* as Lagavulin and Laphroaig. Most of the distilleries produce heavily peated malts with a distinctive tang of the sea. The Georgian village of Bowmore has the island's oldest distillery and a circular church designed to minimize the Devil's possible lurking places. The **Museum of Islay**

Life in Port Charlotte covers the island's social and natural history. East of Port Ellen, the Kildalton Cross, a block of local green stone inscribed with Old Testament scenes, is one of the UK's most impressive 8th-century Celtic crosses. Also worth a visit is the medieval stronghold of the Lords of the Isles, Finlaggan, which is under excavation. Some of Islay's superb beaches support a variety of birdlife, which can be seen at the Royal Society for the Protection of Birds (RSPB) reserve at Gruinart.

Museum of Islay Life

🌐 ◪Port Charlotte
🕐10.30am–4.30pm daily (Apr & Oct: Mon–Fri)
ⓦislaymuseum.org

 13

Ardnamurchan Peninsula

⚑B4 **☗Argyll** **⛴Corran Ferry on A82 from Glencoe to Fort William, or Fishnish (Mull) to Kilchoan** **🅦ardnamurchan.com**

This peninsula and the adjacent areas of Moidart and Morvern are some of the west coast's best-kept secrets. They are characterized by a sinuous coastline, rocky mountains and beaches. Some of the best beaches are at the tip of the peninsula, the most westerly point of mainland Britain.

The **Ardnamurchan Lighthouse Visitor Centre** at Kilchoan explores the history of lighthouses and lightkeeping. The 1846 lighthouse was designed by Alan Stevenson, uncle of author Robert Louis Stevenson. It is one of many built by the Stevenson family throughout Britain.

The award-winning **Ardnamurchan Natural History Visitor Centre** at Glenmore has encouraged wildlife to inhabit its "living building", and wild red deer can even graze on its turf roof. An enchanting wooded road runs from Salen to Strontian, or head north to Acharacle.

Ardnamurchan Lighthouse Visitor Centre

⊕⊗⊜ **⚑Kilchoan** **⏰Apr-Oct: daily** **🅦ardnamurchanlighthouse.com**

Ardnamurchan Natural History Visitor Centre

⊕⊜⊕ **⚑Glenmore** **⏰8:30am–5pm Sun–Fri** **🅦ardnamurchannaturalhistorycentre.com**

 14

Arran

⚑C6 **☗North Ayrshire** **⛴From Ardrossan to Brodick; from Claonaig (Mull of Kintyre) to Lochranza (Apr-Oct only)** **ℹBrodick** **🅦visitarran.com**

Arran is thought to have been populated as long ago as the end of the last Ice Age. The island's Neolithic chambered burial tombs, such as the one at Torrylinn near Lagg in the south, are an indication of this. Bronze Age stone circles can also be seen around Machrie on the west coast. Vikings arrived from about AD 800 and exerted an influence for more than four centuries. After the Battle of Largs in 1263, when Alexander III defeated the Norsemen, Scotland bought Arran from the Vikings in 1266.

Today, visitors tend to come to Arran for outdoor pursuits. Golf is especially popular, with seven golf courses on the island, including 18-hole courses at Brodick, Whiting Bay and Lamlash.

Brodick is the island's only real town. The more mountainous parts offer

Serene Artdoe Beach on the northeast side of the Ardnamurchan Peninsula

some of the most spectacular hill walking in Central Scotland. The Goatfell ridge to the east of Glen Rosa and Beinn Tarsuinn to the west have a rugged beauty.

Robert the Bruce stayed on Arran on his return to Scotland in 1307. His followers had already been harassing the garrison at **Brodick Castle**, then occupied by supporters of the King of England. Legend states that it was from Arran that Bruce saw a signal fire on the Ayrshire coast that told him it was safe to return to the mainland and launch the campaign against the English (*p52*). Parts of the Castle still date from the 13th century, though it has had many later additions.

Brodick Castle

⊛ ⊛ ⊛ ⬛ Brodick
🄲 (01770) 302202 🄾 May-Sep: 11am–4pm (Apr & Oct: to 3pm); gardens all year

15

Bute

🄰 C6 🄾 Argyll & Bute
🚢 From Wemyss Bay to Rothesay or Colintraive to Rhubodach 🚢 From Dunoon 🄸 Rothesay; (01700) 507043

Bute is almost an extension of the Cowal Peninsula, and the small ferry from Colintraive takes only five minutes to cross the Kyles of Bute to Rhubodach on the island. This route is a long drive from Glasgow, however, and most people travel via Wemyss Bay on the Firth of Clyde to the island's main town, Rothesay.

Just 25 km (16 miles) long by 8 km (5 miles) at its widest point, Bute has been occupied since at least the Bronze Age. The remains of the chapel at St Ninian's Point on the west coast date from around the 6th century, while **Rothesay Castle**, now ruined, is mostly a 12th-century structure. It saw struggles between islanders and Vikings in the 13th century, but over the last 120 years, it has played a more placid role as a holiday resort.

GREAT VIEW
Scotland in Miniature

With mountain walks and serene coastal paths, the isle of Arran has it all. The three-mile Glen Rosa to Brodick walk is one of the best on the island, with a stunning view over the Goatfell mountains.

Bute's main attraction is **Mount Stuart House**, 5 km (3 miles) south of Rothesay. This aristocratic house, built in 1877, is set in 18th-century gardens. Its Gothic features reflect the Marquess's interests in mythology, religion and astronomy.

Rothesay Castle

⊛ ⬛ Castle Hill St, Rothesay
🄾 Apr–Sep: 9:30am–5:30pm daily; Oct–Mar: 10am–4pm Mon–Wed, Sat & Sun
🅦 historicenvironment.scot

Mount Stuart House

⊛ ⊛ ⊛ ⬛ Mount St
🄾 Apr–Oct: 11am–5pm daily
🅦 mountstuart.com

↑ Jagged granite ridges of Arran's Goatfell Mountains rising high above the island

16

Loch Awe

C5 | Argyll
Dalmally | Inveraray
loch-awe.com

One of the longest freshwater lochs in Scotland, Loch Awe stretches 40 km (25 miles) across a glen in the south-western Highlands. A short drive east from the town of Lochawe are the remains of Kilchurn Castle, abandoned after being struck by lightning in the 18th century. Dwarfing the castle is Ben Cruachan. The huge summit of 1,126 m (3,694 ft) can be reached by the narrow Pass of Brander, where Robert the Bruce fought the Clan MacDougal in 1308. Near the village of Taynuilt, is the preserved Lorn Furnace at Bonawe, which serves as a reminder of the iron-smelting industry that destroyed much of the area's woodland in the last centuries.

On the A816, to the south of the loch, is **Kilmartin Museum**, displaying artifacts from local prehistoric sites, as well as reconstructions of boats, utensils and jewellery, and providing a vivid glimpse into what life was like in prehistoric Scotland.

Kilmartin Museum
 | Kilmartin
Daily | kilmartin.org

Did You Know?

The first transatlantic telephone cable landed at Oban during the Cold War.

17

Kintyre

B6 | Argyll & Bute
Oban | Campbeltown
kintyre.org

A long, narrow peninsula stretching far south of Glasgow, Kintyre has superb views across to the islands of Gigha, Islay and Jura. The 14 km (9 mile) Crinan Canal, which opened in 1801 and has a total of 15 locks, bustles with pleasure craft in the summer. The town of Tarbert (meaning "isthmus" in Gaelic) takes its name from the neck on which it stands, which is narrow enough to drag a boat across, between the waters of Loch Fyne and West Loch Tarbert. This feat was first achieved by the Viking King Magnus Barfud who, in 1198, was granted by treaty as much land as he was able to sail around.

Travel further south past Campbeltown and the B842 road ends at the headland known as the Mull of Kintyre, which was made famous when former Beatle Paul McCartney, who had a home in Kintyre, added lyrics and commercialized a traditional pipe tune of the same name. Westward from Kintyre lies the isle of Rathlin. It is here that Robert the Bruce learned patience in his constant struggles against the English by observing a spider weaving an elaborate web in a cave.

18

Oban

C5 | Argyll
North Pier | oban.org.uk

Known as the "Gateway to the Isles", this bustling port on the Firth of Lorne commands fine views of the Argyll coast. Shops crowd the seafront around the "little bay" which gives Oban its name, and fresh fish is always for sale on the busy pier. Regular ferries leave for Mull, Coll, Tiree,

Barra, South Uist, Islay, Colonsay and Lismore, making Oban one of the most-visited places on the west coast. Built on a steep hill, the town is dominated by the immense McCaig's Tower, an eccentric Colosseum-like structure built in the 1800s. Other major landmarks are the pink granite cathedral and the 600-year-old ruined keep of Dunollie Castle, once the northern outpost of the Dalriadic Scots. Among Oban's other attractions are working centres for glass and pottery, and Oban Distillery, producers of fine malt whisky. On rainy days a good option is the old-fashioned **Oban War and Peace Museum** which offers an interesting insight into local culture.

At the end of July yachts converge on the town for West Highland Week, while at the end of the month, Oban's Highland Games take place. Nearby Kilmore, Taynuilt and Tobermory, on Mull, also host summer Highland Games.

A few miles north of Oban, off the A85, is the 13th-century **Dunstaffnage Castle** where Flora MacDonald was briefly imprisoned for helping

↑ The beautiful white sands of Balevullin Beach on the windswept island of Tiree

Bonnie Prince Charlie (p54) escape in 1746. Further north at Barcaldine is the **Scottish Sealife Sanctuary**. This centre combines looking after injured and orphaned seals with displays of underwater life. The Isle of Seil is reached via the 18th-century "Bridge over the Atlantic". The **Easdale Folk Museum**, on the tiny island of Easdale off Seil, has displays about the history of slate mining in the area. South of Oban along the coast is **Arduaine Garden**, noted for its rare varieties of spring-blooming rhododendrons and colourful azaleas.

Oban War and Peace Museum
🏛Corran Esplanade ◷Mar-Nov: daily 🌐obanmuseum.org.uk

Dunstaffnage Castle
♿🚹 🏛Connel 📞(01631) 562465 ◷Apr-Sep: daily; Oct-Mar: Sat-Wed

Scottish Sealife Sanctuary
♿ 🏛Barcaldine, near Connel ◷Easter-Oct: 10am-5pm daily; Nov-Easter: 11am-4pm Fri-Mon 🌐visitsealife.com

Easdale Folk Museum
🏛Easdale ◷Apr-mid-Oct: 11am-4pm daily 🌐easdale museum.org

Arduaine Garden
♿🚹NTS 🏛Arduaine 📞(01852) 200366 ◷daily, tours by appointment

 19

Coll and Tiree

🅰B4, A5 🏛Argyll 🚢From Oban 🛫From Glasgow to Tiree only 🚹Oban 🌐visitcoll.co.uk; isleoftiree.com

Despite frequent notices of winter gale warnings, these islands, the most westerly in the Inner Hebrides, often record more hours of sunshine than the rest of Britain. They offer beautiful white-sand beaches and impressive surf. Tiree's soil is 60 per cent shell sand, so no trees can grow. As a result, it is perhaps the windiest place in Scotland. Wild flowers flourish here in spring.

Breacachadh Castle, the 15th-century home of Clan Maclean until 1750, overlooks a bay in south Coll but is not open to the public. Tiree has two free museums, the Trenish Isles Exhibition, about the natural history of this group of islands, visible from Tiree, and the Skerryvore Lighthouse Museum in Hynish. The lighthouse stands 20 km (12 miles) offshore.

← Kilchurn Castle, on a rocky peninsula on Loch Awe

⑳ Mallaig

🏔B4 🏛Lochaber
🚌🚂⛴from Ardvasar (Skye)
ℹFort William; (01397) 701801

The heart of Mallaig is its harbour, which has an active fishing fleet and ferries that serve the Small Isles and Skye. The atmosphere is rather more commercial than leisurely, but it is set in an area of outstanding beauty. The **Mallaig Heritage Centre** is a local history museum covering fishing, railways, steamers and ferries.

Mallaig Heritage Centre
♿🅿 🏠Station Rd ⏰11am–4pm Mon–Sat 🌐mallaigheritage.org.uk

㉑ Rum, Eigg, Muck and Canna

🏔B4 🏛Small Isles ⛴From Mallaig or Arisaig ℹFort William; (01397) 701801

Each of the four Small Isles has an individual character and atmosphere, but shares a sense of tranquillity. Canna is a narrow island surrounded by cliffs and has a scattering of unworked archaeological sites. Once owned by Gaelic scholar John Lorne Campbell,

↑ European shag perched on a rock on the tiny island of Canna

it now belongs to the National Trust for Scotland. It has very few inhabitants.

Eigg is the most varied island. Dominated by the distinctive sugarloaf hill, the Sgurr of Eigg, it has a glorious beach with "singing sands" that make odd noises when moved by feet or by the wind. Here the islanders symbolize the spirit of community land ownership, having successfully led a campaign to buy their island from their landlord.

Muck takes its name from the Gaelic for "pig", which it is said to resemble in shape. The smallest of the islands, but no less charming, it is owned by a family who live and farm on the island. Rum is the largest and most magnificent island, with scabrous peaks that are home to an unusual colony of Manx shearwater birds. The island's rough tracks make it best suited to the active visitor. Now owned by Scottish Natural Heritage and a centre for red deer research, it previously belonged to the wealthy Bullough family. They built the lavish **Kinloch Castle** whose design and furnishings were revolutionary at the time. It has fallen into disrepair, but a group is assessing how to provide a sustainable future for it.

Kinloch Castle
🏠Isle of Rum
🌐kinlochcastlefriends.org

↑ Brightly coloured buildings line the street on Tobermory Harbour

㉒ Mull

🏔B5 🏛Argyll ⛴from Oban, Lochaline and Kilchoan; from Fionnphort, on Mull, to Iona ℹCraignure; (01680) 812377

The largest of the Inner Hebridean islands, Mull features rough moorlands, the rocky peak of Ben More and a splendid beach at Calgary. Most roads follow the coastline, affording wonderful sea views.

On a promontory to the east of Craignure lies the 13th-century **Duart Castle**, home of the chief of Clan Maclean. You can visit the Banqueting Hall, State Rooms and the dungeons that once held prisoners from a Spanish Armada galleon, sunk in 1588 by one Donald Maclean.

At the northern end of Mull is the picturesque town of Tobermory, with its brightly coloured buildings and a kaleidoscope of houses along the seafront. Built as a fishing village in 1788, it is now a

popular port for yachts, and one of Mull's most favoured tourist stops. The harbourside **Mull Aquarium** is Europe's first catch and release aquarium. With its touch pools and cinema, it holds great appeal for kids.

The small and very beautiful island of Iona is one of the biggest attractions on Scotland's west coast. A restored abbey stands on the site where Irish missionary St Columba began his crusade in 563 and made Iona the home of Christianity in Europe. In the graveyard of the abbey, 48 Scottish kings are said to be buried and four historic high crosses can be seen, two of them along the medieval Street of the Dead. Since 1938, when the Iona Community was formed, this has again been a religious centre. During the summer months the abbey has a large influx of visitors.

If you are lucky with the weather, head to **Fingal's Cave** on the Isle of Staffa. A true natural wonder, the cave is surrounded by "organ pipes" of basalt, the inspiration for Mendelssohn's *Hebrides Overture* (1833). Boat trips run there from Ulva and Fionnphort and to the seven **Treshnish Isles**. These uninhabited isles are a sanctuary for thousands of seabirds, including puffins, razorbills, kittiwakes and skuas. Lunga is the main stop for tour boats.

Duart Castle
⊛☺🎧 🅐Off A849, near Craignure 🕒Apr: 11am–4pm Sun–Thu; May–Oct: 10:30am–5pm daily 🅦duartcastle.com

Mull Aquarium
🅐Taigh Solais, Tobermory 🕒Easter–Oct: 9:30am–5pm daily 🅦mullaquarium.co.uk

Fingal's Cave and Treshnish Isles
⊛ 🅐Staffa, west of Mull 🚢Easter–Oct 🕒Timetable varies, check website 🅦staffatours.com

EAT

Café Fish
Super-fresh seafood straight off the boat, and a surprising wine list are on offer here. There's a quayside terrace in summer.

🅐B5 🅐The Pier, Tobermory, Mull 🅦thecafefish.com

Tea Garden Café
For real home cooking, look no further. This quirky café is famed for its pint of prawns, fresh from the harbour.

🅐B4 🅐Mallaig Backpackers Lodge, Station Rd, Mallaig 🅦mallaigbackpackers. co.uk

£££

Argyll Hotel
Crofters and local fishermen keep this cosy restaurant well-stocked with lamb, game, beef and seafood.

🅐B5 🅐Isle of Iona, Argyll 🅦argyllhotel iona.co.uk

The vast wilderness of ↑
Rannoch Moor and
Schiehallion in the distance

㉓
Glencoe

C4 Lochaber Fort
William Glencoe NTS
Visitor Centre, Glencoe;
Open Mar-Oct: 9:30am-
5:30pm daily, Nov-Feb:
10am-4pm Thu-Sun
nts.org.uk

Renowned for its awesome
scenery and savage history,
Glencoe was compared by
Dickens to "a burial ground of
a race of giants". The precipi-
tous cliffs of Buachaille Etive
Mor and the knife-edged
ridge of Aonach Eagach offer
a formidable challenge even
to experienced mountaineers.

Against a backdrop of craggy
peaks and the tumbling River
Coe, the Glen offers superb
hill walking. The Visitor Centre
has details of routes, ranging
from an easy walk near Signal
Rock (from which the signal
was given for the massacre)
to a stiff 10-km (6-mile) haul
up the Devil's Staircase.
Guided walks are offered in
summer by NTS Rangers. East
of Glencoe lies Rannoch Moor,
one of the emptiest areas in
Britain. Take the chairlift at
the **Glencoe Mountain** resort
for a dramatic view.
　　To the southwest, beautiful
Glen Etive leads to the head
of impressive
Loch

Etive, which emerges on the
coast at the Connel Bridge
north of Oban. At the
Ballachulish Bridge a side
road branches to Kinloch-
leven, at the head of a long
attractive loch.

Glencoe Mountain
 Kingshouse, Glencoe
Daily glencoe
mountain.co.uk

㉔
Rannoch Moor

D5 Perthshire

Curlews call and buzzards
mew as they circle above
　　this desolate expanse of
　　wet and wild moorland,
　　dotted with ponds, rivers
　　and small lochs. In the
　　shadow of the summit of
　　Schiehallion, Rannoch
　　moor is home to an
abundance of wildlife,
including herds of wild deer.
The Black Wood of Rannoch
clothes the mountain's lower
slopes, and Alpine flora
left by the last Ice Age
flourish on the bare rocky
slopes of 1,214-m (3,983-ft)
Ben Lawers.

MASSACRE OF GLENCOE

In 1692, the Glencoe MacDonalds'
chief was five days late with an
oath of submission to William III,
providing an excuse to root out a nest
of Jacobite supporters. For ten days 130
soldiers, under Robert Campbell, were
hospitably entertained by the MacDonalds
before, in a terrible breach of trust, the
soldiers turned on them and killed them. A
political scandal ensued, but there were no
official reprimands for three years.

26

Blair Castle

A D4   **A** Lochaber   🚂🚌
W visitscotland.com

This rambling, turreted castle has been altered so often in its 700-year history that it now provides a unique insight into the history and changing tastes of aristocratic life in the Highlands. The elegant 18th-century wing displays the gloves and pipe of Bonnie Prince Charlie (p54), who came to gather support for a Jacobite uprising. Family portraits span 300 years and include paintings by such masters as Johann Zoffany and Sir Peter Lely. Sir Edwin Landseer's *Death of a Hart in Glen Tilt* (1850) also features.

In 1844 Queen Victoria conferred on its owners, the Dukes of Atholl, permission to maintain a private army, the existing Atholl Highlanders.

25

Fort William

A C4   **A** Highland   **W** visit fortwilliam.co.uk

Fort William, one of the major towns on the west coast, is noted not for its looks but for its convenient location at the foot of Ben Nevis (p166). The Jacobite Steam Train, which doubles as the Hogwarts Express, runs the magical route from here to the coastal town of Mallaig (p194).

Jacobite Steam Train
🚂 Fort William   **O** Departs 10:15am & 2:30pm (Apr, May: Mon-Fri; Jun-Sep: daily)
W westcoastrailways.co.uk

27

Pitlochry

A D5   **A** Perthshire
🚂🚌   **i** 22 Atholl Rd
W pitlochry.org

Surrounded by beautiful pine-forested hills, Pitlochry became famous after Queen Victoria called it one of the finest resorts in Europe. In early summer, wild salmon leap up the ladder at the Power Station Dam to spawn upriver. Above the ladder are fine views of Loch Faskally,

popular with anglers. Walking trails from here link with the pretty gorge at Killiecrankie. **Blair Athol Distillery** offers guided tours, while the **Festival Theatre** in Port-na-Craig has shows all year.

Blair Athol Distillery
   A Perth Rd   **O** Daily
W malts.com

Festival Theatre
   A Port-na-Craig
O Mid-May-Oct: daily for plays   **W** pitlochry festival theatre.com

---

28

Killiecrankie

A D4   **A** Perth and Kinross
A Pitlochry   🚌 87 or 887
W nts.org.uk

For centuries Killiecrankie, site of a famous battle in 1689, was a staging-post between lowland Scotland and the Highlands. Now it's a peaceful suburb of Pitlochry, and the starting point for a pleasant walk through the scenic Pass of Killiecrankie.

←

Blair Castle's grand ballroom, built for the Atholl Highlanders

Urquhart Castle ruins overlooking the still waters of Loch Ness

29

Inverness

D3 Inverness-shire
Castle Wynd
visitinvernesslochness.com

In the Highlands, all roads lead to the region's "capital", Inverness. Despite being the largest city in the north, the atmosphere is more townlike, with a compact and easily accessible centre. Although it is sadly defaced by modern architecture, Inverness is known for its floral displays in summer, and for the River Ness, frequented by salmon fishermen during the summer, even where it runs through the city centre. On high ground above the city is Inverness Castle, a Victorian building now used as the courthouse. Nearby, next to the tourist information office, is the **Museum and Art Gallery**, with permanent and touring exhibitions. The main shopping area fans out in three directions and includes a lively pedestrian precinct with busking musicians.

Just across the river is the **Scottish Kiltmaker Visitor Centre**. Here visitors get an insight into the history, culture and tradition of the kilt, with audio-visual and workshop presentations of kiltmaking. On the banks of the Ness, **Eden Court Theatre** has a varied programme of local and international performers. Following the tree-lined banks of the river further upstream and crossing a pedestrian bridge leads to the Island Walks. Beyond this, further upstream still, is **Inverness Leisure**, with swimming pools, spas and a variety of wild, spiralling flumes. Thomas Telford's Caledonian Canal *(p151)*, an engineering marvel constructed between 1804 and 1822, is still in constant use and can be viewed at Tomnahurich Bridge. From here, **Jacobite Cruises** runs various summer cruises along the length of Loch Ness – an excellent way to spend a sunny afternoon. Inverness is an ideal base for touring the rest of the Highlands, as it lies within easy reach of most of the region's popular attractions, including the Culloden battlesite *(p200)*, 8 km (5 miles) to the east.

Museum and Art Gallery
Castle Wynd Apr-Oct: Tue-Sat; Nov-Mar: Thu-Sat highlifehighland.com

Scottish Kiltmaker Visitor Centre
4-9 Huntly St Daily highlandhouseoffraser.com

Eden Court Theatre
Bishop's Rd eden-court.co.uk

Inverness Leisure
Bught Lane (01463) 667500 Daily

Jacobite Cruises
Tomnahurich Bridge, Glenurquhart jacobite.co.uk

HIGHLAND CLEARANCES

During the heyday of the clan system, tenants paid their land-holding chieftains rent in the form of military service. However, with the destruction of the clan system after the Battle of Culloden, landowners began to demand a financial rent, which their tenants were unable to afford, and the land was gradually bought up by Lowland and English farmers. In what became known as "the year of the sheep" (1792), thousands of tenants were evicted, sometimes forcibly, to make way for live stock. Many emigrated to Australia, America and Canada. The ruins of their crofts can still be seen, especially in Sutherland and Wester Ross.

Black Isle

D3 Ross & Cromarty
Inverness black-isle.info

The broad peninsula of the Black Isle is largely farmland and fishing villages. The town of Cromarty was an important 18th-century port and many of its merchant houses still stand. The museum in the **Cromarty Courthouse** runs tours of the town. The **Hugh Miller Museum** recalls the life of theologian and geologist Hugh Miller (1802–56). Fortrose has a ruined 14th-century cathedral, while a stone on Chanonry Point commemorates the Brahan Seer, burnt alive by the Countess of Seaforth after he foresaw her husband's infidelity. For local archaeology, visit Rosemarkie's **Groam House Museum.**

Cromarty Courthouse

Church St, Cromarty Apr-mid-Oct: noon-4pm Sun-Thu; mid-Oct-Apr: by appointment cromarty-courthouse.org.uk

Hugh Miller Museum

Church St, Cromarty Mid-Mar-Sep: 1-5pm daily nts.org.uk

Did You Know?

The Moray Firth dolphins are the biggest bottlenose dolphins in the world.

Groam House Museum

 High St, Rosemarkie Apr-Oct: 11am-4:30pm Mon-Fri, 2-4:30pm Sat & Sun groamhouse.org.uk

31 Moray Firth

D3 Moray Elgin morayspeyside.com

Renowned for its wildlife-spotting opportunities, most notably from popular spot Chanonry Point, the Moray Firth is home to a wealth of marine life. Harbour seals, porpoises, white-beaked and bottlenose dolphins and several species of whale, all come here to feed. Learn more about the Moray Firth's resident and visiting sealife at the **WDC Scottish Dolphin Centre** at Spey Bay. Dolphin spotting tours are available.

WDC Scottish Dolphin Centre

 Spey Bay, Fochabers, Moray Times vary, check website Dec-Feb dolphincentre.whales.org

32 Fort George

D3 Inverness From Inverness Apr-Sep: 9:30am-5:30pm daily; Oct-Mar: 10am-4pm daily historicenvironment.scot

One of the finest examples of European military architecture, Fort George holds a commanding position on the Moray Firth. Completed in 1769, it was built after the Jacobite risings to discourage further rebellion, and is still a military garrison.

The **Regimental Museum** of the Highlanders Regiment is in the Fort, and some barrack rooms show the conditions of common soldiers more than 200 years ago. The **Grand Magazine** contains an outstanding collection of arms and military equipment. Fort George's battlements also offer views of dolphins playing in the Moray Firth.

← Dolphins playing in the Moray Forth, best seen off Chanonry Point

33 (NTS)

Culloden

D3 **⚑**Inverness-shire
⛴🚌From Inverness

The desolate battlefield of Culloden looks much as it did on 16 April 1746, when the last battle was fought on British soil. Here the Jacobite cause, under Bonnie Prince Charlie's leadership (*p54*), perished from the attack of nearly 9,000 troops, led by the Duke of Cumberland. Visitors can roam the battlefield, visit the clan graves and experience the audio-visual displays at the **NTS Visitor Centre**.

Roughly 1.5 km (1 mile) east of Culloden are the outstanding Neolithic burial sites at Clava Cairns.

NTS Visitor Centre

🎁🍽️📧♿ **⚑**On the B9006
🕐Daily **🌐**nts.org.uk

34

Strathpeffer

C3 **⚑**Ross & Cromarty
⛴Dingwall **🚌**Inverness
ℹPump Room, The Square
🌐strathpeffer.org

Standing 8 km (5 miles) east of the Rogie Falls, the holiday centre of Strathpeffer still retains the refined charm that made it well known as a Victorian spa and health resort. The town's huge hotels and gracious layout recall the days when European royalty and lesser mortals flocked to the chalybeate- and sulphur-laden springs, believed to alleviate tuberculosis. It is still possible to sample the water at the unmanned **Water Tasting Pavilion** found in the town centre.

Water Tasting Pavilion

⚑The Square **🕐**Easter-Oct: daily

---

35 🚶 🍽️

Cawdor Castle

D3 **⚑**On B9090 (off A96)
🚌Nairn, then bus or taxi
🚂From Inverness **🕐**May-early Oct: 10am-5:30pm daily (last entry 5pm)
🌐cawdorcastle.com

With its turreted central tower, moat and drawbridge, Cawdor Castle is one of the Highlands' most romantic stately homes. Though the castle is famed for being the 11th-century home of Shakespeare's tragic character Macbeth, and the scene of his murder of King Duncan, it is historically unproven that either figure came here.

An ancient holly tree preserved in the vaults is said to be the one under which, in 1372, Thane William's donkey stopped for a rest during its master's search for a place to build a fortress. According to legend, this was how the site for the castle was chosen. Now, after 600 years of continuous occupation (it is still the home of the Thanes of Cawdor) the house contains a number of rare tapestries and portraits by the 18th-century painters Joshua Reynolds (1723–92) and George Romney (1734–1802). Furniture in the Pink Bedroom and Woodcock Room includes work by the 18th-century designers Chippendale and Sheraton. In the Old Kitchen, the huge Victorian cooking range stands as a shrine to below-stairs drudgery.

↑ The Black Water tumbling over Rogie Falls, Ross-shire

STAY

Culgower House
Between Brora and Helmsdale, on the East Sutherland coast, this quaint family home is nestled in wooded hills. Rooms have sea views and breakfasts are a dream.

D3 **⚑**Loth, Helmsdale
🕐Nov-Feb **🌐**culgower house.com

£££

Beach Cottage
Watch dolphins swim in the Moray Firth from this beautifully renovated 18th-century fisherman's cottage with stunning sea views.

D3 **⚑**Stafford St, Helmsdale **🌐**bannock burninn.co.uk

£££

Dunrobin Castle, seat of the Earls of Sutherland since the 13th century →

INSIDER TIP
Panning for Gold

You can pan for gold in Helmsdale's Kildonan Burn, where a lucky few sometimes find a pinch of this precious metal. Rent the necessary equipment from Strath Ullie Crafts.

The castle grounds provide beautiful nature trails, as well as a nine-hole golf course.

36
Dornoch

A D3 **A** Sutherland
≈ Golspie, Tain
⌷ Inverness, Tain
𝑖 The Square **w** visit dornoch.com

With its first-class golf course and extensive sandy beaches, Dornoch is a popular holiday resort, but it has retained a peaceful atmosphere. The medieval cathedral (now serving as the parish church) was all but destroyed in a clan dispute in 1570; it was eventually restored in the 1920s for its 700th anniversary. More recently, the American singer Madonna chose the cathedral for the christening of her son and for her own wedding in 2000.

A stone at the beach end of River Street marks the place where Janet Horne, the last woman to be tried for witchcraft in Scotland, was executed in 1722.

Nineteen kilometres (12 miles) to the northeast is the stately, Victorianized pile of **Dunrobin Castle**, magnificently situated in a great park with formal gardens overlooking the sea. Since the 13th century this has been the seat of the Earls of Sutherland. Many of its rooms are open to visitors.

The peaceful town of Tain to the south became an administrative centre for the Highland Clearances, when the tolbooth was used as a jail. All is explained in the heritage centre, **Tain Through Time**.

Dunrobin Castle
⊘ ⊘ ⊕ ⊕ **A** Near Golspie
☎ (01408) 633177 **☐** Apr–mid-Oct: daily

Tain Through Time
⊘ **A** Tower St **☐** Jun–Aug: Mon–Sat; Apr, May & Sep: Mon–Fri **w** tainmuseum. org.uk

37
Helmsdale

A D2 **A** Sutherland
≈ **⌷** From Inverness

Founded by Vikings, Helmsdale was settled in the 19th century by crofters turfed off their land by the Duke of Sutherland. A flotilla of fishing boats crewed by their descendants still bobs in a harbour surrounded by neat stone houses. The **Timespan Heritage Centre** tells the story of Helmsdale's fascinating history and of the gold rush that followed the discovery of small amounts of the precious metal in the Helmsdale River in 1868. The Emigrants Statue commemorates the many people who fled Scotland and sailed to far-off lands in search of a better life during the Highland clearances.

Timespan Heritage Centre
⊘ ⊘ ⊙ **A** Dunrobin St
☐ 10am–5pm daily
w timespan.org.uk

Helmsdale's Emigrants Statue commemorating Scottish diaspora

Eilean Donan Castle amid the stunning scenery of Glen Shiel ↑

 38

Glen Shiel

🅰C4 🏠Skye & Lochalsh 🚉Kyle of Lochalsh 🚌Glen Shiel ℹBayfield House, Bayfield Rd, Portree; (01478) 612992

Dominating one of Scotland's most haunting regions, the awesome summits of the Five Sisters of Kintail rear into view as the A87 enters Glen Shiel. The Visitor Centre at Morvich offers ranger-led excursions in summer. Further west is the romantic **Eilean Donan Castle**. After becoming a Jacobite *(p53)* stronghold, it was destroyed in 1719 by English warships. Restored in the 19th century, it now contains Jacobite relics.

Eilean Donan Castle

⌖🖼🏛 🏠Off A87, near Dornie ⏱Feb-Dec: daily 🌐eileandonancastle.com

 39

Wester Ross

🅰C3 🏠Ross & Cromarty 🚉Achnasheen, Strathcarron 🚌Gairloch ℹAchnasheen 🌐visitwester-ross.com

Leaving Loch Carron to the south, the A890 suddenly enters the northern Highlands and the great wilderness of Wester Ross. The sprawling Torridon Estate includes some of the oldest mountains on earth (Torridonian rock is over 600 million years old), and is home to red deer, wildcats and wild goats. Peregrine falcons and golden eagles nest in the towering sandstone mass of Beinn Eighe, above Torridon village, with its breathtaking views over Applecross towards Skye. The **Torridon Countryside Centre** offers guided walks in season.

Further north, the A832 cuts through the Beinn Eighe National Nature Reserve, Britain's oldest wildlife sanctuary. Remnants of the ancient Caledonian pine forest still stand on the banks and isles of Loch Maree, sheltering wildcats and pine martens. Buzzards and golden eagles nest above. **Beinn Eighe Visitor Centre** has information on the reserve.

Along the coast, a series of exotic gardens thrive in the warming influence of the Gulf Stream. The most impressive is Inverewe Garden.

Torridon Countryside Centre

🏛 🏠Torridon 📞(01445) 791368 ⏱Apr-Sep: Sun-Fri

Beinn Eighe Visitor Centre

🏠Near Kinlochewe, on A832 ⏱Mar-Oct: daily 🌐nnr.scot

40

Handa Island

🅰C2 🏠Sutherland 🚢From Tarbet, near Scourie; (07780) 967800; Apr-Aug: Mon-Sat ℹScottish Wildlife Trust; (07920) 468572

Just off Scourie on the west coast, this small island is an important breeding sanctuary for many species of seabirds.

In past centuries its hardy people had their own queen and parliament, but the last few were evacuated in 1847 when their potato crop failed. The island was also a burial ground as it was safe from the wolves on the mainland.

The island is now managed by the Scottish Wildlife Trust. Visitors can walk to the 100-m- (328-ft-) high northern

↑ Puffins are just some of the many species found on Handa Island

cliffs to experience the intimidating antics of great and Arctic skuas (large migratory birds) swooping low over their heads. Early in the year 11,000 pairs of razorbills and 66,000 pairs of guillemots take up residence.

Britain's highest waterfall is Eas Coul Aulin, at 180 m (590 ft), best seen from a tour boat out of Kylesku, 24 km (15 miles) to the south of Handa.

41 Inverewe Garden

🅰C3 🅰On A832, near Poolewe, Ross-shire 🕒 Daily (house: Apr-Oct) 🌐nts.org.uk

Over 130,000 visitors a year come to this national treasure. The gardens contain an extraordinary variety of trees, shrubs and flowers from around the world, despite its latitude of 57.8° north.

Inverewe was started in 1862 by 20-year-old Osgood Mackenzie after he was given a large estate of exposed, barren land next to his family's holding. He began by planting shelter trees then created a walled garden using imported soil. He found that the climate, warmed by the North Atlantic Drift from the Gulf Stream, encouraged growth of exotic species.

By 1922, it had achieved international recognition as one of the great plant collections, and in 1952 was donated to the National Trust for Scotland. Now one of Scotland's leading botanical gardens, Inverewe has Blue Nile lilies, the tallest Australian gum trees in Britain and rhododendrons from China. There's colour all year, but the gardens are at their best between spring and autumn.

42 Ullapool

🅰C3 🅰Ross and Cromarty 🚆Inverness 🚌🚢 ℹ️Argyle St 🌐ullapool.com

With its wide streets, whitewashed houses, palm trees and street signs in Gaelic, this is one of the west coast's prettiest villages. Built as a fishing station in 1788, it's on a peninsula jutting into Loch Broom. Fishing is now only important in the winter, when East European "klondyker" factory ships moor in the loch. The major activity is the ferry to Stornoway on Lewis. The **Ullapool Museum** gives insight into local history.

Ullapool Museum

♿♿ 🅰7-8 West Argyle St 🕒Apr-Oct: Mon-Sat 🌐ullapoolmuseum.co.uk

43 Cape Wrath and the North Coast

🅰C2 🅰Sutherland & Caithness 🚌🚢 ℹ️John O'Groats; (01955) 611373

The northern edge of mainland Scotland encompasses the full variety of Highland geography, from mountainous moorlands and white beaches to flat, green farmland.

Cape Wrath is alluring not only for its name but for its cliffs and its many sea stacks, swarming with sea-birds. In

summer, the 13-km (8-mile) road leading to Cape Wrath is served by mini-bus, reached only by taking a ferry from the pier by the Cape Wrath Hotel.

At Durness is Smoo Cave, an awesome cavern hollowed out of limestone. **Smoo Cave Tours** run trips there. Just outside the town, a small community of artists has established the Balnakeil Craft Village, displaying pottery, wood carving, enamelwork, printmaking and paintings. Astonishingly white beaches follow along the coast, and the road then loops round Loch Eriboll, the deepest of Scotland's many sea lochs.

The **Strathnaver Museum** in Bettyhill explains the notorious Sutherland Clearances (p198), the forced evictions of 15,000 people. At Rossal, 16 km (10 miles) south, a walk around an excavated village offers information on life in pre-Clearance days.

The main town here is Thurso, site of Northlands, the Scottish Nordic Music Festival each September.

John O'Groats is probably the most famous name on the map here, said to be the very tip of the mainland, although this is in fact nearby Dunnet Head. Even more rewarding are the cliffs at Duncansby Head and the Pentland Firth.

Smoo Cave Tours

♿ 🅰Durness 🕒Apr-Sep: daily 🌐smoocavetours. weebly.com

Strathnaver Museum

♿ 🅰Clachan, Bettyhill 🕒Apr-Oct: Mon-Sat 🌐strath navermuseum.org.uk

A DRIVING TOUR
ROAD TO THE ISLES

Locator Map
For more detail see p160

THE HIGHLANDS AND ISLANDS

Distance 72 km (45 miles) **Stopping-off points**
Glenfinnan NTS Visitors' Centre (01397 722250) explains the Jacobite risings and serves refreshments; the Old Library Lodge in Arisaig offers excellent Scottish cuisine.

This scenic route goes past vast mountain corridors, breathtaking beaches of white sand and tiny villages to the idyllic town of Mallaig, one of the ferry ports for the isles of Skye, Rum, Eigg, Muck and Canna. In addition to stunning scenery, the area is steeped in Jacobite history.

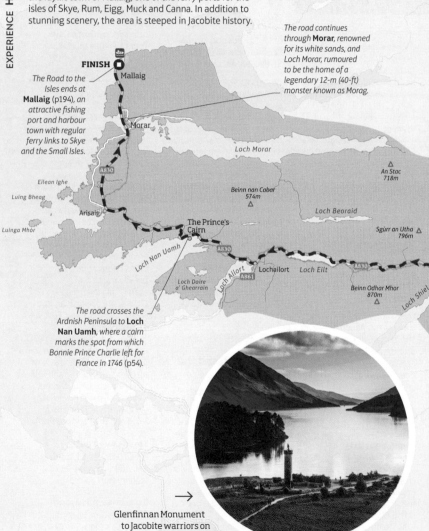

*The road continues through **Morar**, renowned for its white sands, and Loch Morar, rumoured to be the home of a legendary 12-m (40-ft) monster known as Morag.*

FINISH

Mallaig

*The Road to the Isles ends at **Mallaig** (p194), an attractive fishing port and harbour town with regular ferry links to Skye and the Small Isles.*

Morar

Loch Morar

An Stac 718m

Eilean Ighe

Luing Bheag

Beinn nan Cabar 574m

Loch Beoraid

Arisaig

Luinga Mhòr

The Prince's Cairn

Sgùrr an Utha 796m

Loch Nan Uamh

Lochailort   Loch Eilt

Loch Doire a' Ghearrain

Loch Allort

Beinn Odhar Mhor 870m

Loch Shiel

*The road crosses the Ardnish Peninsula to **Loch Nan Uamh**, where a cairn marks the spot from which Bonnie Prince Charlie left for France in 1746 (p54).*

→

Glenfinnan Monument to Jacobite warriors on the banks of Loch Shiel

↑ A woman and her dog on the beautiful white sands of Morar

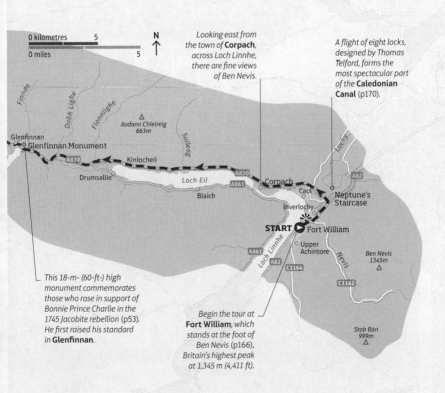

*Looking east from the town of **Corpach**, across Loch Linnhe, there are fine views of Ben Nevis.*

*A flight of eight locks, designed by Thomas Telford, forms the most spectacular part of the **Caledonian Canal** (p170).*

This 18-m- (60-ft-) high monument commemorates those who rose in support of Bonnie Prince Charlie in the 1745 Jacobite rebellion (p53). He first raised his standard in **Glenfinnan**.

Begin the tour at **Fort William**, which stands at the foot of Ben Nevis (p166), Britain's highest peak at 1,345 m (4,411 ft).

NEED TO KNOW

BEFORE YOU GO

Forward planning is essential to any successful trip. Be prepared for all eventualities by considering the following points before you travel.

CURRENCY
Pound Sterling
(GBP)

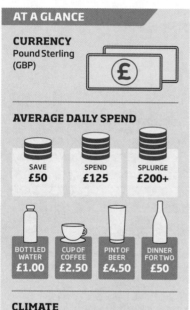

AVERAGE DAILY SPEND

SAVE	SPEND	SPLURGE
£50	£125	£200+

BOTTLED WATER	CUP OF COFFEE	PINT OF BEER	DINNER FOR TWO
£1.00	£2.50	£4.50	£50

CLIMATE

The longest days occur May–Aug, while Oct–Feb sees the shortest daylight hours.

Temperatures average 15°C (59°F) in summer, and drop below 0 °C (32 °F) in winter.

October and November see the most rainfall, but heavy showers occur all year round.

ELECTRICITY SUPPLY

Power sockets are type G, fitting three-pronged plugs. Standard voltage is 230 volts.

Passports and Visas

For a stay of up to three months EU nationals and citizens of the US, Canada, Australia and New Zealand do not need a visa to enter the country. Consult your nearest British embassy or check the **UK Government** website for up-to-date information specific to your home country.
UK Government
🅆 gov.uk

Travel Safety Advice

Visitors can get up-to-date travel safety information from the UK Foreign and Commonwealth Office, the US State Department, and the Department of Foreign Affairs and Trade in Australia.
Australia
🅆 smartraveller.gov.au
UK
🅆 gov.uk/foreign-travel-advice
US
🅆 travel.state.gov

Customs Information

An individual is permitted to carry the following within the EU for personal use:

Tobacco products 800 cigarettes, 400 cigarillos, 200 cigars or 1 kg of smoking tobacco.

Alcohol 10 litres of alcoholic beverages above 22% strength, 20 litres below 22% strength, 90 litres of wine (60 litres of which can be sparkling wine) and 110 litres of beer.

Cash If you plan to enter or leave the EU with €10,000 or more in cash (or the equivalent in other currencies) you must declare it to the customs authorities.

Regulations may be subject to change. If travelling outside the EU limits vary so check restrictions before travelling.

Language

Scotland is a multicultural country in which you will hear many languages spoken. Gaelic is now spoken by fewer than 1% of the population, and most commonly spoken in the Outer Hebrides. Regional accents can be challenging, even for visitors from other Anglophone countries.

Insurance

It is wise to take out an insurance policy covering theft, loss of belongings, medical problems, cancellation and delays. Emergency treatment is usually free from the National Health Service, and there are reciprocal arrangements with other EEA countries, Australia and New Zealand and some other countries (check the **NHS** website for details). Residents of EEA countries should carry a European Health Insurance Card (**EHIC**), which allows treatment for free or at a reduced cost. It is advisable for visitors from outside the EEA, Australia and New Zealand to arrange comprehensive medical insurance.
EHIC
🌐 gov.uk/european-health-insurance-card
NHS
🌐 nhs.uk

Vaccinations

No inoculations are needed for the UK.

Booking Accommodation

Scotland offers a variety of accommodation, from luxury five-star hotels to family-run B&Bs, and budget hostels. Lodgings can fill up quickly and prices are higher in summer, especially in the Highlands and islands and in Edinburgh during the festival season and Hogmanay. A list of accommodation can be found at **Visit Scotland** (p215) and **The Hotel Guru**. Camping is allowed almost anywhere in Scotland, so long as you are respectful of the community and leave the site as you found it. Be sure to familiarize yourself with the Scottish Outdoor Access Code before you set off.
The Hotel Guru
🌐 thehotelguru.com
Scottish Outdoor Access Code
🌐 outdooraccess-scotland.scot

Money

Major credit, debit and prepaid currency cards are accepted in most shops and restaurants. Contactless payments are widely accepted,

though not on public transport. Cash machines can be found at banks and on main streets in major towns, but they are harder to find in remote areas, particularly in the Highlands and islands, where many places accept cash only.

Scottish bank notes are not universally accepted outside Scotland, so it is best to exchange them before leaving.

Travellers with Specific Needs

Most trains and many buses in Scotland are wheelchair-accessible. Accessibility information for public transport is available from regional public transport websites (p212). Many major museums and galleries offer audio tours and induction loops for those with impaired sight and hearing. **Action on Hearing Loss** and **The Royal National Institute for the Blind** can offer information and advice.
Action on Hearing Loss
🌐 actionhearingloss.org.uk
Royal National Institute for the Blind
🌐 rnib.org.uk

Closures

Mondays Some museums and tourist attractions are closed for the day.
Sundays and Public Holidays Many shops close early, or for the entire day.
Winter Some accommodation establishments and other services in rural areas that cater mainly to holidaymakers close from around October until the Easter school holidays.

PUBLIC HOLIDAYS	
New Year's Day	1 Jan
Bank Holiday	2 Jan
Good Friday	19 Apr (2019)
	10 Apr (2020)
May Day	6 May (2019)
	4 May (2020)
May Bank Holiday	27 May (2019)
	25 May (2020)
Aug Bank Holiday	5 Aug (2019)
	3 Aug (2020)
Christmas Day	25 Dec
Boxing Day	26 Dec

GETTING AROUND

Public transport connects Scotland's cities, while trains and buses serve the regions and flights and ferries connect the mainland and islands.

AT A GLANCE

PUBLIC TRANSPORT COSTS

EDINBURGH
£1.70
Single Bus Journey

GLASGOW
£4.10
All-day Subway Ticket

CITY LINK EXPLORER PASS
£49
3 days unlimited travel on Scottish Citylink

SPEED LIMIT

MOTORWAY
70 mph (96 kmph)

NATIONAL ROADS
60 mph (96 kmph)

URBAN AREAS
30 mph (48 kmph)

EDINBURGH URBAN AREAS
20 mph (32 kmph)

Arriving by Air

Three main international airports serve Scotland: Edinburgh, Glasgow, and Aberdeen. All are near their respective cities, with adequate transport links, including tram service between Edinburgh Airport and the city. Glasgow Prestwick Airport handles mainly holiday flights to and from European destinations. Inverness Airport has a small number of flights from Amsterdam in addition to flights from London and other UK airports. Dundee has flights from London Stansted. Other mainland airports include Wick, Campbeltown and Oban. The islands are served by Kirkwall Airport in Orkney Sumburgh Airport in Shetland, Stornoway Airport on Lewis, and smaller airports on Islay, Tiree, Benbecula and Barra.

Train Travel

International Train Travel
Edinburgh and Glasgow are the main hubs for rail travel to Scotland from the rest of the UK. There are connections at London St Pancras International for Eurostar services from mainland Europe. **London North Eastern Railway** then runs from London to Edinburgh, Dundee and Aberdeen. **Virgin Trains** operates from London Euston to Glasgow and onward to Edinburgh with some trains continuing to Inverness. **The Caledonian Sleeper** operates overnight services from London Euston to Glasgow, Edinburgh, Aberdeen, Inverness and Fort William. The **Interrail Great Britain Pass** offers a good deal on travel throughout Scotland and the rest of the UK for 3, 4, 6 or 8 days within a one month period.

Caledonian Sleeper
W sleeper.scot
Eurostar
W eurostar.com
Interrail Great Britain Pass
W interrail.eu
Virgin Trains
W virgintrains.co.uk
London North Eastern Railway
W lner.co.uk

GETTING TO AND FROM THE AIRPORT

Airport	Distance to city	Public Transport	Journey time	Price
Edinburgh	8 miles (13 km)	Airlink 100 Bus	45 mins	£4.50
		Tram	30 mins	£6.00
Glasgow	8 miles (13 km)	Airport Express 500 Bus	15 mins	£8.00
Aberdeen	7 miles (11 km)	Jet Service 727 Coach	30 mins	£3.70

JOURNEY PLANNER

Plotting the main driving routes by journey time, this map is a rough guide to driving between Scotland's main towns and cities. The times given reflect the fastest and most direct routes. Allow extra time for driving in bad weather and beware of rapidly changing weather conditions.

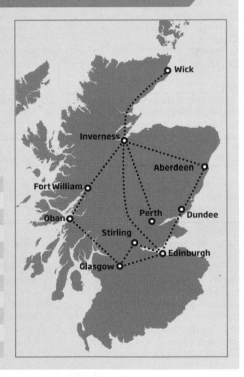

Aberdeen to Inverness	2.5 hrs
Edinburgh to Glasgow	1.25 hrs
Edinburgh to Dundee	1.25 hrs
Edinburgh to Aberdeen	3 hrs
Edinburgh to Inverness	3.5 hrs
Edinburgh to Stirling	1 hr
Glasgow to Stirling	3.5 hrs
Glasgow to Oban	2.5 hrs
Inverness to Fort William	1.5 hrs
Inverness to Wick	2.75 hrs
Perth to Inverness	2.5 hrs

Regional Trains

Lines within Scotland are coordinated by National Rail, with main stations in Glasgow, Edinburgh, Stirling, Perth, Dundee, Aberdeen, Inverness, Fort William and Oban. Thurso is Scotland's northernmost railway station. The West Highland Line terminates at Mallaig.
National Rail
W nationalrail.co.uk

Long-Distance Bus Travel

Long distance coaches connect major towns and cities with each other and with rural areas. Main operators are **Megabus and Citylink.**
Megabus
W uk.megabus.com
National Express
W nationalexpress.com

Public Transport

Public transport in Scotland is a combination of private sector and city-operated services, and fares are relatively inexpensive compared to London and many European countries.

Most cities operate only bus systems. In Edinburgh buses are complemented by a single tram line and in Glasgow by a single subway circuit and a suburban rail network, all controlled by Strathclyde Partnership for Transport (SPT).
Traveline Scotland provide ticket information and timetables for all public transport services across Scotland.
Traveline Scotland
W travelinescotland.com

Public Transport Operators
Aberdeen: First Aberdeen
W firstgroup.com/aberdeen
Dundee: Xplore Dundee
W xploredundee.com
Edinburgh: Lothian Buses
W lothianbuses.com
Glasgow: SPT
W spt.co.uk

Bus
Urban bus networks are generally fast, frequent and reliable. In most cities, a single fare applies for all bus travel within city limits. Multiple trip tickets and one-day travel passes are available in major cities. These can be bought online and stored on your phone. Single-trip tickets can also be bought from the driver when boarding your bus but change is not given so you must pay the exact fare. Public transport in rural areas is less extensive. Timetables are often designed around the needs of local workers and school students, so schedules are less convenient for visitors, with departures early in the morning and in late afternoon or early evening.

Tram
Scotland's only tram line, opened in 2014, connects Edinburgh International Airport with the city centre. There are plans to extend it as far as Leith by 2020.
Edinburgh Trams
W edinburghtrams.com

Subway
Glasgow's SPT subway, the only underground rail service in Scotland, comprises a 7 mile (10 km) loop connecting 15 stations around the city centre. Trains run every 4 minutes at peak times, and it takes 24 minutes to ride a complete loop. Tickets can be bought at any subway station. Single tickets are a fixed price and are valid on any journey. Savings can be made by purchasing a return (£3.20) or an all-day pass (£4.10).

Taxis

Cabs can be picked up at taxi ranks or hailed on the street. London-style black cabs display a yellow "taxi" sign which is lit up when the taxi is free. Fares are metered. "Private hire" cars must be booked by phone:

Driving

Travelling by car is by far the easiest way to explore beyond major cities.

Driving to Scotland
The journey to Edinburgh or Glasgow from London or main English ferry ports via the M1 and M6 motorways takes around 8–9 hours. If arriving by car ferry to Newcastle the A1 brings you to Edinburgh in around 2.5 hours.

Driving in Scotland
Scotland's roads are generally good, with motorways or dual carriageway highways connecting all major towns and cities. In remote areas some roads are single carriageway, with designated passing places. Convoys of slow-moving caravans can slow up traffic in peak summer holiday season. Be aware that weather can change rapidly and driving conditions can deteriorate suddenly at any time of year. Driving in cities is not recommended; traffic is heavy and parking scarce.

Car Rental
To rent a car in Scotland you must be at least 21 years old (some renters insist on a minimum age of 25) and have held a valid licence for one year. Car rental agencies have outlets at main airports and in major towns and cities.

Rules of the Road
Drive on the left. Seat belts must be worn at all times and children must travel with the correct child restraint for their weight and size.

Mobile telephones may not be used while driving, except with a handsfree system, and third party insurance is required by law.

Overtake on the outside or right-hand lane, and give priority to traffic approaching from the right. Give way to emergency service vehicles. It is illegal to drive and park in bus lanes.

On single-track roads which are wide enough for only one vehicle, pull into the nearest designated passing place on your left, or wait opposite a passing place on your right, to allow an oncoming vehicle to pass. You should also use passing places to allow drivers to overtake. Scotland's legal alcohol limit for drivers is lower than the rest of the UK's, at 50 mg of alcohol per 100ml (0.05 per cent BAC). Avoid drinking alcohol completely if you plan to drive.

Hitchhiking

Hitchhiking is a common way for tourists and backpackers to get around on a budget, and locals are often fairly accommodating. Always consider your own safety before entering an unknown vehicle.

Cycling

The trails of the Highlands are perfect for off-road riding,and there are great networks for mountain bikers and gentle trails following old canal towpaths or former railway lines. **7Stanes** trails spanning the entirety of southern Scotland. Find traffic-free city and countryside bike routes on the website of the UK's National Cycle Network, **Sustrans**.

7Stanes
🅦 stanes.com
Sustrans
🅦 sustrans.org.uk

Bicycle Hire

Off road, touring and city bikes, bikes for younger children, and electrically-assisted e-bikes can be rented from companies like **Biketrax** in Edinburgh and **EBS Cycle Centre** in Dundee. **Nextbike** is a cycle sharing scheme with 500 bikes available from more than 60 locations around Glasgow.

BikeTrax
🅦 biketrax.co.uk
EBS Cycle Centre
🅦 electricbikesscotland.com
Nextbike
🅦 nextbike.co.uk

Bike Touring

Several companies operate guided and self-guided bike tours around Scotland.
Wilderness Scotland offers guided cycling tours in areas including the Cairngorms, the Hebrides and the Great Glen, with a support van to carry your luggage.

Wilderness Scotland
🅦 wildernessscotland.com

Walking and Hiking

Walking is an enjoyable way to explore compact city centres such as Edinburgh, Glasgow and Stirling, where key sites are within easy reach of each other, and smaller cities such as Aberdeen, Dundee, Inverness, Perth and Stirling.

Scotland's mountains and glens are easy to reach but bad weather can strike at any time, so planning and preparation are essential. Ensure you have good hiking boots, warm waterproof clothing, a map and a compass. Tell someone where you're going and when you plan to return.

Boats and Ferries

There are no international car ferries direct to Scotland. However **DFDS Seaways** sails from Amsterdam to Newcastle in the north of England, only 100km (64 miles) from the Scottish border. **P&O Ferries** sails between Larne in Northern Ireland and Cairnryan, around 80 miles south of Glasgow and **Stena Line** sails from Belfast to Cairnryan.

For island hoppers, **Caledonian MacBrayne** (Calmac) offers passes valid for 8 days, 15 days or one month on its routes to western isles including Arran, Barra, Coll, Eigg, Harris, Islay, Mull, Raasay, Skye and Tiree. **NorthLink Ferries** sails to Stromness in Orkney from Scrabster and from Aberdeen to Orkney and Shetland. **Pentland Ferries** offers car ferries to South Ronaldsay in Orkney from Gill's Bay, west of John O'Groats. **John O'Groats Ferries** operates a passenger-only service to South Ronaldsay. Smaller, independent ferry services operate between smaller islands and the mainland.

Caledonian MacBrayne
🅦 calmac.co.uk
DFDS Seaways
🅦 dfdsseaways.co.uk
John O'Groats Ferries
🅦 jogferry.co.uk
NorthLink Ferries
🅦 northlinkferries.co.uk
P&O Ferries
🅦 poferries.com
Pentland Ferries
🅦 pentlandferries.co.uk
Stena Line
🅦 stenaline.co.uk

SCOTLAND BY BOAT

Cruising on the Caledonian Canal and around the island and mainland ports of Scotland's scenic northwest coast is a fabulous way to see some of the country's finest scenery in comfort.

Caledonian Discovery
Operating two 12-passenger hotel barges, Caledonian Discovery offers one-week cruises on the Caledonian canal and the Great Glen Lochs.
🅦 caledonian-discovery.co.uk

Hebridean Island Cruises
If you are looking to explore Scotland's Isles in style, these luxury all inclusive cruises tour the Western Isles aboard the Hebridean Princess, an elegant small cruise ship with just 30 cabins.
🅦 hebridean.co.uk

PRACTICAL
INFORMATION

A little local know-how goes a long way in Scotland. Here you can find all the essential advice and information you will need during your stay.

AT A GLANCE

USEFUL NUMBERS

GENERAL EMERGENCY	POLICE (NON-EMERGENCY)
999	**101**

NHS 24 (NON-EMERGENCY)

111

TIME ZONE
GMT/BST
British Summer Time
(BST) runs late March
to late October.

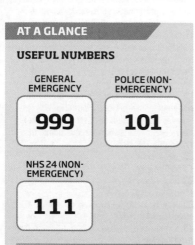

TAP WATER
Unless otherwise
stated, tap water
in the UK is safe
to drink.

TIPPING

Waiter	10-12.5%
Hotel Porter	£1 per bag
Housekeeping	£1 per day
Concierge	£1-2
Taxi Driver	Round up to the nearest pound

Personal Security

Pickpockets work crowded tourist areas and busy streets such as Edinburgh's Royal Mile and Princes Street and Glasgow's Buchanan Street. Use your common sense and be alert to your surroundings. If you have anything stolen, report the crime as soon as possible at the nearest police station. Get a copy of the crime report in order to make a claim on your insurance. Contact your embassy or consulate immediately if your passport is stolen or in the event of a serious crime or accident.

Health

For minor ailments go to a pharmacy or chemist. These are plentiful in towns and cities and in most villages. If you have an accident of medical problem requiring non-urgent medical attention you can find details of the nearest non-emergency medical service on the NHS website *(p209)*. Alternatively, call the NHS 24 helpline number at any hour on 111, or go the nearest hospital Accident and Emergency (A&E) department. You may need a doctor's prescription to obtain certain pharmaceuticals. The pharmacist can inform you of the closest doctor's surgery or medical centre. EU citizens can receive medical treatment in the UK free of charge. Visitors from outside the EU may have to pay for medical treatment and reclaim on their insurance.

Smoking, Alcohol and Drugs

Smoking and "vaping" are banned in all public spaces such as bus, train stations and airports and in enclosed areas of bars, cafés, restaurants and hotels. However, many bars and restaurants have outdoor areas where smoking is permitted. Alcohol may not be sold to or bought for anyone under 18 and may not be sold before 10am, except in airport departure lounges.

Alcohol can only be purchased between the hours of 10am and 10pm, and 12:30pm and 10pm on a Sunday. The consumption of alcohol or possession of an open container of alcohol on

the streets and in public places (excluding a liscenced venue) is illegal. The drink-drive limit (*p212*) is strictly enforced.

Possession of all recreational drugs, including psychoactive substances formerly known as "legal highs" and now classified as illegal, is a criminal offence.

ID

Visitors to the UK are not required to carry ID on their person at all times, but passports are required as ID at airports, even when taking internal flights within the UK. Anyone who looks under 18 may be asked for photo ID to prove their age when buying alcohol.

Visiting Places of Worship

Show respect by dressing modestly, especially when entering churches and religious buildings. Do not talk loudly or use cameras, phones or other mobile devices without first asking permission.

Mobile Phones and Wi-Fi

Do not rely on mobile phones or other devices for navigation or emergency communications in remote areas such as Ben Nevis or the Cairngorms where reception can be intermittent. Free Wi-Fi hotspots are widely available in city centres. Cafés and restaurants will usually give you their Wi-Fi password on the condition that you make a purchase.

Visitors travelling to the UK with EU tariffs are able to use their devices abroad without being affected by data roaming charges. Users will be charged the same rates for data, SMS services and voice calls as they would pay at home. This situation may change once the UK has left the EU. Pay-as-you-go SIM cards are available at newsagents and supermarkets.

Post

Main post offices are found in the centres of major towns and cities. In suburbs and villages, post office counters are often embedded in supermarkets and newsagents. In small communities the Post Office is often also the only shop. Post offices are generally open 9am–5:30pm Monday to Friday and until 12:30pm on Saturday. You can buy 1st class, 2nd class and international airmail stamps in shops and supermarkets (in books of 12) and at post office counters.

Taxes and Refunds

Stores offering tax free shopping display a distinctive sign and will provide you non-EU residents with a VAT 407 form. This is validated when you leave the UK and allows you to reclaim value added tax (VAT) on certain products. VAT is charged on most goods and services and is included in the price shown.

Discount Cards

If you plan to visit as many of Scotland's castles and stately homes as possible, the **Historic Environment Scotland Explorer Pass** provides access to over 70 attractions over a 3-or 7-day period. For those planning to travel extensively within Scotland, Scotrail's **Spirit of Scotland** pass offers unlimited train, bus and ferry transport over an 8-or 15-day period. The **Scottish Citylink Explorer Pass** offers 3-, 5- and 8-days unlimited travel on its extensive coach network, as well as discounts and special offers on accommodation.
Historic Environment Scotland Explorer Pass
W historicenvironment.scot
Scottish Citylink Explorer Pass
W citylink.co.uk/explorerpass.php
Spirit of Scotland
W scotrail.co.uk

WEBSITES AND APPS

Traffic Scotland
Use this app for real-time traffic conditions and road journey times anywhere in Scotland.
visitscotland.com
Scotland's official tourist board website
walkinghighlands.co.uk
A useful tool for planning walks and hikes anywhere in Scotland
mwis.org.uk/scottish-forecast
Weather forecasts provided by the Mountain Weather Information Service

INDEX

Page numbers in **bold** refer to main entries

M

SCOTTISH VOCABULARY

Gaelic is a Celtic language that is still spoken as a second language in the Highlands and Western Isles of Scotland. Estimates put the figure of Gaelic speakers throughout the country at around 60,000. The last decade has seen something of a revival of the language, due to the encouragement of both education and broadcasting authorities. However the majority of people are most likely to come across Gaelic today in the form of place names. Words such as glen, loch, eilean and kyle are all still very much in use. English remains the principal language of Scotland. However the country's very distinct education, religious, political and judicial systems have given rise to a rich vocabulary that reflects Scottish culture. Many additional terms in current usage are colloquial. English as spoken by the Scots is commonly divided into four dialects. Central Scots can be heard across the Central Belt and the southwest of the country. As around a quarter of the population lives within 32 km (20 miles) of Glasgow, West Central Scots is one of the most frequently heard subdivisions of this dialect. Southern Scots is spoken in the east of Dumfries and Galloway and the Borders; Northern Scots in the northeast; and Island Scots in the Orkney and Shetland Islands.

PRONUNCIATION OF GAELIC WORDS

Letters	Example	Pronunciation
ao	craobh	this is pronounced similar to oo, as in cool
bh	dubh	"h" is silent unless at the beginning of a word in which case it is pronounced v, as in vet
ch	deich	this is pronounced as in the German composer Bach
cn	cnoc	this is pronounced cr, as in creek
ea	leabhar	this is pronounced e, as in get or a, as in cat
eu	sgeul	this is pronounced ay, as in say or ea, as in ear
gh	taigh-òsda	this is silent unless at the beginning of a word, in which case it is pronounced as in get
ia	fiadh	this is pronounced ea, as in ear
io	tiocaid	this is pronounced ee, as in deep or oo, as in took
rt	ceart	this is pronounced sht
th	theab	this is silent unless at the beginning of a word in which case it is pronounced h, as in house
ua	uaine	this is pronounced oo, as in poor

WORDS IN PLACE NAMES

ben	mountain
bothy	farm cottage
brae	hill
brig	bridge
burn	brook
cairn	mound of stones marking a place
close	block of flats (apartments) sharing a common entry and stairway
craig	steep peak
croft	small plot of farmland with dwellings in the Highlands
dubh	black
eilean	island
firth	estuary
gate/gait	street (in proper names)
glen	valley
howff	a regular meeting place, usually a pub
kirk	a Presbyterian church
kyle	a narrow strait of river
links	golf course by the sea
loaning	field
loch	lake
moss	moor
munro	mountain over 914 m (3,000 ft) high
strath	valley/plain beside river
wynd	lane
yett	gate

FOOD AND DRINK

Arbroath Smokie	small haddock that has been salted and then smoked
breid	bread
clapshot	mashed turnips and potatoes
clootie dumpling	rich fruit pudding
Cullen Skink	fish soup made from smoked haddock
dram	a drink of whisky
haggis	sheep's offal, suet, oatmeal and seasonings, usually boiled in the animal's intestine
Irn-Bru	popular soft drink
neeps	turnips
oatcake	a savoury oatmeal biscuit
porridge	a hot breakfast dish made with oats, milk and water
shortie	shortbread
tattie	potato
tattie scone	type of savoury pancake made with potato

CULTURAL TERMS

Burns Night	25 January is the anniversary of the birth of the poet Robert Burns, celebrated with a meal of haggis
Caledonia	Scotland
ceilidh	an informal evening of traditional Scottish song and dance
clan	an extended family bearing the same surname (last name)
first foot	the first person to enter a house after midnight on New Year's Eve
Highland dress	Highland men's formal wear including the kilt
Hogmanay	New Year's Eve
kilt	knee-length pleated tartan skirt worn as traditional Highland dress
Ne'erday	New Year's Day
pibroch	type of bagpipe music
sgian-dubh	a small blade tucked into the outside of the sock on the right foot worn as part of the traditional Highland dress
sporran	pouch made of fur worn to the front of the kilt
tartan	chequered wool cloth, different colours being worn by each clan

COLLOQUIAL EXPRESSIONS

auld	old
auld lang syne	days of long ago
Auld Reekie	Edinburgh
aye	yes
bairn	child
barrie	excellent
blether	chat
bonnie	pretty
braw	excellent
dreich	wet (weather)
fae	from
fitba	football
hen	informal name used to address a woman or girl
ken	to know; to have knowledge
lassie/laddie	a young woman/man
lumber	boyfriend/girlfriend
Nessie	legendary monster of Loch Ness
Old Firm	Celtic and Glasgow Rangers, Glasgow's main football teams
wean	child
wee	small